"SCREEN & STAGE MARKETING SECRETS"

The Writer's Guide to Marketing Scripts

by

James Russell

"There should be a written guide so writers can learn how to submit scripts... professionally!"

HERE IT IS

****

FOR YOU
"The Lord has taken me from the pit of despair and has brought me to a high place. As the Lord gave without deserving, so I give to those in need; when I give, I receive and lives are blessed."

FROM THE BIBLE
"Commit your work to the Lord, then it will succeed." Proverbs 16:3

DEDICATED TO:
The Lord: "He healeith the broken in heart, and bindeth up their wounds." Psalm 147:3

TO HONOR:
A loving memory of mother and father.

WITH GOD ALL THINGS ARE POSSIBLE:
Thank God for all things. Trust Him. Believe He is and miracles come large and small. Expect results! This is the way things are.

****

800 PROMISES:
The Lord has declared over 800 promises in the Bible writers will find of great value. Have you read them?

"Screen & Stage Marketing Secrets"
Copyright © 1998, 1999, 2000 by James Russell
James Russell Publishing
780 Diogenes Drive
Reno, NV 89512
Web: www.powernet.net/~scrnplay
E-mail: scrnplay@powernet.net

All rights reserved. No part of this publication may be reproduced in any form or by any means without prior written permission of the author or publisher. Short excerpts for review purposes are permitted.

"Screen & Stage Marketing Secrets"
Written by James Russell
First Pre-press Printed Edition © October 1997.
Updated Printing: November, 1999 (no ISBN change).
First Edition Publication: February 2000 (no ISBN change).
Printed in the USA by Morris Publishing · 3212 East Highway 30 · Kearney, NE
ISBN # 0-916367-11-8
SAN # 295-852X

Sold as information only. Author, publisher and seller assume no liabilities whatsoever. Adult content.

THIS BOOK CAN BE PURCHASED FROM

Any bookstore can order this book by special order, or from:
-- Amazon.Com Books - see internet; www.amazon.com
-- Barnes & Noble - www.barnesandnoble.com or bookstore in your area.
-- Borders Books - www.borders.com or bookstore in your area.
-- Books A Million - www.booksamillion.com or bookstore in your area.
-- Chapters (Canada) - www.chapters.ca or bookstore in your area.
-- Lou's Books, 5647 Atlantic Ave, Long Beach, CA 90805 (213)423-1403.
-- Opamp Technical Books, 1033 N. Sycamore Ave, Los Angeles, CA 90038 (800)468-4322.
-- Varsity Books - see Internet or college bookstore.
-- Walden Books
-- Your local bookstore.
-- We have a bookstore listing on our website.

Any bookstore can order this manual. Just give them this number: ISBN # 0-916367-11-8 and our SAN #295-852X. If all fails you can order from the publisher address above; send $34.95 plus $4 shipping & handling. Overseas orders send $12 for shipping via air mail. A list of booksellers is on our website.

TABLE OF CONTENTS

THIS BOOK CAN BE PURCHASED FROM ... Title Page
THE WAY IT IS ... 1
AUTHOR BIOGRAPHY ... 1
GUARANTEED TO SAVE MONEY AND DECREASE REJECTIONS ... 1
FALSE HOPE ... 1
INTRODUCTION ... 1

CHAPTER 1

THINK THIS BOOK IS EXPENSIVE? ... 2
A NEW WRITING STYLE ... 2
DOING IT RIGHT THE FIRST TIME ... 2
STOP REJECTIONS ... 3

CHAPTER 2

BRIDGING THE GAP TO THE SALE ... 4
WHY THE BOOK IS WRITTEN IN SCREENPLAY FORMAT ... 4
ABOUT THIS MARKETING GUIDE ... 4
HOW THIS MANUAL WILL HELP YOU SELL SCRIPTS ... 6
SCREENWRITING SOFTWARE ... 7
AD-ON SCREENWRITING SOFTWARE FOR MICROSOFT WORD ... 8
PROFESSIONAL STAND-ALONE SCREENWRITING SOFTWARE ... 8
SOURCE FOR SCRIPT FORMATTING SOFTWARE ... 8
STORY ENGINES ... 8
MARKETING SOFTWARE ... 9
TAX DEDUCTIONS ... 9
SELECTING A PRINTER ... 9
STATIONERY YOU MUST USE TO SUBMIT QUERIES PROPERLY ... 10

CHAPTER 3

SCRIPT PRESENTATION – IT'S GOT TO BE PERFECT ... 11
NO COPYRIGHT NOTICE ON SCRIPT TITLE PAGE ... 12
WGA WRITER'S GUILD AND COPYRIGHT ADDRESSES ... 12
STREAMLINING YOUR SCRIPT – NEW RULES TO THE GAME ... 13
NO MORE BEATS AND CUT TO'S ... 17
FIVE BASIC STORY TIPS ... 18

CHAPTER 4

EXCLUSIVE OR NON-EXCLUSIVE MULTIPLE SUBMISSIONS? ... 18
THEFT OF YOUR MATERIAL – DOES IT REALLY HAPPEN? ... 19
THEY STOLE MY SCRIPT! ... 19

STEALING IDEAS – DON'T FRET ABOUT IT ... 20
A WORD ON THE S.A.S.E. ... 22
THE LIFE OF A READER ... 22
BREAKING UP DESCRIPTION ... 23
BREAKING UP DIALOG – HOW TO DO IT ... 32
DIRECTIONAL PARENTHETICALS ... 33
SPELLING OUT NUMBERS IN THE SCRIPT – THE RULES ... 36
DEADLY WORDS TO AVOID IN YOUR SCRIPT ... 36
MORE VALUABLE MARKETING TIPS ON SCREENWRITING ... 37

CHAPTER 5

ADVICE FROM AGENTS ... 40
ADVICE FROM PRODUCERS AND PRODUCTION COMPANIES ... 41
ADVICE FROM READERS ... 43
LIVING IN HOLLYWOOD ... 44
BUSINESS VACATION TO LOS ANGELES ... 45
HOW TO USE COVERAGE REPORTS ... 46
COVERAGE REPORT – SAMPLE FORM TO SCORE HIGHER RANK ... 47
WHAT IS PROFESSIONALISM? ... 48
SEVENTEEN YEARS IN LOS ANGELES ... 49
DO YOU NEED A HOLLYWOOD AGENT? ... 50
BOOKSTORES – FILM / TV / PLAYS / GENERAL INTEREST ... 50

CHAPTER 6

STAGE PLAY SCRIPT FORMAT ... 51
FEATURE FILM SCRIPT FORMAT ... 51
TV SITCOM SCRIPT FORMAT ... 52
MOVIE OF THE WEEK (MOW) FORMAT ... 53
HOW TO FIND TV PRODUCTION COMPANY SHOW ADDRESSES ... 53
A WORD ABOUT FUNNY ... 54
IS IT EASY TO OBTAIN AN AGENT? ... 55
WHEN DO I NEED AN AGENT? ... 56
HOW TO FIND AGENTS ... 56
THE BETTER AGENT: LARGE OR SMALL? ... 58
BE YOUR OWN LITERARY AGENT ... 59
COST OF AGENCY REPRESENTATION ... 59

CHAPTER 7

TARGETING YOUR MARKETING ... 60
GENERATING LOG LINES ... 61
QUERY LETTER WRITING SECRETS ... 61
SAMPLE QUERY LETTER TO AGENT ... 66
MULTIPLE SUBMISSION LOG LINE QUERY ... 68

RESPONSE TIME – LEARN PATIENCE, PLEASE! ... 68
HOW TO FIND PRODUCTION COMPANIES ... 68
SAMPLE QUERY LETTER TO PRODUCTION COMPANY ... 69
RELEASE FORM FOR PRODCO / PRODUCER / ACTOR'S MANAGER ... 69
RELEASE FORM TO AGENT ... 69
HOW DO I FIND PRODUCERS, STUDIOS AND DIRECTORS? ... 70
SAMPLE QUERY LETTER TO PRODUCER ... 70
HOW TO OBTAIN A LITERARY AGENT ... 70
LOCATING A MOVIE STAR TO READ YOUR SCRIPT ... 71

CHAPTER 8

S.A.S.E. IT'S MORE THAN WHAT YOU THINK IT IS ... 72
MAILING SCRIPTS – FOLLOW THE RULES ... 72
A HUGE MISTAKE TO AVOID WHEN MAILING YOUR SCRIPT ... 75
POSTAGE STAMPS – DEAD GIVEAWAY OF AN AMATEUR SUBMISSION ... 75
WORD OF WARNING – SCAMS ... 75
SCREENWRITING CONTESTS
SCREENWRITING MAGAZINES & SCRIPT RESOURCES ... 77
THE INTERNET'S WORLDWIDE WEB ... 79
E-MAIL QUERIES ... 80

CHAPTER 9

STALE TITLES ... 82
MOVIE OF THE WEEK ... 82
COLLABORATION RIGHTS ... 83
MARKETING THE STAGE PLAY ... 84
BASIC TIPS ON WRITING A STAGE PLAY ... 84
MORE USEFUL INFORMATION FOR THE WRITER ... 86
A WORD ON TREATMENTS ... 87
MOVIES YOU MUST SEE ... 87
THOSE WHO MAKE IT ... 89
ADVERTISE YOURSELF ... 89

CHAPTER 10

HOT-SHEET FOR SCREENWRITERS ... 89
STREAMLINE YOUR MARKETING ... 89
ETIQUETTE – DEALING WITH THE DEALERS ... 91
HOW TO OBTAIN A REFERRAL – OPEN DOORS TO OPPORTUNITY ... 92
FINDING A WRITER TO OBTAIN A REFERRAL ... 93
MORE VALUABLE TIPS FOR MARKETING SCRIPTS ... 94
HOW TO MEET PEOPLE IN THE INDUSTRY ... 95
TRADE SHOWS & MEETING PRODUCERS ... 96
SCRIPTS AVAILABLE ... 97

MAILING LISTS AND SAVING $ MONEY $ ... 98
TIPS FOR PLAYWRIGHTS ... 100
PLAYWRIGHT MENTOR ... 101
HANDLING REJECTION ... 101
KNOWING WHEN TO QUIT ... 102
SHOULD YOU WRITE A BOOK OR STAGE PLAY FIRST? ... 103
PRODUCING YOUR OWN FILM ... 103
BOOKS TO READ ... 104

CHAPTER 11

BEWARE OF EXCESSIVE WRITING – IT MAY RUIN YOUR WRITING! ... 104
DANGER ON THE WEB! BE CAREFUL! ... 105
DEVELOPING CREATIVITY – THE SECRET FORMULA FOR SUCCESS! ... 107
A SIMPLE MARKETING PLAN THAT WORKS! ... 110
COMMON IMPROPER WORD USAGE YOU MUST AVOID ... 112
DO YOU NEED A LAWYER? ... 113
GOING BROKE ... 114
SCRIPT TALK – KEEP THE ACTION FLOWING ... 115
STRANGE GOOD NEWS ... 116
AUTHORITATIVE QUERY LETTERS – EXAMPLES YOU CAN USE ... 117
TURNING THE TIDE – BREAKING THE RULES – PACKAGING ... 119
SHOTGUN THE MARKET ... 120
NOBODY WANTS MY SCRIPT – NOT SO! ... 120

CHAPTER 12

WRITER SURVIVAL TIPS ... 120
WRITING SCHOOLS ... 123
COMPUTER BACKUP WARNING ... 124
FIREWALL CHART ... 125
TEST YOUR KNOWLEDGE ... 125
INDUSTRY CONTACTS – USE THIS AGENT & PRODCO FORM ... 125
CHECKLIST – SUBMISSION PACKAGE ... 125
THE LAST WORD ... 126

NO CHAPTER 13 ... 126

CHAPTER 14

INTRODUCTION TO TRAP SHOOTING – YOU CAN MEET PEOPLE HERE ... 126
TRAP SHOOTING WRITING OPPORTUNITIES ... 127
IS YOUR BOOK PUBLISHED? ... 128

CHAPTER 15

AGENTS YOU MAY CONTACT – SPECIAL LISTING ... 128
AGENT & MANAGEMENT FIRM LISTING ... 129
SCRIPT EVALUATIONS – SCRIPT DOCTORS ... 130
OTHER SCREENWRITING RESOURCES ... 131
ADDRESSES OF FIRMS MENTIONED ... 131
LISTING ERRORS ... 136
CONTACTING THE AUTHOR ... 136
TESTIMONIALS ... 136
FORTHCOMING TITLES ... 136

CHAPTER 16

ILLUSTRATIONS – PERFORMING PROFESSIONAL SUBMISSIONS ... 136

- END -

FADE IN:

THE WAY IT IS

"*It is these many 'secrets' revealed in this book that generates success or failure. There are tens of thousands of writers who do not know why their query letters and scripts are rejected. They will continue to receive perpetual rejections, until they comply with the rules in this book. The author did not make the rules, but only reveals them as the Hollywood industry created them, and these rules are called 'firewalls' designed to keep unprofessional writers out of the money.*" -- **James Russell**

AUTHOR BIOGRAPHY

No recognition is desired by the author. Displaying credentials serve no purpose for the reader. What is of most importance is the practical value of the book. Let the readers receive the honors.

GUARANTEED TO SAVE MONEY AND DECREASE REJECTIONS

1. This book will save you more money than the cost of purchase!
2. Many firms mentioned offer special discounts to readers!
3. Cost to mail scripts and queries will be greatly reduced!
4. You will see an increase in requests for your scripts!
5. A list of agents who will give readers of this book <u>special consideration</u>! This alone is well worth the price of the book!

If any of the above do not meet with your satisfaction in 30 days from date of purchase, simply return the book for a full refund of the purchase price. No other publisher offers such a guarantee. All we ask is you tell us why you could not save money and why requests for your scripts did not increase. Fair enough?

We don't believe you will be returning the book, for if you do follow the directions, you <u>will</u> save money and you <u>will</u> see an increase in agents, prodcos and <u>producers</u> requesting your scripts. However, if you do believe it necessary to return the manual, do <u>not</u> return the book to the retailer. Simply <u>write us</u> a letter and we <u>will</u> send you instructions how and where to return the manual.

FALSE HOPE

When you are on the inside looking out, you will look back over your shoulder and see there are many screenwriting products and services and contests that mean well, but are just another means to take the struggling writers' money in the quest for success. This book exposes some, but not all of the pitfalls to avoid. About 1 in 5,000 spec scripts are optioned each year. Though the odds are way better than hitting the lottery, your focus should be to use your scripts as calling cards to obtain writing assignments. This is not an easy business to get into. Likewise, it is not easy to have a book published. Writers have it tough. No book or product can promise success, but I have expectations you will find this book of great value to enhance your writing career! In fact, this book will pay for itself many times over. Follow the advice in this book and you should be well on your way to establishing yourself as a serious and professional writer!

INTRODUCTION

First, to clear the air, this is <u>not</u> a book about technical screenwriting, character development, structure, or mechanics of how scripts are made into movies. It is not a creative writing tutorial, though some tips are presented. It is a bare bones, matter-of-fact, marketing guide and basic instruction manual to help you "professionally" present and market your stage or screenplay script. Practical advice for the playwright and screenwriter!

You'll learn the do's and don'ts peculiar to script writing, related to marketing. For the hard-working aspiring screenwriter, who is having tough luck breaking scripts into the market, you'll learn more than a few tricks to save you money and open doors that have slammed shut. This manual will pay for itself hundreds of times over, year-after-year. Consider it an investment, for that's exactly what it is. Money saved is money earned. And if you sell your script and/or obtain writing assignments, what an investment indeed!

THINK THIS BOOK IS EXPENSIVE? TRY SUBMITTING WITHOUT IT!
Try mailing query letters for five or more years, still not obtaining positive results. Add up the shipping supplies, paper and postage costs alone and it will calculate into *thousands* of dollars. This instructional manual will absolutely save you money, thousands of dollars, no doubt about it -- and may even sell your script!

That's what the book is supposed to do. Take a peek at the subchapter *"Mailing Lists and $ Saving Money $"* to see how much money you'll save. This book pays for itself many times over!

"Screen & Stage Marketing Secrets is a book packed with vital information! No wasted words to fill space! No useless chapters duplicating what other screenwriting books already offer. A powerful marketing tool!"

CHAPTER 1

A NEW WRITING STYLE

You will learn a new writing style developed by the author that is so fast, you'll have to slow down the action! You can use this form to compress a large script and impress industry readers with a tight action-oriented script, exactly what script analysts and executives love to see and read!

One of the biggest complaints from industry readers is the script is too fat with stalled action. Use this new writing style and those complaints are history! Incorporate the compression style with your own voice to enhance your script's power and deliver visual action. However, when incorporating the style, keep your own unique voice and style of writing. You don't want to lose that!

DOING IT RIGHT THE FIRST TIME

You'll learn secrets professionals use. The critical elements to make your script and submissions professionally presented. The tips herein are instantly effective. No theory here, just doing it right the first time. There are a thousand and ten ways to market a script.

We won't be using gimmicks, such as, sending a script disguised as a gift to grab attention. We will bend a few traditions, but never cross over the line to absurdity. Professionalism is the key to success and this book will show you how to conform to the Hollywood rules and standards.

STOP REJECTIONS

If you read the current books on the market (over 35 books), you still would not obtain the practical marketing instructions presented here. If your scripts are being rejected, this guide will help you, but ultimately it's the story you write that makes or breaks opportunities. Let's just be certain your marketing program is not the cause of script rejection!

With proper marketing, more than half the battle is won. Unfortunately, many screenwriters fail at this stage of the game and they have great scripts! You may even have a degree in creative writing or journalism, but if you don't know the rules of the marketing game, you'll strike out. In fact, the more intelligent your writing is, the louder the explosive backfire will be. Twelfth-grade grammar is the rule!

Scripts are not considered literary works of art in the same sense as books. Show-off your writing skills too much and you'll be rejected repeatedly. You have to write to the reader, director, actor, and studio executives. Most are not English professors or editors.

You must write visually and reveal action, and all with concise brevity to maintain the script's inherent timing factors. There is no time to be creative, literally. Just get the story moving and keep it going with as few words as possible. Examples are given in this book.

If you think it is easy, it's not. It is hard to figure it out on your own, but this book will show you how to do it. You can read other scripts and find alternatives, but be very careful, as most scripts offered for sale are shooting scripts or scripts written to be sold as books or formatted for magazine articles. They may not be the original author's script that made the sale in the first place, so don't mimic the formatting of published scripts. All too many writers are making this mistake! You _must_ write the authors script.

The rejection process is simply that, a process. The industry is flooded with scripts and it is quite a feat when you consider just how many scripts there are floating in the mails that even ten percent could be read out of 160,000 or more per year! The film and theatrical stage industry does not want to reject scripts, they simply want marketable scripts.

Problem is, many scripts are marketable though still can't get into the door due to the filtering firewall system. The firewalls are real blockers for most writers. Some writer's, at one point in time, will slip through, but this golden opportunity is ruined due to script/story errors creating more rejections. This book helps you stop the rejections.

Note: A listing of every firm's address mentioned in this book is provided. See, *"Addresses of Firms Mentioned In This Book."* Website URL address are included.

CHAPTER 2

BRIDGING THE GAP TO THE SALE

In screen and stage play writing there are professionals and there are amateurs and nobody in between. You are either in, or you are out! Stuck in the middle of all this are: the agents. They are too busy handling the professional writers, yet they don't want to miss the next big talent to come along with a winning spec script.

In the process lies the dilemma. Authors who want "in" submit scripts that are not up to standards and receive rejections, instantly. Agents and producers are screaming in the magazines about what they want to see in the submitted scripts. Nobody listens. Agents hear the echoes of despair bouncing off the walls from frustrated and confused writers, and are powerless to stop the unprofessional submissions.

There is a huge crevasse in the ice field which communication between the writer, agent, producer and prodco can't seem to bridge. There are formatting books, but they don't fill the purpose of marketing, nor are they intended to. There are film schools and many screenwriting books, but marketing is still in the dark ages for many playwrights and screenwriters.

How do I sell a script? Am I submitting this thing properly? Who is teaching this stuff? We have the screenwriters screaming and nobody hears their echo. A caustic cauldron of screams boiling with flaring tempers of frustration. The writers keep submitting and the agents retaliate with rejection. A full-blown silent war rages on and nobody wins!

Consider *Screen & Stage Marketing Secrets* a rung in the ladder, a plank on the suspended bridge to educate the writer in how to submit scripts, professionally, so they will be accepted and sold! This book is the screenwriter's and playwright's best friend. **Note:** The author may use the word "screenwriter." Please realize it may also identify a playwright.

WHY THE BOOK IS WRITTEN IN SCREENPLAY FORMAT

How many times have you picked up a screenwriting book and found the contents far out of date? That's one reason why we are using Cinnovision's *Scriptware* screenwriting program to format this manual, so flexibility, rapid updates, and expansion for revisions can be made. We would not hesitate to use any of the major dedicated screenwriting programs. The author used *Scriptware* for this project.

Secondly, by using this screenwriting format, you will be exposed to the fonts, headings and styles throughout the book screenwriters must use in the author script. *James Russell Publishing* has attractivve books, but this manual focuses on technical data, a textbook. It's not meant to be a "beautiful book" but rather an "effective book." A book with powerful marketing procedures to get your scripts sold!

ABOUT THIS MARKETING GUIDE

Having read just about every book on the market on screenwriting, there were many questions in my mind still unanswered leading to roadblocks and dead-ends in the marketing process. And to make matters worse, conflicts in opinions left me confused. After much research, trial and error and thousands of dollars spent, I've learned a few tricks of the trade on how to kick through the firewalls and get my scripts to the major players. You can too!

But, let's face facts. Most writers are not business people. Understanding the marketing aspect is essential to selling your product. This will be our primary focus.

Agents are constantly telling us screenwriters (we have ears that lap over)to be professional when submitting scripts and query letters. What is professional? You'll soon find out within these pages. Agent listings and interviews in the screenwriting magazines scream over and over the same ol' things: *"Do this." "Don't do that."* We don't hear them. I've taken the advice of the agents and producers, tested the concepts and compiled this manual, so submissions would comply with expected professionalism.

I've added a few twists to the game to increase the impact of query mailings, to obtain a positive response of requesting the script(s). This manual is a piece of the puzzle, a link in the chain. The writing samples are examples, not absolutes. Feel free to be creative.

Because so many unprofessional people are flooding the market with scripts, more agents are charging reading, processing, or evaluation fees. This is a dangerous trend for writers. It's hard enough to break into the business and now you have to pay to get your heart broken. I felt there is a dire need for a manual like *"Screen & Stage Marketing Secrets"* to help reverse this trend and to assist the new writer in making a professional appearance when submitting scripts and query letters. There's a lot of confusion out there!

As you already know, literary agents are Pandora's box: valuable, yet at times, useless. They can't do all things for all people. This business of writing and selling screenplay, teleplay, and stage play scripts is a crazy endeavor. It is easier to create and manufacture a new product and launch it to the general public than it is to sell a script. I developed an industrial chemical and sold it to industry and the public, so I know the difference. I am also a successful book publisher and know much, of course not all, about marketing.

Scripts are harder to sell! The information in this manual will make it easier for you to sell your script, much easier than what you are likely doing now! You will avoid the major pitfalls amateur writers tumble into only to receive perpetual rejections from the industry.

The purpose of this manual is not to guarantee you will sell your script, for that is an intangible not in my control, but this manual can get your screenplay into the hands of those who have the power to recommend and buy scripts! The trick is to get past the intentionally erected firewalls and get past the reader.

To do so, you need to know the "inside secrets" on properly formatting the script, and formatting does not always mean format; the logical placement of slug lines, dialog, etc. It can mean writing style, too! Even mistakes made on the envelope you mailed your script in can result in a rejected, returned script. It happens, more than you know.

For some, the information herein may be basic, for most, it will open your eyes to the errors in your own scripts. Certain words used in scripts scream, "AMATEUR" and the reader passes like yesterday's sunset. I bet you have tens-to-hundreds of these errors in your scripts! It took me months to discover and edit them out. When I did, the scripts were vastly improved and so many requests for scripts came, I had to turn down requests!

This book will show you how to banish these script-killers to the graveyard and make your screenplay a clean read. This manual will show you how to present a professional submission, which is critical if you wish to stand any chance of selling a script. Best of all, your scripts will advance forward in the Hollywood maze of script overload and open the door of opportunity for you. That I can guarantee. It is the first step to obtaining agent representation or a production deal.

There comes a time to face the drudgery of the business, marketing. The entertainment business is a business, and you'll have to knuckle under to the task; conducting your marketing efforts as a business. And you can't watch all the movies and plays, read all the scripts and books the world has to offer. The time comes you must sit down and just write, and not just scripts; but query letters, synopsis, log lines and cover letters, and this book is going to help you do these tasks in a very big way.

HOW THIS MANUAL WILL HELP YOU SELL SCRIPTS

No miracles. This book will show you how to obtain an agent with sheer determination and a generous dose of helpful advice. If you don't secure an agent, it's no big thing. You can still market and sell your scripts without one and get an agent at the snap of your fingers (no kidding).

You'll learn how to slam your scripts through the firewalls to producers, story editors, actors and production companies. Included are actual samples of powerful query letters, request to submit letter, release form, log line submissions, and more, with tried and tested step-by-step advice on marketing your script. You will see less rejections!

The book will show you the inside secrets of why readers, story editors and agents reject scripts, not story structure and character development problems, but errors that will send your script into the rejection pile by the time the reader reads the first page or two.

If you don't know these little tip-offs and how to avoid them, success can be difficult, about as hard as tying a rock to a cloud! When you cut out these dangerous words, you will see a marked improvement in the responses from agents, prodcos, producers and readers. No ifs ands or buts about it. It's not hard to do, once you catch the drift.

Remember: Seemingly tiny errors can undermine your script no matter how well-written the story. This is a fickle business. Play by the rules or you lose. But what are the rules? The book will be showing you a few rules related to entertainment industry marketing. This manual and one more book you must read, *The Screenwriter's Bible* will put you on the right path, fast. Every screenwriter needs the know-how to structure the story and the knowledge to market the script. Most screenwriters fail one or the other, or both. That's right, one book and this marketing manual are all you need to get the ball rolling. Everything else you read is gravy to help you deepen your writing, develop characters, learn about the business, etc.

Marketing is more important than having a good script. After all, a great script goes nowhere if it is not read! Many fine stories are rejected, due to poor marketing presentation and formatting errors. It's a fact of life. Most writers learn the hard way from ruthless rejection. Lucky for you. You have a head start I and many others never had. So let's start the process now.

I'm assuming you already have written a script or two. If not, you'll need to at least get to this point, but not always. If you can write a good treatment you can sell that too, but it's a hard-sell, if you can't demonstrate to the potential buyer two things:

1. You are not a one-script wonder. (Someone who only has one script.) Most agents/buyers want writers who have at least two or more completed scripts to demonstrate ability.

2. You must demonstrate you have the ability to take your treatment to a marketable finished form. If you have at least one completed screenplay, teleplay, or stage play, that demonstration is realized.

Write and complete a script. The more the better. That's my best advice. With this said, let's begin.

SCREENWRITING SOFTWARE
Lets begin with the basics of software. This manual is written with "*Scriptware for Windows*" a product of Cinovation, Inc., 1750 30th St., Suite 360, Boulder, CO 80301-1005 (303)-785-7899. Ask for a competitive upgrade, if you use any other story building/formatting software with script formatting features (Blockbuster computer program qualified). It'll save you a hundred dollars or so. Most software companies have free demonstration programs, so try them before you buy.

There are a few more companies selling script formatting software. Which ones do the pros use? Any and all. They all get the job done. Save yourself a ton of grief and buy one of these programs. Using a standard word processor to format scripts will cause you tons of grief. They can't cut the mustard. Pages repaginate improperly leaving slug lines hanging, etc. Fatal errors for a reader to see giving them justification to toss your script into the rejection heap. Errors in formatting are not tolerated.

The add-on screenwriting program are available, but Microsoft Word has a habit of not printing what you see on the screen and shifting elements; especially hanging slug-lines at the bottom of the page. That's why book publishers use *PageMaker* or *Quark* software programs as they lock the pages tightly. That's why you should use a stand-alone dedicated screenwriting program. Opinions may differ.

Dedicated programs have more features and plenty of conversion options, generate reports, increased flexibility and are perfect for the professional. For the same reasons, that's why you need to use a dedicated full-featured scriptwriting program. They cost more, but are superior. For those who just want to dabble without making the investment, the add-on programs serve this purpose well. You can buy them for as low as $20. If the pages do not float, the program can be of value and will get the job done.

Advice: Pay now or pay later! Make life easier on yourself. It's hard enough writing without playing around with software not perfectly dedicated to the job at hand. You may outgrow the add-on software needing to update to a dedicated professional program. Will the pro program recognize the data file to import your script? Will it do so, flawlessly?

AD-ON SCREENWRITING SOFTWARE FOR MICROSOFT WORD

-- Cyber Film School / Impact Pictures, Dept. S, 30 Mountainview Ave., Toronto, Canada M6A 2L3   Offers Scriptmaker program for $20.

PROFESSIONAL STAND-ALONE SCREENWRITING SOFTWARE

--Cinovation, Inc., 1750 30th St., Suite 360, Boulder, CO 80301-1005 (303)-785-7899.
-- *Final Draft*, Inc. Dept. E, 16000 Ventura Blvd, Suite 800, Encino, CA 91436 (800)231-4055 (800)-231-4055 Web: www.finaldraft.com.
--Hollywood Screenplay Software, Ballistic Computing, Dept. A, 8 Pima Court, Oakland, NJ 07436 (201)651-0746. 20% discount for readers of this book.
--Movie Magic Screenwriter, Screenplay Systems, Dept. A, 150 E. Olive Ave. #203, Burbank, CA 91502 (800)84-STORY.
--Script Thing, Script Perfection Enterprises, Dept. 1-J, 4901 Morena Blvd. Ste 108, San Diego, CA 92117 (800)450-9450. 15% discount.

SOURCE FOR SCRIPT FORMATTING SOFTWARE:

-- Scriptshop.com, Dept. B, P.O. Box 11742, Atlanta GA Orders Only Phone(770)234-4000. They offer a discount: Film section: $15 off 4th item.   TV section: $12 off 4th item.

STORY ENGINES

A powerfully effective story engine that is incredibly easy to use is, *Blockbuster*. I like *Blockbuster* because it is capable of importing a first draft written in *Blockbuster* into *Scriptware,* which saves a ton of typing hours.

-- John Truby's Writer's Studio, Dept. J-9, 1737 Midvale Avenue, Los Angeles, CA 90024-5512 (800)338-7829. Blockbuster is easy to learn and use and very effective.
-- Screenplay Systems, Dept. A, 150 East Olive Ave., Ste 203, Burbank, CA 91502(818)843-6557. The *Dramatica* program is complex to use and may be of great value to the highly-intensive story writer. You don't need to use story programs, but they help and I recommend them as they are part and parcel to the advanced-level writing function.
-- *Writer's Blocks*, Ashley Software, Dept. R, 27758 Santa Margarita Pkwy #302, Mission Viejo, CA 92691. 800-229-6737.
--Collaborator, Dept. 1-J, 4335 Van Nuys Blvd., PMB#205, Sherman Oaks, CA 91403. 10%.

Before you buy any story-building software, ask if the copy protection scheme allows for the computer hard disk to defrag during disk maintenance. If not, reconsider (author's opinion) as it is a pain having to uninstall the program or risk program corruption.

MARKETING SOFTWARE

You need a contact manager database program to develop query letters; mail merge letters for mass mailings; log agent and prodco (independent production company) addresses, names, titles; track responses; print envelopes, mailing labels, etc. *"ACT!"* is a great program for marketing, and it's no wonder it is used heavily in industrial sales departments. Any computer store or catalog house can order you a copy. It's not cheap, but it works very well. You can use it for personal use, mailing Christmas cards, etc. It's a contact manager with a solid database. You can purchase *"ACT!"* direct from the creator: Symantec, 10201, Torre Ave., Cupertino, CA 20559 (800)707-3000. Ask if you qualify for competitive upgrades that can save you a hundred dollars or so.

If you can't afford *"ACT!"* there are other competing products that may get the job done. Buy "ACT!" if you can. It's a proven, reliable, flexible product that works! *Gold Mine* is another popular program, but the author has never used it, as of this writing.

Note: Regardless which program you use to generate mail-merge query letters, you must sign each letter by hand with blue ink. See Fig. 1-3. Don't use a printer to dab on the signature. Nobody likes it. Even if your laser printer can imprint color ink, don't do it. How many times have you opened a letter and felt "tricked" seeing a signed letter in blue ink that is not real? Believe it, this is good advice to increase responses.

TAX DEDUCTIONS

Quickbooks or *Quicken* are fine software packages for accounting. I prefer Quickbooks, but Quicken will do the job. You can take tax deductions for computer and programs, books, magazines, printer, stationery and paper, toner, disks, software, postage, envelopes and supplies, etc. You will survive an audit if you keep receipts and have the "intent" of making a profit. You may not make a profit for many years, but as long as you "intend" to, and conduct your business in a professional manner you should have no problem. You simply file Federal tax deductions on Schedule C.

You don't need an accountant or tax preparer to use a computerized tax preparation program. **Note:** Don't mix personal expenses with business in the accounting software or the IRS will clobber you on an audit. They look for this mixing and could disallow your business as a hobby or cut your deductions and will bill you for tax due. That's why I use Quicken for personal use and Quickbooks (you don't need the expensive professional version) for business transactions only.

SELECTING A PRINTER

You'll need a laser printer with 300 d.p.i (dot per inch) print clarity. A 250 sheet capacity paper tray is fine. Any higher resolution than 300 d.p.i. is overkill. Don't use a dot matrix printer. The print must be clean and easy on the reader's eyes. The ink jet may work, but is the print a tad fuzzy? Usually is. Crisp laser-printing is the only way to go. Don't skimp on print quality!

You don't need a color printer to print scripts, and don't ever print any other color but black ink into a script! A color printer can come in handy if you have a touch of color in your query letter stationery, but it's often cheaper(and more professional)to buy the stationery than print it, due to toner cost.

STATIONERY YOU MUST USE TO SUBMIT QUERIES PROPERLY

For excellent quality, stationery supplies contact: Paper Direct, Dept. A-6, P.O. Box 1514, Secaucus, NJ 07096-1514 (800)272-7377. The catalog has many exquisite multi-colored items. Ask for samples.

Advice: Don't get too fancy with splashy colors. If you look at top agent and prodco stationery, you'll notice it is plain and simple with a dash of color, not a splash (in most cases). Yours should be too. Don't use brochure/mailers. Plain stationery letterhead from Paper Direct's selections such as Strategist, Blue Carrara, Acropolis, French patina, Enterprise, Green Marble, Foundation, Aristocrat and Monarch are good choices. A dash of color, yet not overbearing.

Keep in mind you don't have to use this expensive stationery for mass query mailings. Just a soft, light colored paper works fine. You can buy 500 sheets for about $15 at any office supply store. Something similar to Wausau Papers, Astroparche, is fine. Try lavender. This tip will save you a few hundred dollars, easily. Once you receive a response to send a synopsis or script, you can type a cover letter with the fine stationery.

Save your best stationery for cover letters and communications, not mass mailings; otherwise, it will cost you a small fortune (see Fig. 1-24). Some may disagree with this approach, as first impressions count, so try both methods. My experience tells me it's a waste of money. Moreover, you don't need matching envelopes, so save yourself money here. Plain old white #10 business letter size (See the illustrations describing dimensions of a #10 envelope).

You also don't need business cards, but it wouldn't hurt to have some on hand to pass on, not to send in the mail to agents or prodcos, but to hand to persons you meet who know people in the entertainment industry. You never know when you'll need that card!

Note: If you think sending colorful stationery and beautiful envelopes to agents and production companies will give you a great first impression and an advantage, you are dead wrong! The mail filtering firewall system will segregate these fancy letters into the "some other day" or "never respond" pile. Your envelope should simply be plain white #10 size, with a traditional "business postage stamp" applied. A professional mailing is a business mailing. Corporations do use fancy stationery, but in this business, less is more! More on this later.

When to use fine stationery? **1)** Cover letter when mailing a script. **2)** Follow-up communications. **3)** Responding to ad listings in screen writing magazines. Even if there are fifty agents and prodcos listed in an annual survey of agents seeking scripts, this is not considered a mass cold-call mailing.

Keep in mind that the Release Form is always printed on plain white paper because it is a legal document. Any stationery you use for any mailings should never distract from the message or fade the print into a hard to read blur. Do this and you will receive a rejection.

Have you ever wondered why many agents never respond to your query letters? Look at your presentation. It's likely so amateur looking, it's no wonder the agent simply tosses it into the trash. Hollywood and Broadway is a cruel business. With over one-hundred thousand unprofessional submissions being made each year, you can see how easy it is to simply discard on sight envelopes that scream "amateur."

CHAPTER 3

SCRIPT PRESENTATION - IT'S GOT TO BE PERFECT

The script is printed on <u>white</u> 20 pound, 8 1/2" by 11" paper (though acceptable, overseas size A4 paper is not recommended). No matter how nice it may look, do not used colored paper, it must be white. Do not use fine linen paper. Use standard copy paper.

Amazingly, people send in scripts on fine linen stationery or lightly colored paper. Do not do this, as the reader will immediately recognize the script is definitely amateur. This error is made because firms that sell scripts often use an attractive blue or other colored paper stock to make the script look nice. The buyer then assumes colored paper is the norm for script format. This advice also includes the cover of the script, no bright colors.

Rule: no fancy colors!

The script covers should be plain-Jane type stock with nothing written on the cover. See Fig. 1-1. You can use a manila (vellum) color card stock. You can use white, but not black. Never be cute and use florescent or brightly colored covers. It's a sure sign an amateur submitted the script. Readers will see alright, but will frown and leave it for someone else to read and nobody will read it! It just gets shuffled around, eventually lost, trashed, or ultimately passed on with a rejection letter, unread.

Has this happened to you? Why do writers use fancy script covers? They believe it will stand out from the stack of scripts. It does. It says, *"Don't read me!"* Some firms actually sell "color covers" to make your script stand out from the pack. These are businesses who sell paper, not scripts to Hollywood. It can be very confusing for the new writer when seeing such advertising. *"Gee, maybe I should be using colored script covers?"* Now you know the answer.

Punch three holes in the script and covers and affix them with two brass brads, one in top hole, one in bottom hole. Use Acco #5 solid brass fasteners stock #71505. They are heavy gauge brass 1 1/4" long and is the standard size for movie screenplays. Smaller brads are used for 30 minute teleplays. Any office supply store can order them, if not in stock. You can use three brads if you want, but many writers only use two, one on top, one on bottom, center hole empty. See Fig. 1-1. Using 2-brads is often a tip to the reader the script is from a professional (part of the firewall system).

Don't use any other type of binding or fasteners, no matter how nicely they look. Any deviation is a clear sign of an amateur. Some firms advertise fancy bindings to submit scripts. Do not use them! Stay with the brads. Why use two brads when three makes the script easier to handle and read? It's just one of the fickle things about Hollywood.

Readers are accustomed to handling scripts with only two brads.

So why have three holes punched in the script? Because someone may want to insert another brad somewhere down the line. You can use three brads, but most pros only use two. It's a small tip-off that if you use two, you may be professional. Interesting isn't it? It's a device to inform the reader at a glance which scripts are likely professional and which are not. And it makes good sense if you saw a pile of fifty scripts that needed to be read, you would look for the professional scripts first. If you want your script read, follow these little rules.

The best three hole punch you can buy is the Acco Model 650 (or later model). It'll punch holes with ease through the entire script at one stroke of the handle. It's expensive, approximately $235. You can use economical $30 punches, you'll just have to insert 30-sheets, or less, at a time. Any office supply store can supply you with a variety of paper punches. Paper Direct has a special catalog featuring office equipment. They have a paper punch for $130 with 128 sheet capacity and a small 30-page punch for $35. Also, mechanical envelope sealers and tri-fold paper folders if you prefer convenience. Why must scripts be bound so? Because the spine will be titled by the reader/prodco, if the script is accepted. Brads make disassembling the script to make photocopies easy to distribute to actors, director, etc. See Fig. 1-1 for an example.

NO COPYRIGHT NOTICE ON SCRIPT TITLE PAGE

Don't put the copyright or WGA# on the title page of the script. See Fig. 1-2. We know we are told to so by the U.S. Copyright Office, but some agents and producers feel it's intimidating that you feel they will steal your script. There is another good reason. If you place the copyright symbol with the date, your script is telling everyone who reads it, *"I'm an amateur sending you an outdated script. Please reject me!"* Another filtering system and firewall to be aware of.

Hollywood is a town of taboos and even goes against common legal procedures. It's not necessary to put the copyright on the script's title page, okay? Just register your script with the WGA and with the Library of Congress <u>before</u> you submit your script to <u>anyone</u> and it's still protected. You <u>do</u> not need to be a member of the WGA to register scripts. Ask for their brochure on script registration services and their booklet titled, "General Information." By the way, when you submit a script to a production company the release form will normally be asking for the WGA and the Copyright numbers, anyway.

If you live east of the Mississippi River you still register with WGA West. When you write to the Register of Copyrights, you ask for "Form PA." They have a free guidebook all about copyrights. Ask for it. They all have websites. Here are the postal mail addresses;

WGA WRITER'S GUILD AND COPYRIGHT ADDRESSES
--Writer's Guild of America, Dept. J, West 7000 W. Third St., Los Angeles, CA 90048-4329.
--Writer's Guild of America, Dept. J, East 555 W. Fifty-seventh St., New York, NY 10019.
--Register of Copyrights, Washington, D.C. 20559 (202)707-3000 or (800)688-9889.

When you send your script to the WGA for registration, you send it unbound. No staples, no covers, no binding, no brads, no holes punched in paper, etc. Just flat sheets of paper inserted into a bubble or padded envelope. When you send your script to the Register of Copyrights in Washington, D.C. for copyright registration you put covers on it and use three brads to bind the script. You can use any binding method for registering the copyright.

The WGA number should be on your release form and synopsis. Fig. 1-3 shows a General Release form, Fig. 1-4 a synopsis. You would only list one title and WGA number when sending one script with a release. If you're sending two scripts to a prodco, you send two separate releases. Fig. 1-3 is a release form to mail with log lines. It can be used as a release for a script, just list only one script in the heading. Copyright number is not necessary.

Hollywood wants to see the WGA number more than the copyright number. In fact, agents and producers won't even look at a script that is not WGA registered. It's just the way it is. They don't want to get sued. That's why you insert the statement, "All scripts WGAw registered" in your multiple submission query letter or, "Script is WGA registered." The little "w" means it is registered on the West coast. This procedure puts everyone at ease knowing you are professional and have registered your scripts.

Before we begin with actual script writing examples, we are breaking a rule, using the double dash (--) [aka: double hyphen] to identify where the author picks up after reading dialog or directions. This is to avoid confusion, so you'll know the scriptwriting end point. Since this screenwriting software will not insert bullets or other symbols, the double dash was our only practical choice. There is a purpose for using the double dash in scripts. See the subheading: *Words Not To Use In Your Script* on how to use them.

Lone Eagle Publishing has a book titled: *This Business of Screenwriting* It explains how to protect yourself as a screenwriter. See Lone Eagle's contact information at the back of this book.

STREAMLINING YOUR SCRIPT - NEW RULES TO THE GAME
Times are changing so you need to keep up with the trends. Readers have less and less time on their hands (it's never been an easy job) and there are more scripts than readers, especially qualified readers! More white, less ink on the script. The reason is to make the read easy and to motivate executives to read the scripts!

This means most scripts circulating in the loop will need to be rewritten to conform... another filtering device! When readers see the script does not conform, they know instantly not to select that script to take home to read.

Much of what you read in classic screenwriting books and what you learned in film school regarding formatting will need to be revamped to fit the new form. It's easy to do. Don't overlook this, as it is an effective first-glance firewall filtering device.

Get rid of CUT TO, MORE, CONTINUED, FADE-IN (use on first page only) and FADE-OUT (use on last page only), DISSOLVE TO, etc. When dialog is broken across a page, using the parenthetical (cont'd) is okay.

Example:

> FADE IN:
>
> **EXT. JENNIFER'S KITCHEN - DAY**   PRESENT
>
> JENNIFER ANNE STUPIED (38) stumbles to sink, washes face forgetting to turn on water. She stumbles into kitchen table.

-- **Note:** Assume this above entry is the first page. FADE IN: is used. A full slug line EXT. JENNIFER'S KITCHEN - DAY is used. First slug in the script indicates time: PRESENT or DETROIT, SEPTEMBER 2010.

Note: Did you see the error in the slug line? There can be no exterior kitchen! Did you see the other slug line error? The slug line is in bold type. You can't do this! All type is to be non-bold. Uppercase is used for slug lines but never bold. There should be no bold type anywhere in the script!

> JENNIFER
> Who's moving my kitchen?
>
> Her daughter, NANETTE (16) stands by entry, disgusted.
>
> NANETTE
> It was my birthday yesterday.
>
> Nanette turns away, Jennifer yawns.
>
> JENNIFER
> Uh. I think...
> (more)

-- **Note:** If Jennifer's dialog is split in half from prior page it's okay to use (CONT'd) or (more) in the character cue on the next page. The old method was to use CONT'D OR CONTINUED at the top or bottom of the page along with CONTINUING (or more) by the character name.

Next page. No CONT'd at top or bottom of page.

> Jennifer stares hard, finger to her chest.
>
> JENNIFER
> (cont'd)
> What about <u>my</u> birthday?
>
> Nanette frowns with surprised shock.
>
> JENNIFER
> (continuing)
> Nobody thinks of mine... nobody!
>
> Jennifer collapses to floor, pills spill from her nightgown. Beside her under the table is DIANE MAGILL (45) with a wine bottle clutched in folded arms, snores loudly.

-- **Note: Following Example is the Same Page.** You can still use continuing when character breaks across description lines as shown here below if you wish, but it is not necessary. Eliminate the "more's and cont'd" as much as possible. It's just a waste of space and interrupts the reader's thoughts. Let your script flow!

                    JENNIFER
                    (cont'd)
          Hello, Diana.

    Jennifer passes out, table tumbles, she lands on Diane.

-- Use <u>full</u> slug lines on each scene heading.

Example:

          INT. JENNIFER'S ATTIC - DAY

Not:

          JENNIFER'S ATTIC

  -- The latest trend is to use triple-spacing to begin a new slug line instead of double-spacing to give a more airy, cleaner appearance.

  -- Using action in parentheticals is now accepted to save the need to write a description entry. This is so readers and executives will read the brief action since they only read dialog and not descriptions when they read a script. Just make sure the action is really necessary when you use it. Excessive use is considered the work of an amateur.

Example:

                    JENNIFER
                    (trips to floor)
          Ow! Help!

                    NANETTE
                    (gasps, stubs toe)
          Now look what you've done!

                    DIANE
                    (angry)
          She needs help. Help her! You
          worthless daughter!

                    JENNIFER
                    (to Nanette, rubs toe)
          Help, mama!

-- As you an see in the above example, excessive use clutters the dialog, making it harder to read. It would be better not to use this as frequently as shown. Try this,

Example:

                    JENNIFER
               (trips to floor)
          Ow! Help!

Nanette gasps, stubs toe.

                    NANETTE
          Now look what you've done!

                    DIANE
          She needs help. Help her! You
          worthless daughter!

                    JENNIFER
               (to Nanette, rubs toe)
          Help, mama!

-- Description is pared to bare bones.

Example: Don't use.

          Jennifer tosses about the floor in pain but realizes Nanette
          will not help her, so she rolls about on the floor writhing
          in agony always peeking to see Nanette's reaction.

Use this.

          Jennifer sees Nanette is remote. She writhes in exaggerated
          agony for sympathy.

-- Plot point twists for the three-act structure are occurring faster now. Instead of page fifteen, shoot for pages eight to ten. Page twenty-two to twenty-five to begin act two and page eighty to eighty five to start act three.

* Script length is shrinking too, with 105-pages to 110-pages is considered maximum now. It used to be 130, then it was reduced to 120 and now it's 105 to 110. So now all a reader has to do is pick up a script, flip to the last page and, if the page count is 115 or 120, chuck it back into the rejection pile. The reason for the reduced page count is money. Saving ten to fifteen minutes of filming production time will save millions of dollars. Of course, this is not always the case as scripts of 115 to 120 pages will still be read and purchased.

* Fewer main characters are desired. Reason? Cost and to focus more attention on the lead character. It is easier to add characters to a script than to delete them, if more are needed.

Most of the information you read in this manual will be right on the mark, such as condensing your writing to a high-visual concept using a brief punchy-action form, less dialog, less direction, less of everything is more in this business. I've rewritten many of my scripts from the advice I've received from the old screenwriting books to the new form and the coverage scores and acceptance skyrocketed. Yours will too! See subchapter: *Coverage Report - Use This Sample Form To Score Higher Rank.* Fig. 1-28.

Now don't get side-tracked. Many screenwriters purchase shooting scripts from script retailers on the latest movie releases and will not see these new formats and may feel it is not necessary to comply. If you are already an established writer with an historical track record you can write any darn way you please and the industry will accept that. If you're on the outside looking in? You better conform to the new rules or you'll be shivering in the cold hoping someone will invite you inside (and that won't happen).

Just letting you know about these changes is well worth the price of this book in itself. How much money would you have wasted by not following the new rules? Thousands of dollars over the years and the accumulated pain of horrendous rejections.

Stay informed of the new trends. You can do this by subscribing to the many screenwriter's magazines. Basically, once you do catch the drift of condensing everything you possibly can in your scripts, streamlining your writing to eliminate unnecessary weight and maintaining a diligence to keep lots of white space on each page, the rules may change but your script will likely fit right in with the changes anyway. Nothing like doing it right the first time.

Most of these changes are really not new when you think about it. Every screenplay book tells you to cut out the fat. Writers don't listen, so the industry changed the rules to cut these writers out of the market! Think "Lean and Mean" when you write. Think "Action" and you'll do just fine. Never write what you can't see on the screen! An old rule everyone breaks. It's no longer forgivable. Following the instructions in this manual and rewriting your script from 120 pages to 110 will be a breeze, and it'll be a more powerful read.

NO MORE BEATS AND CUT TO'S
Here's an example:

>   NANETTE
>   Mother? I don't approve of your
>   behavior!
>   (beat)
>   What you do embarrasses me to no
>   end to my friends. Leave my
>   boyfriends alone!
>
>   JENNIFER
>   Now, darling.
>   (beat)
>
>   DIANE
>   You call yourself a daughter?
>   It's a mother's right... to test
>   drive a siblings lovers!
>
>   CUT TO:

-- Leave out the beats and cut to's, there is no need for them in the author's script. If you are hired to write a production script, then that is another issue. This includes, "dissolve to" "smash cut," etc. You can place a beat, when it is imperative to do so, but you can use the characters (--) or (...) to obtain the desired result. The point here is to stop trying to control the actors and director! And to make your script read clean and mean.

FIVE BASIC STORY TIPS

This manual is not intended to take the place of a technical screenwriting book. Here are some points to check on your script before you submit. There are no hard and fast rules, though these are considered important.

1. The story should be focused on the journey of one central character. Subplot characters are okay too, but "less is more" still applies in the expensive world of making films. Keep the cost down. Generally, each scene should be focused in some way on the antagonist (enemy) or protagonist (hero). Remember what Mark Twain said, *"If I had more time I would have written less."*

2. The main character should have a compelling need and desire with an opposing character equally intelligent and powerful to obstruct the goal. Both must have strong needs and desires that conflict with each other. This drives the action. Keep clashing them together.

3. The main character usually needs a side-kick mentor to exchange dialog in order to reveal character and action. It could be a true friend or a friend who is really working for the opponent.

4. The main character is always in a tight spot or something bad happens to make him/her fail, struggle and fail again. "The poor thing!" This creates audience identity with the character. The audience (and reader) must care about the hero. A human weakness helps to create sympathy and/or understanding.

5. A final conflict and resolution to the struggle with both characters visually confronting each other in a very big way. All hell breaks loose here. The main character need not change but the better stories always show the hero changing for the better. Hollywood loves a happy ending!

Certainly there are many more elements to consider, but if you at least make sure you have these five, your story should end up with interesting twists and a good read. Later, when you rewrite, you can add in all the other elements. Screenwriting books and computer programs can help you do this easily, this book is not a screenwriting how-to book, just a marketing guide. Read books on how to develop stories and character.

CHAPTER 4

EXCLUSIVE OR NON EXCLUSIVE MULTIPLE SUBMISSIONS?

In the publishing industry for books and magazines it is considered a huge error to mass-mail query letters. It can be done as long as you mention the fact multiple submission is taking place in the query, but it lowers the impact and results.

For screenplays and stage plays you can mail mass queries without any hard feelings whatsoever from just about anyone in this business. So, go right ahead and do it. However, once you do find an agent you want, and want badly, it won't hurt to make an exclusive submission giving the agent 60 days to make a decision to accept or reject the script. If you do this, you should mention the exclusive status in your cover letter. See Fig. 1-25 and Fig. 2-4.

You can also do this with prodcos. It just may help open a door. Some agents may mention on their release forms the submission must be exclusive for the period of time they are to review the script. Don't give everyone exclusive treatment or your scripts will gather cobwebs and... well, just get out there and put those mass-mailing queries on the road.

THEFT OF YOUR MATERIAL - DOES IT REALLY HAPPEN?

Anything's possible, but it's highly unlikely any agent, actor, prodco, or producer will steal your script. They are more concerned about being sued! That's why they have the firewalls and filtering system. Many will not even read your script unless you have an agent. The agent makes sure everything is legal and filters the wheat from the chaff. But if you follow the query letter format given in this manual, it will open doors for you. You'll be surprised just how much more receptive these letters will make the recipients respond to you, requesting your scripts!

It is possible theft of your ideas can take place, but if you wish to keep your script home so nobody can read it, go right ahead. All I can tell you is to forget about theft. Just get your script out there. But, before you do, register your script with the WGA. That is a must! If theft takes place you will have the WGA to verify the completion date. Also, copyright the script by registration with Office of Copyright, Washington, DC. Use form PA. It's easy to remember the form title. It means, "**P**oor **A**uthor". Only kidding!

You will certainly need to sign a production company release form. When you read the release, it will appear you are giving the producer or prodco a license to steal your work. Not so. A firm that asks you to sign a release is not likely to steal anything. So just sign the release and get your script in the mail. It's routine procedure. After you've read a few you'll know if something mighty strange is taking place or not. Never seen a bad one (yet) that doesn't protect the author's rights, too.

What if you signed a weird release from some unknown producer and later found that you gave your script away for free hidden in legalese language? I've never heard of it happening. Anyway, in the eyes of the law a bad contract can never be made good. If any theft does occur, it will likely happen in a few countries overseas. Book and software publishers have the same problem with nations that do not adhere to copyright law, but that does not stop us from publishing. Right?

THEY STOLE MY SCRIPT!

You go to see a movie and see a scene that is just like yours. *"My gosh! They stole my idea!"* Not likely. I call this the "Edison Effect." At any given point in time and space, ideas are floating about the universe. When you conceived your idea, some other writer snatched the same idea. It's real. Alexander Graham Bell and Marconi had similar ideas with other inventors. So did Henry Ford, Diesel, and the list goes on. History is full of patent conflicts. Your idea is not unique, no matter how much you wish to believe so. Do not concern yourself with theft. Just keep writing, register the scripts and get them in the mail. We are all in the same boat.

If you send an agent or prodco a script, and you even included a S.A.S.E. and months go by and your follow-up letters are ignored. You call and that too is ignored. *"Oh, my gosh. They have my script and for all I know they are circulating it to other writers and reworking my ideas."* Forget it. It's likely not happening at all. The script was likely trashed or misplaced or an employee who requested the script left the firm and nobody knows anything or nobody wants to get involved. Just leave it alone. Don't hire a lawyer. Don't file threatening letters. Just let it be and go about your business casting your net in bluer waters.

You will send out scripts and some won't return. It's not theft. It may make you feel terribly uncomfortable and your imagination may run wild with suspicions, but forget about it. It's not worth the grief you put on yourself, and it's not worth having your name plastered around that you are litigation-happy. Scripts do get lost. It really happens.

As long as your script is copyrighted and WGA registered you are protected. Theft is very rare. There are instances in which a lost script resurfaces somewhere years later and gets optioned. So as long as your script is floating around, sleep tight. Don't be paranoid. Okay? Theft happens once in awhile, often by accident, but is still quite rare.

STEALING IDEAS - DON'T FRET ABOUT IT

As a general rule of thumb, the only thing you are really copyrighting is the "expression of content" not specific content. The story title, genre, characters, ideas and even scenes may be similar, and if small changes are made to make each -- just a tad different -- there is no infringement on your copyright. This is how theft can take place, legally.

Everybody's in the same boat, wondering if their scripts will be stolen, so just get in and row. Get your scripts in the mail. Theft is really rare anyway. Some writers will steal ideas, but you are not submitting to writers. Sure, wannabe writers may steal the script from the agent using friend and relative contacts, but professional writers are not going to steal anything from your script. And if they do? Well, there's not much you can do about it, as trying to prove it can be near impossible. You have to prove that writer had direct access to your script.

Every writer steals ideas from others and from the movies. It's not a carbon copy in most instances but a scene that triggers an idea for a new story or a better way of expressing a scene visually. Everybody is bouncing off of one or another, exchanging ideas whether consciously or subconsciously. Film schools unwittingly encourage this practice, since they are showing films to reveal how scenes work. Habits are passed on thereafter. Each movie you see you are learning to steal an idea. Everybody is learning from the ideas of others. That's what textbooks do, give knowledge from other sources. So, we all learn borrowing ideas and knowledge from each other.

Here's the good news. Writers who steal ideas usually have bad scripts anyway and they go nowhere. Best advice? Use your own imagination when developing scenes. Use your own creative powers. If you get stuck with writer's block? Sometimes going to see a movie similar to your script's genre will give you an idea to unblock yourself.

Another method used for idea theft is when unscrupulous producers, directors and illegitimate production companies advertising for scripts in the major trade magazines and newsletters seeking scripts. Everybody sends a script then never hears from the firm or person again. Who cares? Since your work is registered with the WGA and Copyright Office, it should be of no major concern to you. But you should not have sent your script out in the first place! Here's some advice;

1. When you see an ad from an unknown producer, director, etc., asking for scripts, check the ad for the producer's name. No name? Red flag #1.

2. Is there a full street address or just a post office box? No street address? Red flag #2.

3. Is this the first time you've seen this ad in the past two years? If so, it's red flag #3.

4. If the ad is saying "send scripts" that is red flag #4. Especially when a producer, director, actor's agent or production company is advertising, since they are not requesting a release form!

5. An ad with only a phone number to call and no address? This is red flag #5. It is likely the person you talk with will be soliciting to you a movie deal. After you submit the script to them, they call you informing they can do the deal, but the script needs rewriting, and they only use ABC Scriptwriting Consultants, or whatever, for $1,000. It's a hustle to get you to part with your money. The movie deal never materializes.

Let's assume the advertisement is still pulling your strings and you want to submit? Simply send a query letter. Legitimate firms will respond, others will not. What if you send the script and never hear from them again? They don't return your phone calls or lie to you on the phone? They never respond to follow-up mailings? They moved? Forget it and move on.

You could file a brief "issue of concern" to the magazine or newsletter explaining the situation. The magazine may or may not give you the firm's phone number, address, or person's name, etc. All you can do is put a "paper trail" on the firm to report the activity. Overall, it's not even worth doing that. These firms change names and simply do it again.

Who are these people? Pitchmen. They are idea sellers. They steal ideas, pitch them for sale and move on to the next script idea. Ideas are not copyrighted, only the unique expression of the idea. If you send a query letter, the pitchmen may have your idea just from that alone, especially if you send a synopsis.

When dealing with unknowns, just send a simple "request to submit script" query giving no details. Pitchmen hate paper trails! They won't respond to the query. But don't let these scams stop you from submitting your scripts. There will always be scams of one sort or another and you should not become petrified by them. Register your work and keep on submitting to legitimate firms.

A WORD ON THE S.A.S.E.

It is mandatory and not an option for the writer to fail to send a #10 size S.A.S.E with query letters. It is not mandatory to include a S.A.S.E. when sending a script, but mention this fact on your query letter that you do not want your script returned. You certainly don't want the agent or prodco to think you forgot to include the S.A.S.E. or are ignorant of business protocol. See Fig. 1- 15 and Fig. 1-14.

There is no reason why you should even include a "Script S.A.S.E." unless you really want your script returned as a security blanket. It would be better to not have it returned, as it may accidentally fall into the right hands! A rejected script about to be trashed somehow finds its way to a producer or executive and a green light is turned on. Anything can happen in Hollywood!

New rule in the making: No script S.A.S.E.'s required! Since the postal service is enacting an anti package-bomb regulation, heavy movie and play scripts can no longer just be plunked into a mailbox. The agent or producer must now stand in line at the post office to mail it back to you. This could really leave a bad impression upon you, depending on the mood of the mailer. However, follow specific instructions by the agent or prodco. If they want the script S.A.S.E., send it. One thirty minute TV script is light weight, so the S.A.S.E. is not a hassle to mail.

Other good reasons not to have your script returned? It is likely outdated, since you have rewritten it, and the cost to print a new script is just about as expensive as postage to have it returned to you. Scripts are returned in damaged condition, so print a new, clean script for each submission! And, stop worrying about it being stolen. There is nothing you can do to prevent it, and it rarely happens.

THE LIFE OF A READER

Years ago, writers used typewriters and it was not easy to format a perfect script. Today, people go to the movies and say to themselves, *"I could write a better movie than that."* Now everybody is in on the act, submitting scripts due to the ease of computers and their spell-checking software. Consequently, thousands of scripts, 160,000+ per year arrive in Hollywood. Swamped is the word. So multi-level filtering is required to discard the weeds. The first and most critical filter is the unseen reader, whether you have an agent or not. This is the major firewall.

When you write your script and send it out to an agent, production house, producer, or director, it will be read by a reader who will make the first level judgement for the firm to accept or reject the script. So, it is imperative when you write your script to entertain the reader. Keep this thought in mind and your battle is nearly won.

Another problem is that many readers are simply incompetent in evaluating the true essence of the story you have written. Incredibly, most are not trained to do this. So make your story compelling to the point they can easily read it and understand the plot. It has been said more than once that readers are disgruntled writers looking for an excuse to reject the script.

The truth is, they are looking for reasons to reject the script regardless of their competency level. However, each one is looking for a story that will entertain them. If your script is a good read, you have your foot in the door. And just because twenty readers didn't like your script doesn't mean it's a bad script. Plenty of hit movies were rejected for many years until someone with "brights" said, "Yes." *Star Wars* was one of the them, so were *Terminator I and II*. Amazing, but true. The filtering system is highly imperfect.

Now why would a reader want to reject a script? Readers are paid $30 to $50 to read and give coverage (written evaluation) on a script. If the reader recommends a script it had better be good, otherwise the reader may be looking for another job. So there is risk in saying "Yes." [Hmmm! Getting paid to reject scripts. Seems we are in the wrong business?]

Readers have a tough, demanding job. They often go home at night with five scripts to read. That's a lot of reading to do in one night. How do they do it? Easy, just read the dialog. They can tell from the dialog if the story is flowing properly and if the dialog is exciting to read. If so, the reader will scan some of the directions you've written. Never knowing where the reader will pick up on the directions, all of it had better be brief and visual.

More or less, every reader is direly searching for new talent or a script they can recommend. Opinions differ on this, but they do want to find that sparkling gem. Every reader is looking to be entertained and hoping, just hoping, one of the twenty scripts they read each week will turn them on and transport them into another world.

Imagine if you had to read twenty scripts each week, year after year. Would you be so patient to forgive formatting and misspelling errors? Be honest. Frankly, they can't. So why do we continue to send them sloppy scripts? One reason is because we just don't know how to write scripts that entertain and meet marketing factors. Another reason is the script is too heavy.

EXAMPLE:

> JOHN stands on the edge of a fabulously high skyscraper with the sun blazing in his face. MARY stands, looking mean, then steps forward with an object in her hand that glistens in the sun. As she passes by the camera a shadow forms. John suddenly sees the object. We see it is a knife. He begins to leap off the skyscraper, then leaps.

-- What is wrong with the above direction paragraph? It is more than four lines in length. You could split the paragraph in two, but it's still too heavy with many errors. A reader would toss the script into the rejection can at this point. It screams amateur. So why bother reading the rest of the script?

-- Key words that should <u>not</u> be used are; fabulously, stands, looking, object, camera, suddenly, we see, begins.

SOLUTION:

> JOHN's at the edge of the skyscraper squinting in the sun. MARY approaches, knife in hand. John leaps off the building.

-- See how easy that was? We don't need to explain about the shadow. We know John can't see well because he's squinting, but at some point he does see well and leaps off the building. Let the director fill in these blanks. If shadow must be in the line, use "shadowy knife in hand."

More tips on specific words never to use in your scripts, later. For now, read your script and see if you can cut the directions down in size. **Basic rule:** Directions must be "action" oriented, not static descriptions. You are not writing a book. Let the set designers do their job. Your job is to tell a story "visually" to please the reader.

We all try to write great stories, and they are not all great. Just do the best you can do with the skills you now have. Keep the costs down as much as you possibly can when you write your stories. Low and medium budget increases the odds of a purchase. If you're working on a Jimmy Bond Jr. film, then go for the splash and fireworks. Even then, why travel the world? Jimmy could stay is Los Angeles and save lots of money.

Rule: Huge budget movies are made by established professionals. Few are bought on spec by unknowns (but it does happen).

DIALOG:

Here's an example of Mary speaking to John.

> MARY
> Go ahead and jump, John. You're
> going to hell where you belong.
>
> JOHN
> Leave me alone. You know I don't
> love you anymore. I hate you and
> the world. There is nothing left
> for me to live for. Please,
> please, listen to me. It was an
> accident. I didn't mean to do it,
> put the knife down.

--The above conflicting dialog is not only confusing and lousy, it is unnecessary because the directions told the story visually. Go ahead, read the directions again. We know John doesn't love her, he's afraid of her. He doesn't love the world or himself because he's committing suicide.

A man on the edge of a building being chased by a woman with a knife would plead for mercy, but it's wasted dialog and silly because we have it written in the script he will jump. Frankly, nothing need be said. So get rid of Mary and John's dialog.

If you want to punch a tad of comedy or purpose in this scene you could use the following line of dialog just after John leaps to his death.

>   MARY
>   One down, two to go.

Now we know Mary is a brutal killer and she has an agenda. We are set up to wonder who the other two people may be. It pushes the story forward, reveals her character and gives vital information. That is the purpose of dialog.

See where you can eliminate useless dialog that fails to push the story forward or reveal character in your scripts. Chop out the fat. Make the script lean and mean with lots of fast action.

If you slow down the reader it creates turmoil and the revenge is a rejection slip. It's a cold-hearted business. But remember, suspense should also be an integral element in fast action scenes, so we (reader or audience) are not quite certain what will happen next to the characters.

There are plenty of books on how to write dialog. What we need is actual examples of good and bad dialog. Keep reading, they are coming. You will see how easy it is to combine emotion, action, power and purpose to dialog.

When you see a movie, the dialog can often be yucky breaking all the rules. This doesn't mean you should do this, as the original authors' script was rewritten to appease somebody else but the audience.

Stay with the basic rules described above and your dialog will have power, purpose and meaning. Chit-chatting talking-heads on screen drag the story down. Use a direct approach to set up the story if dialog must be excessive.

Here's a direct approach example of a hit woman for the mob. We start it off with her looking into the camera. Notice that no camera shot advice is given; CLOSE IN, PULL BACK, TIGHT ON, etc. Never use camera angles in an author script!

EXAMPLE:

MARY stares at us casually filing her nails.

>   MARY
>   I'm not a bad girl. It's just a
>   job, like any job. Sure I have
>   bad days, but if I felt like
>   taking a day off I'd be pushin'
>   daisies just like my customers.
>   Working for the mob is exciting.

Still too stuffy. So let's try this,

> MARY
> (continuing)
> The Mafia isn't evil. It's a business of integrity, built on trust and honor. If you transgress this sacred reverence, you'll deal with me. I kill. That's my job. Now people believe that's murder. The local supermarkets are in the killing business. Butchers too. Why would you care if I killed a cow or a rat? What's the difference?

-- The above dialog is longer than the first, but it's telling us a lot more about Mary's character and her purpose. From this point we just go right on into the story. You can later use another method called the Voice Over(V.O.) to get the story moving. For example, we want to know who Mary works for and her next mission. We can do it like this.

EXT. LUCIANNA'S CAFE / NEW YORK CITY - DAY

Tough-skinned SALVO LUCIANNA (60) exits a limo with bodyguards. He argues with FRANCESEE CAPOTE (40).

> MARY (V.O.)
> Salvo Lucianna, that's my boy. Takes no trash from underlings. Now, that pork-chop, Francesee Capote? He's got a date with me, he don't know it yet.

Lucianna pins Capote against wall.

> MARY (V.O.)
> (continuing)
> Funerals makes me depressed, so I don't go.

-- See how one or two voice overs riding over the action can eliminate tons of dialog in your script in the first fifteen pages. The purpose is to jump-start the story and get right down to business. There is no need to explain page after page why Mary is a hit man for the mob. The audience will want to know, so somewhere in the script you can put a tad of back story in like this,

> MARY
> At least you had a mother. It's scum like you who create people like me.

-- This dialog tells much that Mary had a hard life on the streets with no guidance and she's envious of other people who have had a better life than her.

See if you can simplify the back story in your script. You'll likely eliminate a few pages and add in more pages of exciting action in its place.

WORDS NOT TO USE IN YOUR SCRIPT

As promised, here are the ugly words, the dangerous words to use in any script for the visual arts. Any reader who sees these words will likely frown. Story editors will reach for the antacid pills and reject the script. If any of these words are in your scripts, get 'em outta there!

1. No passive words or words ending with: is, ing, are, ed, begin to, start, have, had, have been, will be, etc.

Example: John is about to turn the corner, and will be, when he's seeing Mary beginning to move at him with the machete.

Solution: John turns corner as Mary moves toward him with machete. Sometimes, "ing" has to be used, but try to minimize them.

2. No asides or editorial talk in description: If you can't see it, don't write it. Show don't tell.

Example: If John could, he would run from Mary, but something is holding him in place. Something I will reveal later in the story.

Solution: John's belt is snagged on the machine, he struggles to free himself as Mary closes in for the kill.

3. No similes. Words such as: like, as, as if.

Example: Mary tenderly placed the roses in a vase as if she loved them.

Solution: Mary gently slips red roses in a blue vase. (Color is visual so use color in descriptions if the color has significance to reveal a mood or intensify something.)

4. No mysteries or surprises. Introduce characters by name and age when they appear. The director needs to know who is who in the script. The audience will not know who they are unless it is explained in dialog or a visual location or occupation or action is described.

Example: A rugged character we've never seen before creeps along the alley ready to pounce on John.

Solution: Tough guy JACOB BLAKE (45) creeps up on John in the alley.

5. No suddenly, incredibly, disappears, amazingly.

Example: Suddenly, John spins around and incredibly Jacob disappears.

Solution: John spins around. Jacob is gone, hidden behind a trash bin.

6. No camera angles or camera directions. Your script is an author's script, not a shooting script. Let the director do his job.

Example: Camera swings low and tracks John as Mary kicks him in the butt.

Solution: Mary kicks John in the butt.

7. Never put in these words: we see, we hear, we notice, we know, we are, etc.

Example: We are at Central Park. We see John and Mary argue as we hear the sirens blare.

Solution: John and Mary argue MOS as ambulance siren screams o.s. (o.s. means a <u>sound</u> off screen. We never see the ambulance, though we do hear it. It is mostly used for sounds not made by character voices and is used in description. Normally, you don't have to use o.s. at all. V.O. is mostly used for <u>voices</u> in dialog.

Remember, no surprises for the director. Let him/her know who is screaming. MOS means no voice and it is always capitalized. We see them argue but hear no voices.

Example:

                    MARY (MOS)
              Shouts to her dog.

-- Screenwriting books will explain these devices.

8. No excessive use of multiple punctuation?!, semicolons (;) or ellipses (...).

Example: John's in deep trouble! Jacob and Mary have him boxed in.

                    JOHN
          All right! You win! Why can't
          you leave me alone?! You...
          you... know I'm innocent-- I've
          been setup!

Solution:

      John's jaw sinks as Jacob and Mary close in.

                    JOHN
          All right, you win. I've been set
          up. I'm innocent.

-- See how the fat was melted out of the directions and the dialog? Less is more. The ellipses (...) is used when the character has a change of thought. The double hyphen dash (--) is used when the character is abruptly interrupted. It was used improperly in the above example.

Example:

>   JOHN
>   Mary, I... look. I was wrong,
>   okay? I didn't mean to --
>
>   MARY
>   Shut up!

-- There is very little need for ellipses, double hyphens (double dash), and exclamation points. You can use them, but make sure they have a purpose. Some writers go hog wild and the character sounds like a babbling moron. All things are good, in moderation.

A rule you should try to retain is only one or two of the above devices per page, if at all. Anything more could be excessive. If one page has a few of them, try to go the next page or two without any. Eliminate as many as you possibly can. Actors also don't like them. If your character is supposed to be confused and seeking change of thought you could use them, but it's better to just mention that fact than bust up the dialog throughout the script to make it difficult to read.

S-s-s-s-stutter-ing is also an overused item. Though i-i-t c-c-c-an s-s-s-erve a p-p-p-p-urpose, it is difficult to read and upsets the reader, something you don't ever want to do.

Note the double dash (--) in dialog. This is used to indicate conversation is abruptly interrupted.

>   MARY
>   You -- Bozo! How many times have
>   I -- Get away, shoo! You are not
>   the same man I married.

-- The example above is in total error. You should use ellipsis for change of thougt interruptions, not the double dash! The example that follows reveals John being interrupted by Mary using the double dash, and Mary having a second-thought pause with a change in her tone of voice using the ellipsis.

>   JENNIFER
>   Now wait a minute here --
>
>   SAMANTHA
>   You listen to me, darling.
>   Betrayal is never forgiven... you
>   knew the rules.
>
>   JENNIFER
>   Know what your problem is... huh?
>   Huh? You should be happy, that's
>   what!

> SAMANTHA
> I'm not happy unless I'm pissed off!

-- The ellipsis (...) is used to reveal an interruption of thought and the double-dash (--) is used to interrupt the conversation. The underlined word (not) is used to inform the actor to emphasize a word and is often used in punch lines for jokes, but it is wise to use them sparingly, if at all. The double dash can also be used in direction to break up series of shots.

> SERIES OF SHOTS
>
> -- Mary enters clothing store, exits with bags of goods.
>
> -- John runs along railroad track, train hot on his tail.
>
> -- Mary hails a taxi, not one stops.
>
> -- John leaps off railroad bridge, splashes in river.
>
> -- Mary hurls shopping bags at traffic. Cops chase her.

9. No large blocks of descriptive action.

Example:

> Mary flings ice pick into John's face as Jacob fires up his blowtorch, melting his nose. John's screams echo into the alley. DON CORMIER (40) taking out his trash, hears the screams, races to assist, freezes, sees entire alley explode in flames blocking his entrance.

Solution: Just split the dialog in two logical points. No more than four lines. Remember, less is more.

> Mary flings ice pick into John's face as Jacob fires up his blowtorch, melting his nose. John's screams echo in the alley.
>
> DON CORMIER (40) taking out his trash, hears the screams, races to assist, freezes, sees entire alley explode in flames blocking his entrance.

Solution: It's still not quite right. Let's rewrite it.

> Mary flings ice pick into John's face as Jacob ignites a blowtorch, melting John's nose. Screams echo.
>
> DON CORMIER (40) takes out trash, hears John's scream o.s., races to assist, freezes as alley explodes in flames.

-- It's tighter now and easier to read with plenty of visual action. Get the idea? You could eliminate the o.s. Notice we eliminated two words ending in "ing" and the word "sees."

You don't have to copy this punchy style of writing. You can if you want to. It is a valid form. The author has received many complements from readers and studio executives for doing so and the writing form has placed high in screenwriting contests using this abbreviated action-oriented form of writing.

Use your own flair if you wish, just try to cut unnecessary words and keep the action moving forward. Remember, one page = one minute of film time. If script is heavy with description or dialog, the page timing will be out of synchronization. But regardless of writing style, out go the "ing" "ed" "we see" etc., words.

Consider the "I Spy" comic in Mad magazine. No words are used. It's all action and tells a story like a silent movie in a very brief amount of time. If you write briefly, you can be as visual as the comic cartoon. It's this sort of visual writing readers are seeking. Easy to read and full of meaningful action to push the story forward.

10. Always use complete slug lines (scene headings) and let the description point to the next slug line if at all possible. See if you can find the errors here.

Example:

>   INT. GENERAL HOSPITAL OF NEW YORK
>
>   JOHN is rushed to the emergency room.
>
>   INT. EMERGENCY ROOM
>
>   JOHN's clothing smells of burned flesh, still smoldering from
>   the blazing inferno he endured.

-- The slug lines above are not complete. We don't know if it's day or night. Emergency room is repeated, once in directions and again in the slug line. Audience can't smell burned flesh watching the movie. We know he's been burned, as we saw this in the previous scene, so there is no need to add in the words, "...the blazing inferno he endured."

Solution:

>   EXT. GENERAL HOSPITAL / NEW YORK - NIGHT
>
>   JOHN is rushed to,
>
>   INT. EMERGENCY ROOM - NIGHT
>
>   JOHN's clothes smolder.

-- See how easy that was? Less is more. The reader knows where we are, it's night, and the action is brisk and precise. The first slug line above was changed to EXTERIOR to give even more of a panic mode to the scene. There is no need to describe hospital or paramedic characters, the ambulance, weather conditions, etc. Keep your script lean!

11. No "CONTINUED" or "CONTINUING" at the top and bottom of pages. This was acceptable years ago, but times have changed.

12. No titles at top of pages. Only the page number, please. Top right side. See examples in the illustration pages of this book.

13. No scripts over 120 pages and no less than 90 pages. Less than 90 indicates the story isn't complete for a feature film. More than 120 reveals there is too much clutter in the script for a two hour movie. The new trend is 110 to 115 pages. Remember, one page per minute is the timing sequence for screenplays. A sitcom is 40 to 46 pages per 20-minutes (approximately 2 pages per minute for 1/2 hour show).

Note: Commercials take up ten-minutes, or more. Each TV show will have its own format and pacing requirements. A stage play is a tad longer than a screenplay and can go 120 to 135 pages for a two-hour performance with intermissions. MOW's a.k.a. Made for Television Movie are usually 90 to 100 pages (90-minutes for two hour movie commercials take up 20 to 30 minutes of time.

14. No endless dialog (called "I" pages) or pages with no dialog. If dialog is important, break it up with descriptive one-liners like this.

BREAKING UP DIALOG - HOW TO DO IT

INT. EMERGENCY ROOM - NIGHT

Mary barges in, shoves nurses aside. John's eyes wide.

                MARY
    Hello, my love. I have something
    for you.

Mary reveals a hypodermic needle.

                MARY
        (continuing)
    Relax. You won't feel a thing,
    babe.

John screams into his oxygen mask as Mary injects his jugular.

-- If that gave you a chill, then that's how you want to write your lines so the reader can feel the story actually happening. Be vivid and daring. You can always tone down the script later or after you sell it. Gory stuff gets people's attention wether they like it or not. Here we were merciful. We could have written the needle was stuck in John's eye! The story is a bloody nightmare. Mary's a cold witch. Do you get the picture? Let's switch to comedy in the following examples.

-- Continuing is <u>not</u> necessary in dialog above.

-- Break the <u>action</u> with dialog if dialog can push the story forward, reveal character or vital information.

-- Break <u>dialog</u> with visual action.

See how the above paragraphs are broken down to make it easier to read? Lots of white space here. That's how you write your script. Readers will love you for it and they'll read the script because it's so easy and pleasing.

15. No spelling errors. Grammar should be at 12th grade level. Here are three books you should read; Strunk & White *The Elements of Style*, *The Elements of Grammar*, and *Woe Is I*. All are small, easy to read books. Contact Writer's Digest Book Club or any bookstore.

Note: Keep in mind missing words seem to vaporize into space, so check all your query letters and scripts for these red demons, they stand out like a sore thumb. Be very afraid of missing words and letters, spelling and grammar errors. Everybody makes these mistakes, even proofreaders and editors! Nobody is perfect. But you can't afford to make these mistakes, okay?

16. Capitalize sounds like, BANG. You can use exclamations on sound effects, BANG! There is no need to cap the sounds of boom, bang, crash and clunk if you don't want to, but most writers do it as standard practice. Capitalize when important characters are first introduced in the script with age following, JOHN STANFORD (45).

The author capitalizes each important character in each scene, but you don't have to do this; it's his style. Do not capitalize minor characters like, a crowd of PEOPLE walk by or a WOMAN gawks at them. It's okay if the person has important significance, but it can distract the reader if overused. Writers make these mistakes because they read shooting scripts where all characters are capped, then assume this is the correct way to write an author script.

17. Get rid of the personal direction parentheticals, or use them sparingly. Professional actors despise them. Give them the freedom to create the motivation and expression. If you are writing a stage play and intend to debut the project in a local theater, then more description and directions may be necessary as the actors are sometimes amateur and will need the guidance.

DIRECTIONAL PARENTHETICALS

Not a good idea to use too many. Use only when you believe the actor needs guidance. General rule? About ten per script. Some producers want as many as you can write! Your spec script should have few. It is considered a bad move to give any advice to actors in a script! When you need to, here's an example.

Example:

                    JOHN
               (looking at Mary)
          Why is it every time I try to talk
          to you, you slap me?

                    MARY
               (eyes squinting)
          Because, I love you.

Solution:

John turns to Mary.

>   JOHN
>   My mother never told me marriage
>   would be like this.

Mary delivers a cynical expression as she grabs a rolling pin.

>   MARY
>   That's because we are girls, John.
>   Girls are not meant to be
>   understood. Now take out the
>   trash like a good boy.

John stoops to pick up trash, drops contents to floor. Mary stares with anger.

>   JOHN
>   (eyes roll up)
>   You constipated again?

>   MARY
>   (hands to hips)
>   I want to be constipated! My
>   entire life I've been --
>   (remorse)
>   Flushed away into oblivion by
>   people like you
>   (anger)
>   who are never constipated, ever!

-- As you can see, parentheticals are really not needed and the action is breaking up the dialog. A tad of subtext is in Mary's dialog prior to dumping the trash. What she's really saying is, "Shut up and obey me."

Many readers look for subtext, dialog that is saying something that means another thing. In essence, we should even eliminate, "Girls are not meant to be understood." Read it again with the deletion. Sound better?

You can use parentheticals, especially when three or more characters are speaking, but the script will read so much better if you refrain at all costs to not use them. Just a handful per script will do.

Example:

>   JOHN
>   Men have a higher purpose in life
>   than to serve the whims of women.

>   PARROT
>   Awk! Dumbo, speaks.

                    JOHN
                 (to parrot)
            Shut-up.

                    MARY
                 (to parrot)
            You're a good girl.

     Mary kisses parrot. John fumes.

                    JOHN
            I'm speaking to you.

                    MARY
                 (to John, sharply)
            Look at my feet when you speak to
            me!

-- Parentheticals come in handy if properly used. Just don't use them
to try to tell the actor how to act. Even the word "sharply" could be
removed. The actor may be able to pull off the line with more comedy by
speaking in a whisper or exploding with rage. Give them freedom to
create. In parenthesis, don't capitalize words (except character names)
and don't put in periods. A comma is okay. Also, a parenthical should
never roll over to the next line. It must be brief as shown.

   The comedic dialog above is not a joke and some readers would not
catch the significance, but an actor would, and they have the power to
get movies made! The dialog allows the actors explosive creativity to
execute the comedy scene. A strong superiority struggle is taking place
which generates powerful comedy.

   Writers make the mistake of trying to direct the director and
manipulate the actors. Just write your story and let the cast do their
job. Certainly, we do tell actors what to say and do in the script, but
let them determine <u>how</u> to do it, because after you please the reader,
you must please the actors; otherwise they will pass on the script and
your movie gets rejected or slides into development hell. That's also
why you put no camera angles in your script. It drives directors up the
walls!

18.   If you must direct the camera, do it like this.

     Wall clock ticks onward as John scrubs the floor.

                    JOHN
                 (to himself)
            Who made her boss, anyway?

     Parrot smiles. Mary listens by the entry.

                    MARY (V.O.)
                 (mimics parrot)
            Awk! You married the bitch.

-- This tells the director time is of the essence, so put the camera on
the wall clock, then to the parrot, to Mary, then to John. The director

knows what he's doing; it's his job to interpret the scene. Yes. Parrots can smile with special effects (SPFX) No need to write in <u>sound</u> effect (SFX) as it is obvious. Use these sparingly, if at all. I <u>try</u> never to use them. All they do is distract the reader. I'll use them in a stage play as it helps point out the booms and bangs, but not always.

19. When writing numbers in dialog or directions a general guide is to spell out all numbers less than one-hundred and numerically display numbers over 100. You can spell them all out, but be consistent in character's dialog throughout the script.

SPELLING OUT NUMBERS IN THE SCRIPT - THE RULES

Example:

>   MARY
> Don't jump a sixteen-foot cliff
> over a one-thousand foot canyon.
> Think, man. Think!

The next example is okay as it applies to the rule (see #19 above).

>   JOHN
> For the second time since five-
> twenty a.m. I've asked you to give
> me 200 dollars so I can buy
> underwear.

-- Now when you look at both examples above, it's not consistent. So pick the one you like and stay with that style throughout the script. Some readers are very picky about these little things. Now you know.

DEADLY WORDS TO AVOID IN YOUR SCRIPT

20. More words to avoid in directions: because, anyway, however, that, could. So-called useless words. Readers will pick up on these errors and when they do, your script feels heavy to hold in hand. When that happens the script is put down.

Example:

> John trips because trash is on that floor. He could move
> left to avoid Mary, but he doesn't anyway, because the parrot
> is wildly flying back and forth blocking his only exit.

-- Try it this way.

Solution:

> John avoids Mary and trips on the trash. Parrot repeatedly
> swoops upon John blocking his exit.

-- Let's get rid of the "blocking" word, and others.

> John avoids Mary, trips on trash, blocks exit. Parrot swoops low.

-- Can be confusing so let's try a longer description.

> John trips on trash as he avoids Mary's flailing hands. His exit blocked by trash, parrot swoops and rips a piece of John's hair, OW! OUCH!

-- No good. We are back again with the "ing" and "ed" words, though description is longer it reads better. How do we get rid of the "ed" word? We can't use "sealed" "foiled" "obstructed" so we do this:

> Mary's hands bat John as he trips on trash. No escape. Parrot swoops, rips John's hair, OW!

-- Avoid the "ing" and "ed" words. It's okay to use them, just do so sparingly. If you can work them out of the description, your writing will get higher marks with readers, and that's exactly what you want when marketing your script.

One major agency became so fed up with these "ing" "ed" and "other useless wordage" infections, they won't even read a script if it has any past tense structured wordings... a pure rejection no matter how good the story! At least they are honest about it. How many readers have trashed scripts because of this disease and the poor writer never knew why the scripts were rejected? Thousands of writers. May be your script too!

MORE VALUABLE MARKETING TIPS ON SCREENWRITING

1. Be aware of costs when writing your script. If you have locations in Rome, Africa, Canada and Sahara desert, try to change locations to Washington DC, Los Angeles Zoo, Mohave Desert. Be aware of the logistical aspect of shooting a film; it costs money. The less money it costs, the higher the odds of your movie getting made. Think low budget.

Keep in mind night scenes cost more than daytime scenes, four times more. Water scenes are very expensive, especially under water. Water in the background is okay. Explosions cost a small fortune. Could a standard gasoline fire do the same as the explosion? Do we need a fire? Minimize your locations, too many speaking characters 10+, firearms, stunts, night scenes, bad weather and crowd scenes, animals and children, etc. Screenwriting books generate more tips on reducing costs.

2. Don't follow trends. If theaters are showing Westerns, don't write a Western to enhance your odds. There is a method you can use. The Hollywood Reporter lists films in production. Here you can see a snapshot of what sort of films will be presented next year, and what Hollywood is most likely wanting today. The author noticed prison movies were being made, and jail-related scripts were eagerly requested when queried to prodcos. This method does work. But it is not recommended to see what is currently in demand and then try to write a script to match the market.

The market will always outpace you and nobody knows what the blockbuster market will be next week, never mind next year. It's nice to know which direction the market may go next year, but if you try to out-guess the market, it will prove to be a big let down and a waste of your time. If you already have a Western and you notice prodcos are doing Westerns, you have "reacted" to the market, not gambled with it. By all means get your script in the mail!

It doesn't hurt to have multiple genre scripts in your portfolio so you can respond when opportunity knocks. Many professionals advise to specialize in one genre. Opinions vary as everyone is right. There is no argument on specializing and becoming the best there is in that field you choose. Sometimes you have to branch out and try a few to see what genre you can do best. When you find it, then master it.

Hollywood Reporter, Dept. A, 5055 Wilshire Blvd., Los Angeles, CA 90036 (213)525-2000 Ask for a sample issue. You may want to subscribe or ask your library to do so. Ultimately, you should not time the markets, because if you're writing solely for the money and your heart is not into the story it will show up in your writing.

3. If you want a lesson in screenwriting try writing a 2-hour, 120 page low budget script or a stage play where everything must happen in a confined space. Who said screenwriting was easy? If you write big budget scripts, the story had better be compelling to a wide audience. Locations, night scenes, and explosions must have a greater purpose other than just visual effects. Good examples are the Star Trek, Babylon Five, and Deep Space Nine television series. Confined space, but the story is always good along with all the special effects and costumes that actually do little to tell the story, but add visual intrigue. TV writers should get more respect as they write tight.

Pitfall: Don't write a story just because it is presumed that is what Hollywood is looking for now. Write what you believe in; otherwise, it shows up in the script as being just a writer trying to make a fast buck. It usually doesn't work. Write a story from the heart. That's what really counts and opens doors. You don't have to time the markets.

4. Most scripts are just rehashed stories of another film. People get ideas and believe they can make a new movie based on a film that was very successful. Hollywood has seen it all, so don't try to hoodwink them. Yes, it is done, but usually by the prodcos and established writers. Be original in your scripts. Show them something that was never before seen on the silver screen. A story so unique it generates interest. Make your own heat! Then again, Hollywood likes movies that are "similar" to past movies that did well at the box office. Find a happy medium here. Add a new angle or twist, but be original.

5. When calling out for music in your script, be aware if you do call for numerous top-40 artists, a producer will likely pass as the royalty costs will be expensive. It's better to imply like this so the producer sees options and suggestions;

> John and Mary dance to music similar to "Newborn Friend" by Seal.

6. Character description should be visually brief.

   Example:

   MARY BEE CANARY (29) is beautiful, wearing fine clothes, bright red lipstick and hair shine women would kill for. In fact, she is a killer.

That's too much description and tells us nothing. Actresses are beautiful, will wear fine clothes, lipstick, nice hair, and we can't see she's a killer on the screen. Here's a better way to do it.

   Solution:

   MARY BEE CANARY (32) has the face of an angel with an attitude of a tiger.

7. If the trend is less violence, write less violence. Violence must have a specific purpose in the story anyway. Too many scripts have violence just for visual effect but no real relevance to the story. Why kill when you can maim or use threat to kill? You could financially ruin a person instead of killing. Research alternatives to death.

8. All genres -- action, comedy, thriller, etc. -- can sell, but think of the market base when you write a script. Horror has a small market compared to romantic comedy. If you write the expensive action film, you've limited the market to only the large studios. If you write lower budget, hundreds of prodcos and producers are now available and will be much more receptive to looking at your script. **Solution:** Write both. Have some low and high budget scripts in your portfolio of available projects. Don't write a high-budget screenplay then mention in your query or cover letter you can rewrite it to low budget or visa versa.

9. Important redundancy. Before mailing your cover letter, query, log lines or script, proofread them for errors. Always enclose a S.A.S.E. with all submissions. This could be just a standard #10 size S.A.S.E. or the larger size for the script (if you want the script returned). If you don't want the script returned then use the #10 size S.A.S.E. Be habitual about this. Check the script pages to insure they are numbered properly (no blank sheets inserted by printer error or missing sheets). Is the ink/toner printing dark and fresh? Don't send a muddied script. Check all pages to insure the printer printed each page crisply. Staple nothing to the script. Don't use staples on mailing envelopes. Use clear packaging sealing tape You don't want the recipient to cut their fingers or hands. Always include a release when sending a script (most agents don't need a release though some do) and mark the envelope indicating the script is requested and a release is enclosed. Don't use splashy stationery or script covers. Bind the script with brass brads. Follow the established rules.

10. Do not put any camera angle shots in the script and never number the scenes. Most scripts sold to the public are *shooting* scripts, not *author* scripts. Many books tell readers to read scripts to learn how to write scripts and fail to inform the reader not to copy the format of the shooting script! This is why so many agents keep telling writers in

magazine interviews not to number the scenes or reveal camera directions.

11. Don't get carried away with underlining what you believe are key words to emphasize in character's dialog. Often, if you read the script aloud you can remove many underscores. Use them to assist in hitting a word in a joke or to identify a word with a double meaning. They are okay to use, just don't get carried away. Words are not capitalized or bold in dialog (Help!) as they can be in direction (**HELP!**) Best **not** to bold any word in the script.

12. Some crossover of dialog in direction is allowed, but keep it to a bare minimum.

Example:

>   Little Beany screams, HELP! The baboon growls and nips his heels.

-- Using this technique saves space in a script to maintain pacing. If you wrote like this,

>   LITTLE BEANY
>   Help!
>
>   BABOON
>   Grrrr!

-- Every time a character yelps a plea, the script will grow heavy in page count. At the same time, valuable story content is consumed by the wasted space. For this reason you can add small elements (one word) of dialog in action (direction).

You can crossover sounds that are normally in direction to dialog like this.

>   LITTLE BEANY
>   (hears explosion,)
>   I'm gettin' outta this forest.
>   (branch snaps)
>   Uh-oh, it's that crazy baboon
>   again. It must be female.

-- Again, don't get carried away with these permissible breeches of the rules. They are meant to be used as space-saving tools of convenience, not abused. Keep 95% of your action with action and sound effects, and keep dialog, dialog.

CHAPTER 5

ADVICE FROM AGENTS

This is what agents say they want from a query letter: "Include S.A.S.E." "Register script with WGA and Copyright Office." "Include a brief synopsis." "Include theme, plot, character. I want to know the subject matter." "Include a personal biography of yourself." "A resume would be fine to see." "Query should include something different." "Proofread. A spell check does not proofread." "Keep it short." "Don't Fax queries." "Tell me right away if this is a screenplay, teleplay, book manuscript or whatever. Tell me the genre." "You should have several scripts in your portfolio before submitting." Hold on... there's more...

"Give me a single sentence log line or at most one paragraph." "Be concise and to the point." "Include a one page treatment." "One paragraph describing the plot." "Be professional." "Send query letter and brief synopsis." "Check grammar and spelling." "Query should be smart and simple." "Be patient." "Screenwriting is like playing the lottery. Keep playing with patience." "What's the premise?" "We do not accept unsolicited scripts." "We are looking for memorable characters and plausible situations." "Script must use the correct format." "A brief description of oneself and the project." "No cutesy letters." "Don't call." "Be prepared for criticism and be polite about it."

Here's more:

Agents and production companies want to share a few tips about how they spot amateurs; "Using too much dialog." "No clear protagonist." "Poor descriptions (exposition) fail to help me see the story." "No more than 120 pages no less than 100." "Excessive violence and profanity." "Inefficient long-winded dialog." "No inciting event in the first 10-pages." "No momentum to the script." "Synopsis fails to express the core concept of the movie." "Lack of visual writing technique." "Send a query with S.A.S.E. and not the script or you waste your postage and our time." "Don't send colorful script covers or cute cover letters." "No handwritten notes in the script, please!" "No spelling errors." "Unbusiness-like cover letters." "Have your work critiqued before submitting." "Too many writers are in a hurry and it shows up in the script. It may take years of rewriting to perfect a script." "Wordy narrative and dialog. Screenplays are not books. Learn to write tightly with less words." "Where's the story? So many scripts have no real story."

ADVICE FROM PRODUCERS AND PRODUCTION COMPANIES

This is what prodcos and producers advise: "Don't write to make money." "Don't send unsolicited scripts." "Send us a query letter with a release or write to us requesting permission to submit." "Have your script evaluated first before sending it to us." "Don't call us. Write to us first. We'll call you if interested." "Include a resume or bio." "Write a story you personally feel strong about." "Write something that grabs my attention but keep it straight-forward and to the basics." "Query should show conviction. Give me a brief pitch." "Write a great story." "Query should be original and innovative." "Query should show intelligence." "No cigars, please!" "Query should show brevity and specifics." "Quality script with good dialog." "Rewrite the script." "Don't write a mixed-genre script." "Perseverance does pay off. Keep plugging away." "Your ideas should be original. Don't copy other films." "Tell me why I would want this script." And there's more...

"Always believe in your project." "Query should include a brief synopsis." "Include a resume." "Don't send script until it has been read by a dozen people." "Script should have strong story beats, open with a bang and have a good villain to challenge hero." "Query story should explain who, what, where, when, how and why." "Query should reveal professionalism." "I'd like to know your past credits and experience." "We want quality writing, not just high concept." "Tell me how many screenplays you have written." "Develop a good catchy log line and query."

Note: Most have the same requirements as agents. Certainly, you can't comply with all the demands, but you can write your query to satisfy most concerns. When you write your query and synopsis, read the advice above and incorporate the concepts.

And when you thought this was enough, here's more:

"Be professional in all aspects. We need more professionals in this business." "I want to see a professional presentation." "Use the correct format for the medium you are writing for. Too many writers are making this mistake." "Does the script have mass audience appeal?" "No camera directions in the script, none whatsoever." "Do not send me a shooting script. They are useless to me." "Get the story across quickly in all your writings." "Cut back on the dialog and directions. I want to see more white on the page." "Don't send anyone a script in a plastic or fancy binding. Use the industry standard. Three hole punch, simple cover with two or three heavy brads." "I don't want a manuscript. I want a script. Send your manuscripts to New York." "No typos, format problems." "I want to be pulled into the story right away so I can't put the script down."

And more:

"Too many scripts have unoriginal ideas. Be creative! Don't copy what you have already seen in the movies." "A synopsis should be brief. No more than one page, if that." "Keep your query letter right to the point." "I believe a log line tells me more than a full page synopsis." "Most writers have no screenwriting education so I look for this in query letters. Even attending a seminar will perk my interest." "Novice screenwriters fail to learn how to write visually. We can't sell those scripts." "Screenwriting is a visual medium not a verbal one. Learn how to write visually." "I like a brief synopsis of three to six sentences." "If the script has a good log line I'll request the script." "Don't label and date the script as a first or second draft." "I want a release form, synopsis and S.A.S.E. when I request a script."

Note: Agents do not require a release unless they specifically ask for one. Otherwise, do not send them a release as it indicates amateur status. Most all production companies must have a script and a release.

And more, too:

"Indicate on envelope that a release is enclosed; otherwise we are not going to open that envelope due to liability problems." "Don't send us a script we never requested. Those tricks will backfire on you." "A huge error in many scripts is the first opening scenes are all back-story. Open with a bang and establish the character and story by page ten." "Always, always, always include an S.A.S.E. Otherwise, don't bother sending us a query or the script." "Don't be argumentative. Control your emotions. You're going to get a lot of criticism in this business so be professional about it." "There should be a book written so screenwriters can learn how to submit scripts professionally!"

You have that book in your hands right now!

Most agents say, *"Send the best example of your work."* What is best? You may believe all of your scripts are great! Send the script that has ranked the highest in a screenplay contest, or simply send what you feel may be the best for this agent. An agent who specializes in comedy would not be interested in an action genre contest winner.

ADVICE FROM READERS

Screenwriting magazines publish great interviews with script readers. It pays to subscribe to the magazines. Here's what readers want to see.

"Stop using college-level writing." "Don't use asides." "We don't want a scene, set, prop or character list. Screenplays are not theatrical plays." "I want mystery starting on the first page and every page thereafter." "Never include a glossary of terms. Write the script so we can understand it." "Don't send anything with the script like, cassette tapes, gifts, special notes for the reader, etc. We only want the script." "Don't bore me. Entertain me." "Format your script properly or I will certainly have to reject it." "Spelling errors will give you a fast rejection. I can't recommend it no matter how great the story may be." "Buy books on how to write screenplays and read the magazines. That's my best advice."

And more:

"Good writing is hard to find. Take the time to write properly." "It is not my job to reject scripts, but to find good scripts. Tell me a good story that keeps me on the edge of my seat." "Pay to have your script evaluated before sending it to agents. You may be surprised what happens!" "I want snappy dialog and strong visual directions. This means plenty of action." "I want to see the main character in deep trouble with no way out." "Don't send me a script that mimics another movie. You story must be original." "I like unpredictable dialog." "You should consider writing for low-budget films. High budget is a hard sell." "Develop a great character with a serious flaw and the rest of the story usually takes care of itself."

And more:

"I can tell when a script has been rewritten too many times. You should not spend a lifetime rewriting the same script. Write a new one." "Each scene should create greater danger for your character." "What does your main character want? What or who is opposing the desire? Now that generates a powerful script!" "I can't stand writers who try to impress me with their writing. I don't care about flair, I want a good script!" "Take a rest break. I can see your desperation in the script. Later, come back and write calmly with intelligent plotting." "Write stories on subjects you know well. A secretary is not a fighter pilot. Take flying lessons, then write!" "Write something that has never been written before. Be different."

We could fill the pages in this book just on the advice of readers alone, so we stop here. A method of writing a good script is to learn how to think as the reader does. Ask yourself "What would a reader think of this page and this situation?"

LIVING IN HOLLYWOOD

You don't have to live in Hollywood to sell a feature film script, MOW, or a stage play (Yes, prodcos do buy stage plays). There is no doubt Los Angeles and New York City are where the action is for film and TV work. These hubs are where film and television writers are represented, interviewed, pitched in meetings and hired. Nevertheless, it can be to your advantage not to live in Hollywood or New York. How is that?

If you think you can knock on doors, it won't work. The industry has multiple firewalls to stop entry. Even the telephone won't be of much use. The best way is by mail. Your letters will get into the door, and they will be read. Your scripts will be requested and that is the opportunity. In fact, living in Hollywood can subject you to a barrage of delightful bullpoop, where everyone is lying to each other. It's a Wild West atmosphere and Hollywood is built on lies and hype. Everybody has a script and a production deal, etc.

Hollywood is a very strange place where deception reins supreme. It's called the "Hollywood High." Everyone is high on fabrications and delusions. Everyone is working on a screenplay, but nobody has a script! Or everyone is producing a dozen screenplays but can't even deliver one completed script to be read. Welcome to Hollywierd!

That scenario is also what happens with some chat sessions in the Hollywood social haunts. There are plenty of unfinished scripts in Hollywood. Literally tons of them sitting on desks in every agent and prodco story analyst's office.

Only the people with produced scripts make good money? No. Many writers earn great livings just on option money, but at least they do have a tangible script to see and read. Don't go to Hollywood unless you have some scripts to bring, regardless of what you may hear otherwise.

If you read in the news a new screenwriter, plumber or auto mechanic made a million dollar deal based on an idea, treatment or synopsis... it is true. It's the exception to the rule, that is _why_ it is most certainly making news! And it may only be a promotion ploy to attract major talent and players into the act. There are methods to the madness.

Certainly, if you hangout at "hot spots" to meet producers and actors by chance and slip them your business card it could open a door, but it will likely go nowhere unless you follow up with the person's agent or manager. However, it is still preferable to go through an agent or do it yourself by mail. I can't go into detail here. Screenwriting books explain this personal relationship form of alternative marketing anyway. No need for duplication.

You can stay where you are and write features, movie of the week (MOW), stage plays and sell them. TV sitcoms, soaps, episodic drama (Law And Order), anthologies (Tales From The Crypt), serials (NYPD Blue) are another animal. You can send samples of your work and may even sell a few episodes once you are known. But if you want to be a television staff writer you'll need to relocate. Sell your TV script first, then later move to L.A. if you are invited. Did I say that?

It's hard to sell a TV Script from an unknown writer, but not impossible. If you're young, go west and have fun. There are books on the market how to tackle the TV market. The Journal of the Writer's Guild of America-West, will give you the scoop on the TV market in their "*Written By:*" magazine. You can expect to see about 120 shows seeking scripts. See the WGA herein for addresses.

Be aware the competition for TV work is fierce and very hard to break into, but not impossible. Selling a MOW may be easiest of all the TV programs to sell. It may even be easier for you to sell your feature film screenplay or stage play than it would be to sell a television script. One never knows. It all depends on your talent, who you meet or know, and where your interest resides. Film & TV jobs can be found in a magazine that lists current positions open in all areas and levels: *Entertainment Employment Journal*, Dept. 2-A, 5632 Van Nuys Blvd., #320, Van Nuys, CA 90036. And of course the Hollywood Reporter.

Keep in mind, just because a show does not accept submissions, it doesn't always mean they won't. (Boy, they are going to hang me for saying that.) the same is true with literary agents that are closed to all writers with no recommendations or references. Each can be coaxed to accept a script breaking their own rules! Try a query letter. Never send a script, never, unless asked to do so.

If you want TV work, please consult a book that specifically deals with the subject so you will understand how the business operates. You simply send queries as you would market screenplays. Never send treatments or a script... always query first. If you break this rule you will make enemies very fast.

Now, if you want to pitch high-concept script ideas to the studios and obtain rewrite work, you will have to move to LA. No question about it. Once established (you have box-office successes under your belt) you can relocate out of LA as long as you have a strong agent in the Hollywood area pulling for you. But if you are selling a spec script, you can live anywhere you want. It takes longer, usually, but then again, living in LA does not assure a sale.

The sad truth is, most screenwriters will never sell a script. Only those who are extremely dedicated and stubborn enough to never quit. These people will eventually sell a script and 90% of those will never see their story displayed on the silver screen. They get optioned and are forgotten. But they keep on and on until it happens, usually after many years of tiring effort. This is not an easy money business!

One thing you must learn is that you must keep writing even though you are not selling and keep on submitting your scripts over a long period of time, years! You will read of someone writing a script and selling it for million or two, but there is likely many years of writing without a sale behind the scene.

BUSINESS VACATION TO LOS ANGELES

Why not take a vacation to Disneyland? And while you're at it, make it a business trip! Before you leave simply write to agents and tell them you are planning to be in LA in the near future and would like to schedule an appointment to introduce yourself and your screenplay. When you get a half-dozen who are receptive to the idea, then set your schedules up, buy a ticket and fly. It's a person-to-person marketing tactic and can be fruitful to open doors for you.

At this time make sure you tell the agent you would be willing to fly out to LA to attend meetings, if required. The studios will pick up the tab if they are serious about your project.

Now assuming these efforts failed, you had a great vacation and a tax write-off to boot! You don't have to do this, but it's something you should consider at some point in your screenwriting career. Don't fly out uninvited, okay? The firewalls still exist and you won't get past the secretary. Write your letters and obtain invitations first. It's also a professional way to do business.

Don't expect to hear, *"Come on out now... we need you badly!"* If you do, I wouldn't go. You're being conned by some cruel person who probably hates writers (monsters do exist). You will likely get a response such as, *"If you do arrive in the LA area please schedule an appointment for further consideration."* That's all you need to crack open the door of opportunity.

Some good advice is to make certain you have had your script reviewed by a reliable firm or agent to make your script shine. Winning a respectable screenplay contest or placing in the first fifty ranking could be a valid key to open the locked doors of Hollywood. It will do you little good if your script(s) can't get good coverage marks by the Hollywood readers (a tough bunch to appease).

You can pay for coverage by script analysis firms and established screenwriters who offer the service. Point is, when you do arrive to meet agents in person you'll have some big gun scripts with the ammunition to back it up. Then your trip to LA may very well be worth taking.

HOW TO USE COVERAGE REPORTS

A good marketing tactic is to pay to have your script evaluated by a reader/editor. Make the necessary changes and resubmit for another evaluation. Or, if the first evaluation came in okay, then copy this coverage and include it with your query letter. This knocks down firewalls and your scripts will be requested. There are many firms performing coverage evaluations and it's not cheap. Some charge over $500 per script. Some as low as $90.

Did you know? You can send along with your query letter a copy of an excellent coverage report to enhance your query in a big way. If the coverage report is from an agent or prodco, block out the company name. If it's from a script doctor, you can leave the name on the report. At the same time, include a copy of your script's winning certificate of high ranking in a screenplay contest. After all, this is an informal coverage report not to be ignored and reveals demonstrated ability and talent to rank high in screeplay competitions. Now you have a strong calling card and agents will take a look at your work and give you a chance!

Note: Coverage reports can be a handy tool to open doors that are otherwise shut tight. Agencies that are normally closed to writers will be impressed with these coverage reports. They will break their general rule of not accepting submissions from unknown writers and request your script!

Do not send a huge package of material in your query letter. If you have a lot of information to send because you won many contests, have lots of good coverage reports, etc., simply list these on a single page query mentioning the agent may obtain copies upon request.

You can ask professional working screenwriters to give you coverage on your script. Negotiate a fee or free. If you can get a top-gun writer to do this for you, and the coverage comes out good, it's almost like getting a referral! Best bet? Use a script doctor first to delete the errors out of your script so it is polished, then contact a well-known working writer to give the script coverage. You will be amazed how fast doors may open for you!

COVERAGE REPORT-USE THIS SAMPLE FORM TO SCORE HIGHER RANK

See Fig. 1-28 for a sample of a coverage report. Before sending in your script you may want to use this coverage report for your own self analysis of the script. However, it is best to have someone else read the script and fill in the coverage report for you. This could be friend who understands screenwriting, as you are too close to the story to make an objective evaluation. Do not send an agent a copy of a coverage report that is completed by an unrecognized authority.

The purpose? It's a preliminary evaluation that will ultimately give you a much higher reader's score when you do send the script into the marketplace. That is, if you are not using the services of a script doctor, this evaluation process will be second best and way better than not performing the analysis at all.

SAMPLE LETTER TO OBTAIN COVERAGE REPORT

See Fig. 2-2 for a sample letter you can use to request a copy of the coverage report. It is usual and customary that coverage reports are never sent to the screenwriter and most writers believe they can never get a copy of the report. This is not true. You can obtain copies of these coverage reports, but not from every agency or production company. However, some will, if you ask. The key is to make your request properly so the agency will know the report will not be misused. The sample letter in Fig. 2-2 is all you need. The good news is, it works!

Getting your hands on a copy of a coverage report is a blessing with a curse. The blessing is you will know what is going wrong with your script in relation to the marketing appeasement in the reader's opinion as to the script's selling potential. Story elements will also be spelled out, usually defects, of course. The curse is that you may be shocked and stunned by the sheer brutal evaluation process. You will see just how unmerciful these readers can be! This is why you are not supposed to see the coverage report and they are not given to writers. They are internal documents and they must have free expression to get the job done.

Agents are under no obligation to give you the original reader's coverage report, even if you paid the agent a reading fee for a script evaluation. Point is, do not demand the coverage report be sent to you. Odds are, most agencies are not going to give you the report under any circumstances. These reports can cause trouble when writer's read them. Some writer's are so insulted they fire off retaliative letters of rebuttal, make nasty phone calls, etc. However, you can obtain coverage reports from some agencies, if you are deemed professional in the agency's eyes to handle it.

The sample letter you may use in Fig. 2-2 will get the job done, but notice the comment boxes on the page warns you to keep your promises. Be forewarned, if you send your letter and you receive an insulting coverage report, you promised never to rebut or contact the agency again on the matter. If you break this promise, you will never get this agent to ever even look at your query letters and you could end up with a bad reputation. One day, when you are closing a deal, the broken promise may arise in an informal background investigation and the deal will not close. Agents talk to each other, so keep that in mind. Always keep your promises. This holds true when asking for writer referrals, don't break your promise. Be professional!

WHAT IS PROFESSIONALISM?

If you are professional in your dealings you will see greater results. Professional can mean many things. You may be a pro writer, but to the industry, professional means behavior! It's how you present yourself and how you react. A professional follows the rules, whatever the rules may be. A professional does not get angry, argue or complain like a child. The pro stays cool, calm and collective while everyone else is acting crazy!

This book focuses on being professional in marketing endeavors, that's all. Follow the advice in this book and you will be deemed professional by the industry. You will see a major increase for requests of your scripts and you will likely get an agent and sell your scripts, if you stay professional and work hard being so.

There are three levels of professionalism in this business:
1. Submitting materials in a professional manner.
2. Writing scripts professionally.
3. Being professional.

Most writer's fully understand and know how to write scripts that meet industry standards. Writers with great scripts fail to understand the marketing process. It is here they are deemed unprofessional and it is a crying shame such writer's receive persistent rejection for not following industry protocol. Then we have the writer that submits professionally, writes professionally, but is just totally unprofessional in attitude and behavior. Work on all three levels if you wish success to come to you. Don't gossip, don't bitch and complain, don't be rude, don't be a bloody pest and most of all, keep your promises.

The best way to envision what a professional should look and act like is to see a judge in a real courtroom. The self-assurance and absolute sense of authority radiates. It is how your written correspondence letters should reflect along with your verbal conversation -- a sense of professionalism is present.

When you are asked by an agent to submit, do not delay. If you are asked to write an assignment, get the job done -- not on time, but before it is expected! Performance is the signature of a professional. Believe it or not, there are many writers who are talented, but are so unreliable and flaky they soon find themselves out of work.

Professionalism is highly respected in this industry and at the same time, unprofessionalism is strongly punished. It is very hard to remain sane in this industry as a writer. The demands are incredible and the insults you will receive are beyond describing. There are cruel people in this business (and good people, too). You have a right to go home, pull your hair out, scream at the walls and smash wine glasses against the fireplace(like they do in the movies) but you have no right to explode or reveal your feelings to others. You have to hold it all in while you are being insulted and demoralized.

That is the life of the professional writer in the entertainment business. If you can't take the heat, then don't get into this business!

The good news is that it is easy to be professional. You simply roll with punches, bend with the wind, flow over the dam. This does not mean you have to be a pushover, just that you do not have to reveal your inner feelings by expression of your heartfelt emotions. Integrity to yourself is yours. You may never be able to stop others from trying to compromise you, but you can control yourself and stay true to who you really are, inside. With that core within, you can make the right decisions.

It also helps to have "professional" writing friends to help you stay on track, with a psychologist as a backup. People can only take so much heat before they melt. Don't think you are Superman, you can break. By understanding that this business is insane from the beginning and that nothing and nobody makes sense, you will remain safe and sane and earn a good living. If you can learn to laugh at all the stupid, idiotic things that are going on around you and trying to infest you, you'll survive!

SEVENTEEN YEARS IN LOS ANGELES
Having lived in Los Angeles for over 17 years, here is what you can expect. If you've never been to Hollywood you may be in for a shock. It's not a pretty sight (don't believe what you see in the movies, a screenwriter wrote the script and we know how they exaggerate things).

Sunset Strip and Hollywood Boulevard is a perpetual mass of people and not the kind you may want to associate with. The buildings are not so fantastic to the eye. Get the picture? The Universal Sheraton Hotel is a good bet (movie industry people loiter here all the time and you could make good contacts). Universal Studios is a stone's throw away, too. It's a safe area compared to other places in LA.

When driving, stay on the brightly-lit main streets and freeways. Leave very early for any appointments as the freeways really are parking lots! June is always overcast... every day, but the weather is mild! July, August and September can be sweltering hot, but the evenings are so balmy you just bathe in the air.

October is the best month as it's never hot or cool... just right, and many of the millions of tourists are gone (but not all I can assure you of that). Use eye-drops if the smog stings your eyes. It won't be bad in October, but it's going to be thick as smoke in the summer. You get used to it after a few days, years!

If you must travel in the summer consider staying anywhere on the coast. Santa Monica, Marina Del Rey, Redondo Beach, etc. Venice is a crazy place, so not a good place to bed down as you'll get no sleep. The weather is always cooler and there is considerably less smog along the coast. And don't forget to bring money, as it is expensive to live in LA. If you plan to come out West in a motorhome, be prepared to find there will be no RV spaces. Any that exist will be full.

You can find spaces up Soledad Canyon in the Santa Clarita Valley near, near Acton, California. You will also find spaces near Magic Mountain (Castaic Lake area). Many people do not know this, now you do. Consult Woodall's or Good Sam's RV park directory. The commute is very reasonable. And if you feel like you've missed a step when you're walking or notice things moving... it's just one of those daily earthquakes (tremors). You'll get used to them, too! Enjoy your stay in LA!

DO YOU NEED A HOLLYWOOD AGENT?

Yes and no. It depends on the agent's connections to Hollywood's power brokers. It's always a good idea to get an agent in the Los Angeles basin area. Second best is the outskirts in the surrounding valleys (San Fernando, Santa Clarita, Simi Valley, San Bernardino Valley, Orange County are a few to mention). Third best is anywhere in Southern California. Fourth best anywhere in California. Get the idea? Out of sight is out of mind, so having an agent in California and closer to LA is better.

The best chances of success is to live in LA so you can attend meetings, pitch sessions, get to know people in the industry, whatever. It's certainly an edge. But it's not an absolute in feature film marketing. If you can get an agent in LA, you can stay or you can leave. Bottom line, if your script is good and you get past the firewalls, it will sell. Many screenwriters flourish in New York, Chicago, Tampa, etc. Most are established writers. In television? You have to be in LA to work full-time, but you can sell spec scripts from anywhere, especially if you have an agent in the LA area.

You may want to consider hooking up with an agent nearest your town and start a business relationship. Jumping straight to Hollywood/LA agents usually results in closed doors, as most require a referral by an agent or established writer, producer, actor or other powerful person. You never know just who has the connections to Hollywood. Certainly there are agencies in most major cities who have some juice. Ask other writers in your area who these players are and focus on them. See the subchapter on how to obtain a referral. See Fig. 2-3.

BOOKSTORES - FILM / TV/ PLAYS / GENERAL INTEREST

--Applause Theater & Cinema Books, Dept. 0, 211 W. 71st St., NY, NY, 10023 (212)496-7511.
--Book City, Dept. T-7, 308 N. San Fernando Blvd., Burbank, CA 91502 (818)848-5615 they sell scripts.
--McFarland & Company, Dept. A, Box 611, Jefferson, NC 28640 (910)-246-

4460.
--Samuel French Theater & Film, Dept. S, 7623 Sunset Blvd., Hollywood, CA 90046 (213)876-0570.
--ScreenStyle Software & Books, Dept. 1-A, 3010 Hennepin Ave., #278, Minneapolis, MN 55408. (888)627-8812. 10% discount to readers of this book.
--Stage & Screen Book Club, Dept. S, 6550 East 30th St., P.O. Box 6309, Indianapolis, IN 46206.
--Writer's Digest Book Club, Dept. J-5, P.O. Box 12948, 1507 Dana Ave., Cincinnati, OH 45207 (513)531-8250.
--QPB Book Club, Dept. S, Camp Hill, PA 17012-0001 (717)6976443.
--Of course, the major chain bookstores has writing books.

Screenwriting magazines advertise bookstores. A comprehensive source of bookstores, screenplay competitions, agents, prodcos, software, etc., is the *New York Screenwriter's Annual Screenwriter's Guide*. It's free for subscribers of the magazine. You'll find it valuable.

QPB Book Club also sells VHS movies and sitcoms in the Mixed Media catalog, books not often available from other sources. We also have books for writers on our website. See Title Page for our URL address.

CHAPTER 6

STAGE PLAY SCRIPT FORMAT

One day you may write or may already have written, a stage play. There are three formats, but only two you can pick from.

1. The published version is what you will see in the actor's hands at the theater rehearsals. Publishing companies sell them in this format. We won't even discuss it. If you want to see one, just visit any performing arts theater. If you never saw a live play, do so. It's an education that will certainly help you write screenplays. Theater is three dimensional, film is two. Attend try-outs and rehearsals. It's also lots of fun.

2. The standard screenplay format is acceptable, but

3. The format you should use is illustrated as Figure 1-5. Scriptware, and other computer formatting programs have the format already built in.

When you write your stage play, keep the market in sight. What are the odds of a large production play from a new writer hitting Broadway? Nil to none. But, if you write a small play with only one or two quick set changes with less than 8, not more than 10 actors, the market opens up to thousands of small theaters in the USA alone! Also, keep in mind working professional actors are not available in all cities so the acting shouldn't be extremely demanding. Keep the set props to a minimum. Many theaters are not-for-profit and must have items donated.

FEATURE FILM SCRIPT FORMAT

The feature screenplay is illustrated as Figure 1-6. The Movie Of The Week (MOW) script is the same as the feature film format. Each network has their own commercial break sequences so don't bother inserting commercial breaks in the script unless you are requested to do so. However, you should keep notes where commercials should be in the script. The commercial break must come where the story is hanging, after a twist, so the audience will not change channels. Watch a movie of the week and your wall clock and you'll see the timing of the commercial breaks and hooks. One page = 1 minute.

With <u>all</u> scripts, the title page is not numbered. You can number the pages like I've done in this manual; - 17 - or plain old 17. Don't put # or No. symbols on the page. For script title pages you can write to the WGA and ask for samples of their approved format.

TV SITCOM SCRIPT FORMAT

The TV sitcom script is illustrated as Figure 1-7. Again, each production company may have a specific format, but you can't go wrong with this one (Fig. 1-7 is the "TV-2" format in Scriptware).

It is said you shouldn't write sitcom episodes and submit them to agents. Sometimes, true. However, you can write a sitcom and send it to the producers of the show (after you query and they request the script). Then again, it is said you shouldn't send in a sitcom to the producers for the show they produce. True. Confused yet?
There is a method you can use.

1. Write a sitcom based on another show.

2. Send a query letter to the producer asking if you can submit a sample script for evaluation of your writing skills, along with a pitch list of log line story ideas you can write for them.

3. You can write a personal congratulations letter to the writer who wrote a great episode you really liked. Writers don't often receive fan mail. At this point you should tell the writer you are a writer and would like to keep in touch. If the response is positive, then ask if you can submit some story ideas. How do you find the writer's address? Easy. Call or write the Writer's Guild and ask for the mailing address or phone number of the writer's agent. Mail letter to agent requesting to forward mail to writer. Keep letter brief and sincere. Hint about a job. If you're too forward and moving too fast the writer may feel used and it ends. The industry is infested with users and abusers. Sincerity is a valuable asset.

4. You can take the huge long-shot step and write a back-door series and hope for the best. This is a feature film, a one-hour pilot, with at least three sitcom episodes. Shop it around to literary agents, television producers and the major networks. It's about the only way an outsider can develop a new sitcom. Do you really have the time to do all this? That's the question you must decide. Most people won't do it and I don't blame them. It's a hard sell. New sitcoms are most always brought on by writer/producers with established credits and proven accomplishments (is this why many sitcoms are lame and uninspired with poor acting and weak dialog?) but if you feel lucky, nobody say's you can't try. Success often comes by surprise. Just be aware the probability of success is low. It's a buddy system of the good ol boy network.

5. Move to Hollywood because in sitcom work you'll need to be there, as scripts are written on site by hired staff. Some are bought from writers who live in any state or place on the planet.

6. You can write to the show's producers and simply ask if they accept submissions. Ask for a copy of their guidelines. The door may be open. Some shows are and some aren't. If your query letter is good, they may make an exception and let you in to submit your ideas and/or script. Usually they will pick one of your log lines or a synopsis of a story and hire you to write it, or something like that. Every show is different.

7. Most TV writers must write at least one script to use as a calling card and demonstration of writing style and ability. You can develop story ideas as brief log lines or treatments and query them to agents and show producers.

8. Keep in mind TV shows are very low budget, especially sitcoms. You'll see very little off-site filming and few special effects. Know the show you want to write for and know it well, especially the characters. Know them as well as your best friends.

9. Subscribe to *Written By:* magazine. It lists the TV market open for submissions. This is where you begin the marketing process, or end it, leading to a direct sale.

MOVIE OF THE WEEK (MOW) FORMAT

MOW format is a seven-act structure. I don't show one here. Why? Because you can simply write it in standard screenplay format. Many agents and producers are not adverse to standard screenplay format for MOW's. So why bother with the seven-act format? Typical MOW script page count is 90 to 110 pages. No need to insert any commercial breaks into the script.

There are formatting books on the market on how to time the twists in the story for these commercial breaks, and each prodco will want these twists at unique times for their programming formulas.

The beginning writer may enhance the chance of a sale by writing a MOW rather than a feature film, especially if you obtain the rights to a person's story. The market for cable TV is generally better than the large primetime networks.

You can read magazine articles to find out what these firms are looking for... HBO, The Disney Channel, USA, TNT, Lifetime, Showtime, etc.

HOW TO FIND TV PRODUCTION COMPANY SHOW ADDRESSES

Your library will have books on locating specific companies. You can also obtain them through trade publications. Write to:

--Lone Eagle Publishing, Dept. A, 2337 Roscomare Rd., Suite 9, Los Angeles, CA 90077 (800)345-6257. (310)471-496.

The *Hollywood Reporter, Hollywood Scriptwriter* and the *New York Screenwriter* magazines have TV production company listings, though not as extensive as Lone Eagle Publishing. For more addresses and job information, write to the *Entertainment Employment Journal* as they list open positions.

Also, see, WGA *Written By:* magazine as they publish in the journal a monthly "Television Market List" featuring submission contact information on current weekly prime time television programs. You'll need this if you want to break into TV work and sell a script.

The best source is the *Written By:* magazine for open listings, but one must consider the competition will naturally be fierce. I recommend reading books on how to enter the television markets, as TV may not be as open to writers as the feature film industry (some will argue this point). No TV prodco will accept unsolicited scripts and you shouldn't ever send a script. Send a query letter. Many won't even accept a query letter as they have their own in-house staff of writers. Regardless, it is worth trying. Nothing is impossible in this business.

Getting in is like obtaining any traditional employment:
1. Network with people to get you hired on as staff or have someone on the inside pulling for you to submit a script for consideration.

2. Send resume with a cover letter asking to submit a sample script to demonstrate your writing ability.

3. Responding to advertisements in screenwriting magazines mentioned above. Fig. 1-15 is an example of cold-call query letter to a sitcom show.

4. Write well.

5. Compelling storyline, or it better be funny if a sitcom.

A WORD ABOUT FUNNY

Now funny is a funny word and the writer's task is far from funny. What is funny? Nobody really knows! In sitcoms, jokes are ironed out by the writers as a team, usually, and stage-tested. Even then, not everyone likes all sitcoms on TV. In features, it's a crapshoot to extremes. Your script may make you, family and friends laugh as the reader yawns.

Then again someone writes a stupid script and it gets made into a movie and it bombs at the box office big time. How could that happen? Are there shady deals being made in Hollywood? Best advice? Write what you want. Write the funny the way only you can, for that is being unique and that can sell.

I wrote a comedy and the director wanted to make some minor changes. He butchered the script's story to the point there was no story left and he ejected every funny punch. I'm talking zero jokes! I dismissed the director after he absolutely would not listen to reason and refused to adhere to the original agreement.

We first agreed we would perform a test market debut to a small audience and work on the laugh volume from there. If the audience laughed we would leave the scene alone. If they didn't, we would make changes. "No problem" was his reply. So we tag on the actors and do a reading with the original draft and it's so funny the actors can't get past page three without breaking in tears.

This "experienced" amateur director wanted to bully-in and take over the show, change all the scenes to his own "religious" theologies...

which included, by the way, putting "angel made" purification liquids in our food as we ate to turn us into living fellow angels! These are the sort of persons you may meet in the entertainment industry... nut cases, schizophrenics, impulsive, compulsive idiots! However, you will meet very intelligent people, too, who will lie to you with a smile. Now, that is funny! Too bad it's a true story.

The bottom line. What is funny? Nobody knows except the audience. Comedy is not just jokes as in sitcoms and night show monologues. In film and stage it's an undiscovered field still, and that's why there are no formulas and no guarantees at the box office. You can learn all the theory you want from comical professors but to write funny... they can't teach you that!

IS IT EASY TO OBTAIN AN AGENT?

Under the best of conditions the answer is, no. Agents are reluctant to take on first-time writers, so fewer and fewer do so. It is difficult to break in, though not impossible. A writer may have one or two scripts and query hundreds of agents and receive hundreds of rejections. Why is this? Because there are writers with a dozen scripts or more competing.

The more scripts you have completed, the higher the attention span of the agent. This is why I use the multiple submission log line approach. See Fig. 1-8. It screams, "*Hey, look at this!*" So even if you only have two scripts, start using this approach. You may not agree, others may tell you not to do it, but I say from long experience it obtains positive results. Try it and see for yourself what happens.

If your writing is brief and visual, the story is good, and the structure is acceptable, somebody will represent it. Trouble is, it's hard to get anyone to read your material. With the competition pounding at the doors you need to try unconventional creative approaches to the market without being unprofessional.

And don't forget, the conventional approach of sending agents a single query focused on one script with a synopsis and resume still opens doors the old fashion way, if it is written to grab attention... the magic bullet we all seek to discover.

Whatever you do, don't copy a query letter from some other author, make it fit your story and think it will fly. It will fly into a trash container! Agents know all these little tricks and they have seen it all. You may copy a format, but not the voice. Use your own voice to grab attention. In more than a few instances it's not the query letter composition alone, but pure good timing and luck that gets a script in the door.

Many new writers have obtained agents just from subscribing to the screenwriting magazines, responding to agents seeking scripts. A method you can use is to contact a TV or film writer's club and join (most cities have them). Someone may have an agent and introduce you through a personal recommendation. That will certainly open doors. If there are no writer's clubs, then just keep your query letters flowing in the mail. Be aware that for most, patience is of utmost essence. It's a slow grinding process that can take years even if you have an agent circulating your scripts to make a sale.

There is no reason to sit back and wait for an agent to come along. Continue to market your own material to producers, prodcos, etc. The key is developing a mailing list of agents, producers and prodcos. This requires hard work and years to develop such a database, but if you start now you'll have a list for future use. You'll be glad you did. To accelerates the process, you can buy a mailing list.

The goal is to have, on any given day, your script(s) in the mail somewhere "out there" being looked at. That is the purpose of this manual; to get your scripts read. Uncountable blockbuster movies spent years circulating the markets before being accepted. It's true! You want your script perpetually circulating, too, with or without agent assistance, and get your script in the door and read. That is the prime purpose of this manual, to open the locked doors!

It is not easy to obtain an agent. They already have dozens to hundreds of writers but there is always room for one more! Problem is, the writers who are trying to get in are flooding the agent with so many unprofessional queries they simply close shop to all writers hoping to escape the deluge of drudge trying to get in. The key to obtaining an agent is in your hands right now. This book has the advice to allow you to step up your submission package to professional rank. When agents see this package, compared to what they normally receive, it grabs their attention, *"A professional submission, let's check on this!"*

The main purpose of this book is to give you the keys to good marketing and clean up your script so it reads powerfully. The next phase is the story must be compelling and that's when the book shoves you out of the nest and you begin to fly on your own.

WHEN DO I NEED AN AGENT?

You don't need a literary agent to market and sell your script to the independent prodcos who contract through the major studios. You can go directly to producers, directors, actors, etc. It's not as daunting as you think it may be.

If you follow the advice in this manual, you'll be mailing scripts, and that's great news. When you do obtain an offer to option or purchase your script, that is the time to hire an agent. You don't want to do any deals with anyone you do not know and trust.

It's easy. Since you have a sale, any agent will handle the legal contracts for you and get you more money than you would otherwise. At this point, you can just about get any agent you want with one simple phone call or letter. The agent will protect your rights.

The agent should be a signatory with the WGA, as the major studios will only deal with them since the agent agrees to abide by the WGA rules and standards. To find out, simply ask the agent or call the WGA for verification. Hollywood even have firewalls to keep out agents!

HOW TO FIND AGENTS

1. Subscribe to the *Hollywood Scriptwriter*, Dept. S, P.O.Box 10277, Burbank, CA 91510 (818)845-5525.

2. Subscribe to the *New York Screenwriter*, Dept. S, 545 8th Avenue,

Suite 401, New York, NY 10018 (800)418-5637.

3. Order *Writer's Digest's Guide to Literary Agents*. This book lists many agents open to writers. *Writers Market* book does, too.

4. Order a copy of the Writer's Guild of America's (WGA) list of signatory agents. WGAe address listed at end of manual. Cost is approximately $2.50. You can download a list from the WGA internet home page.

5. Purchase the *Annual Agency Guide* (Approx $30 + $5 shipping) from; The Writer's Network, Dept. Z-1, 289 South Robertson Blvd. Beverly Hills, CA 90211. Listings include Agent's name, address, phone/fax, genre specifications, submission requirements, interviews and advice on queries, pitching, marketing. Or write for a catalog to Lone Eagle Publishing, Dept. A, 2337 Roscomare Rd., Suite 9, Los Angeles, CA 90077 (310)471-4969. They publish film, studio, agent, casting directors guide books.

6. See subchapter heading in this manual "How To Use Coverage Reports." I've listed a few literary agencies that not only perform coverage, but are geared to represent the new writer, and those struggling to get an agent but have been direly unsuccessful.

7. When you mail a query letter to an agent, keep it one page, short paragraphs with lots of white space. Anything more they won't read. This holds true for most business communications. Busy people have little time. A query letter is not to sell the steak (script) but to sell the "sizzle" (heat, excitement, interest) for the reader to request and read the script. See Fig. 1-16, 1-17 for a sample of a query letter pushing two scripts. In this example, include a one page synopsis. See Fig 1-4. If the reader likes your query s/he can go on to read the synopsis. If that generates curiosity, the script will be requested. You can just send a query without the synopsis if you wish. Try both methods.

8. You can query agents by three means. **1)** Send a log line listing as shown in Fig. 1-8 to advertise completed multiple scripts. **2)** Send a single page query letter only as in Fig. 1-15, 1-16, 1-17. **3)** Send a single page query letter with a one-page synopsis. See Fig 1-16 and Fig 1-4. **4)** Send a letter seeking representation with a log line listing and/or a resume if you wish. See Fig. 1-8.

9. In reference to paragraph #8 above, you can query producers and prodcos by using item #1 and #2 but always include a <u>release</u> in the submission. See Fig. 1-3 for a release. You don't send them item #4. You can mail a one page request to submit letter as in Fig. 1-18. Generally, use a query letter as shown in Fig. 1-18 or simply send log line listings, Fig. 1-8, with a release, Fig. 1-3, when mass mailing to producers and prodcos.

If an agency, producer or prodco advertises for scripts, you may include a cover letter explaining how your script fits their needs. See Fig. 1-10 for a cover letter responding to an advertisement. Note that you have included a cover letter, log line list, release and synopsis of the script that fits their needs. You may not want to deliver the script even though the prodco asked for it to be sent,. that is, send the script if the addressee is reputable.

Just because an agency says they do not accept unsolicited material does not always mean they will not do so. If you have a good reason as to why you want the specific agency to take on your project, that could be the exception to open the door. Just saying, "*You're the greatest and the best and I want you to represent me*" isn't enough and should never be said that way anyway (some people actually do this). If you have a script that is perfect for the director that agency represents you may be able to convince them to take a look see. Odds are you'll earn a rejection letter, but what if you don't? Try it.

Everybody is out there banging on doors and all the agents are wearing earplugs. It's a tough business, a business of rejection. Get used to it. Learn to adapt to the competition and try new things to generate attention. If you know a writer who is represented by an agency, a referral by the writer will absolutely open the door to representation. See Fig. 2-3 for a sample letter you can send to a writer.

If you live in Nebraska and know no writer, just keep mailing queries until you do. It will happen, in time. The *Writer's Digest Magazine* and *Writer's Market* book lists agents looking for new writers. Some charge fees, but it's often a path a new writer may have to take if all else fails. Then again, representation is never free for anyone. Most agents reimburse the charges to the client/writer when a sale is made.

10. See, "How to Find Producers" subheading in this book. A listing of resources are given to help you locate agents, producers, directors, studio executives, etc.

THE BETTER AGENT, LARGE OR SMALL?

A large agency has intense contacts, but it's a huge machine representing famous authors, actors and writers. Consider the fact you'll be lost in the shuffle. A new writer just doesn't stand much of a chance of being aggressively marketed when the most the agent will make is 10% on a $80,000 to $400,000 sale. The actor will command $20 million! Do the math.

A smaller agency may not have the pull with major studios, but can devote more time to market you to independent prodcos, which are often funded by the majors. A small agency can be a good thing. The bottom line? Are your scripts good? Is the agent marketing them? Any sales? If a small agent can sell your script or secure options, step-deals, and get your picture made, then I'd say you're doing just fine.

So which agent is best for the new writer? Any agent! What other choice do you have when nobody else will represent you? Buy your ticket with the agent and go for the ride and see what develops. There are two endings to this scenario; heaven or hell. Purgatory was abolished by Hollywood.

Every writer has nightmare stories to tell regarding agency relations. When things go bad, don't get depressed, it's just another phase in the process. A stepping stone in your career path. You are not alone!

Warning: Just because the agent is signatory to the WGA does not mean they are super-duper fantastic agents and incredibly honest and sincere.

There are goofball agents, too, in signatory status. Eventually these agents are dropped from the list, sometimes, but use your common sense! Agents are evil subservient demons working for the King of Hell with a highly focused mission to make your life as miserable and demeaning as one can possibly imagine. Of course, this is a joke. Isn't it?

BE YOUR OWN LITERARY AGENT

I'm not saying to print business cards and form an agency, though you (or your spouse) can do so, but it is highly recommended not to try to cheat the filtering process. To sell scripts you can't sit back and rely on the agent to find writing assignments and sell your scripts. Often, you will need to make the rounds, performing query mailings. When a positive response arrives, notify your agent to follow up and send your script.

A word of advice: When you snag a lead like this, tell your agent the producer or prodco is only interested in your script. *"ABC Productions request that "Mystic Forest" screenplay be shipped to Mr. B. C. Thomas, V.P. of Development."* Why? Because the agent could send a shopping list of scripts to the production company and your script (or synopsis, treatment, etc.) is lost in the pile. All the effort and expense comes to nothing. The agent makes a commission and represents many writers. So why just send your script? Be specific.

There is a book titled *How to Be Your Own Literary Agent*. It's a book on how to get your book published and dealing with publishers. This manual has some good ideas to research and somewhat applicable to the film, TV and theatrical markets. $13.95 includes S&H. Richard Curtis, Box 11-J, 75 East End Avenue, New York, NY 10028.

It's hard work selling scripts and it is expensive to market them. The postage and office supplies add up to impressive figures by year's end. See Fig. 1-24 revealing actual costs.

COST OF AGENCY REPRESENTATION

It's not free. Getting an agent is challenging under the best of circumstances, a nice way of saying, *"Good luck, you'll need it."* No kidding. You need perseverance and sheer determination in between the tears of rejection. But once you do get one to take you on, it may cost you money.

Some agencies charge reading fees, most don't. Some agents charge no fee, they only make money when the script sells. Some charge a flat fee to market the work and will reimburse you if the script sells. Some use a piecework fee. They charge you for everything they do, photocopying scripts, postage, phone bills, etc., reimbursable if the script sells. The cost can be $20+ per script submitted.

So what do you do? Pay the fees! Having an agent can open up doors for you. Just mentioning the fact in a query letter adds a more credibility, status and impact to your letter. If all works well, you'll be laughing all the way to the bank. If not, you're out some money, so you eat sandwiches for a while until you recover the losses.

There are some ways to control costs. You can ask the agent not to "shotgun" the market by sending out two-dozen scripts. You can ask to supply the scripts by using a local printer. If you ask a printer for a discount on printing ten or more scripts, you may get a 40% price reduction.

Example: At the normal price of five cents per page on a 110 page script you will pay $5.50 per script. You can easily get a discount to three cents. You're cost is now $3.50 per script. That's a lot better than what the agent will charge you for time and labor!

You can also ask the agent if you can supply the mailing envelopes and purchase them at a shipping supplies wholesaler at one-half cost of retail. But, tread lightly. The agent may not want to bother with such nonsense. It doesn't hurt to ask, but if the agent is not moved by your offer, leave it alone and go with the program.

Most agencies will charge 15 percent for domestic sales and 20 percent for foreign rights when they sell your script. If the commission fee is outrageously higher than these figures, think twice before signing on. The new writer simply does not have many options. You sometimes have to take what you can get. Overall, it is better to have an agent than not, so sign on and hope for the best.

There are writers who have never had an agent and are successful. So, just because you can't get an agent, don't focus all of your energy trying to get one. Write good scripts, good query and cover letters, polish your synopsis letters and keep your scripts circulating. With or without an agent you are self-employed. Never forget it. You must stay busy writing and submitting. Marketing is still your job!

CHAPTER 7

TARGETING YOUR MARKETING

It is often suggested you should only target agents with script genres they represent. This is a problem if you try to follow the rule too closely. Why? There are very few agents that only specialize in one genre. What is ironic is the same agent that says, "*We only want comedy and drama*" will be listed in other directories as "*All genre, except horror.*" Yes, it is best to always send a script genre to an agent that represents such, but don't let it hold you back from sending your log lines or queries of other scripts.

Why? Even dedicated genre agents often change, horses in the middle of the stream, prior to being listed in next years annual agency surveys! You could get a jump on the competition. One rule is pretty firm. If you do write horror genre scripts, you have to be very selective. Not many agents will represent fantasy or horror. However, most agents will take on a good action, drama, comedy or western.

Rule of thumb: Try to submit only scripts and queries to genre specific agencies, but don't let it hold you back from submitting other genre log lines if the agency is listed elsewhere under a different genre.

When dealing with producers, the strict genre rule often applies. Producers usually specialize and are focused on making films they feel most competent to pull off. So don't send a comedy script/query to a producer who specializes in drama. Okay? You will find many sources of information to target your market throughout this book.

GENERATING LOG LINES

A log line is a single sentence describing your entire story. Impossible to do, but this is what Hollywood requires. You'll need to practice writing log lines as it is a bit trying to get the log line close to perfection. You need to boil the entire story down to one sentence like this.

You have a screenplay where grandmothers form a military assault team to take back a city powered by criminals. The script is full of action scenes at 120 pages. The log line would be; "Grannies attack a crime infested city." Look for the core value of your storyline and the log line comes easier. The shorter your log line is, the more powerful it will be. Now it's your turn.

Question: What would be the log line of a movie of; professional con artist gamblers conspiring to cheat Las Vegas slot machines?

Your Answer: _____.

Answer: Gamblers cheat Las Vegas casinos raking in millions.

A log line is not a paragraph, it is a "single line" simply as shown above (Fig. 1-8 is an exception to the rule). It does not wrap into two lines on a page. If an agent or prodco requests a log line and you send them a double-sentence or two lines, you are asking for a rejection -- and you will likely get what you asked for. They want professional writers! You must make your submission professionally presented to be taken seriously in this business. Hollywood is flooded with writers who want to get into the screenwriting business. The firewalls they erect to keep unprofessionals out has no mercy on those who fail to comply with professional standards. If you follow the rules in this book, your submissions will scream "professional" and this professionalism will get your scripts read and sold.

Read the section in this book on multiple submission log lines. You should use this technique if you have many scripts to submit. Some agents hate multiple submissions, but many do like them. You can't please everyone, but I do show you how to do it, professionally!

A log line should be presented on each query letter you send, right at the top of the letter before you write your first paragraph to the agent. See examples in the illustration section of this book. Why? Because the agent will need to fill-in the production company submission form and release agreement that asks for the log line!

Do you want your agent or their secretary to inaccurately fill in the log line section and make a poor showing? As you can see, there are reasons for everything in this business. Even the simple log line and how it is written and presented in your query letter has a huge impact on success or failure.

QUERY LETTER WRITING SECRETS

An entire book could be written on this subject alone. Examples of query letters are in the illustrations and are referenced in this manual. I just want to add a few extra tips here for consideration when responding to agent magazine listings, those huge listings often called "Agency Surveys."

You have likely noticed each agent seems to want different items. Some want a bio. Others don't. Some want a statement of commercial marketing potential. Other's don't, et,al. It could drive you nuts trying to appease each agent's specific requirements. What to do? Strike a happy medium.

Read the listings and the comments. Look for the common theme. Design a query letter to come close to pleasing all. Of course, that is impossible to do, but it's better than sitting down for weeks at a time writing one hundred personalized query letters.

The idea here is to design one query letter as a template in the ACT! contact database program to appease all agents. This will save you many hours of work. You just enter the agent's name and address and the program will automatically fill in the essentials. Hit the print button and go. Very efficient. Use this method when you query a large number of contacts.

There are times you may want to mail your query with all the desired elements the agent requests in a listing. This is where you can design a cover letter to attach to the query! Again, this cover letter is a template you design in the ACT contact database. You can paste it into the same file page so when it prints both the cover letter and the query are produced. I use this technique when I am querying only a few production companies who run ads in the trades. I can type in a paragraph or two in the cover letter to meet the requirements. It's all performed very quickly and professionally. All writers have their own methods.

Reality is, regardless of what you read pertaining to what an agent wants in the listing, you don't have to send it! If your query letter or log line submission is good, they will request the script. Certainly, if you can send each element desired it will be a plus in your favor, but it's not any guarantee you will receive favorable treatment.

1. If an agent wants a biography? If you have an impressive bio send it with all your submissions. If you're just starting out? Don't send a typical resume! The industry is only interested in screen, stage, magazine or book writing credentials. If you don't have that? Then add a paragraph to your cover letter or to the query letter listing any screenplay contests or courses you have taken in writing. If you don't have that? Don't send a bio. Ranking in any screenplay or play contest in the top one-hundred should be mentioned and can be inserted in the log line paragraph itself. Or you may simply add a short paragraph at the end of your query letter mentioning any seminars or writing courses you have attended.

2. Agents are keen on seeing a query that mentions the writer has taken industry-related academic courses or has attended seminars. If you have not taken any courses? Consider doing so. If there are no courses available? Contact Truby's Writer's Studio for the mail correspondence video and cassette tape series. The Internet also has courses and colleges are offering distant learning courses, too. Don't forget to at least try to get your scripts ranked in screenplay contests. It's good for the bio and good for the script.

3. As long as your script is presented professionally and your query letter is short, concise, to the point... it will work. Avoid long query letters filling the entire page, unless you are listing log lines. Nobody wants to read an entire one-page story of your script. The query should tease, not explain details. Less is always more. Keep pruning your long query letter until you can get it down to one six-line paragraph. Anything more and you risk boring the reader. You can send a full page if you want. I often do and obtain good results, but not as good as a log line listing.

4. Do not mention anything in the query, or in any of your writings, of how well your script will do in the marketplace. Never brag, *"This script will make you millions of dollars."* This will give you an instant rejection as being a total amateur (believe it, people really submit such query letters). Even agents don't know how a script will float in the market or what script will be worth millions, and they are in the business. How do you know? Your heart tells you, but even good films bust at the box office. Also, stay away from making side-deals, *"I'll give you 50% commission instead of the 10% you make now!"* Total amateur! By law, agents can't charge more than 10% (laws and commission rates in California can change). If you want to sell your script (or a book manuscript to a publisher) you had better get professional about your query letters, fast. There are books at the bookstores to help you write effective results-getting queries. Read them!

5. Agents want reliable writers they can work with for the long-term career. Don't mention in your query letter, *"I am reliable and I will not leave you for another agent."* Forget it! It won't work. Can you see the trend in paragraph #4 & #5 here? Don't try to get personal and chummy with the agent. They don't want that at all. It's offensive in the business climate. Stick to business; the business of communicating a good story in the query letter.

6. Realize not all query letters will work with every agent or producer. It is often said writers should avoid sending impersonal letters to agents. Magazines will tell you to get on the phone and call the agency to find out who to send the script to. That's okay if you live in Los Angeles, but it is not practical if you live in Kansas or London. The phone bills will eat you alive. You can send a letter with an S.A.S.E. postcard to the agency requesting a contact name if you want to. It's always acceptable to send a query to a "name" or "title" not a "Dear Sir."

Example: For screenplays, "Dear Story Editor" works just fine! For stage plays, "Dear Artistic Director" also works just fine! Both may technically be wrong, but in the real world it works and you'll still get good results. The key is addressing the letter with the proper title. A production company, "Dear VP of New Acquisitions." A producer is obviously "Dear Producer." A movie star? Better use the name and send the letter to their agent, not to the star's home (you could break this rule and find success, if you have a strong script).

Some agents, producers or production companies will toss the non-personalized letter in the trash or reject it, but they will do that anyway in many cases regardless if you put a name on the query. Unfriendly firms will always be unfriendly. I'm not saying to ignore the rule. If you can find a contact name, by all means do use the name. If you find a firm you really want to establish a relationship with badly? Get the name.

If you are simply responding to an annual survey of 70+ agent listings and the agent does not list his/her name? Send a "Dear Story Editor" query. Why? What are you going to do? Send out a bunch of letters asking for the contact name while everyone else is busy sending in queries and getting their scripts read while you wait for a name to arrive? You may wait weeks to months for that name or, it may never arrive or arrive so late the person no longer works there!

Over a period of time you will compile a database of your own and you will insert names as you find them. For now, the important thing is to get your queries in the marketplace. You will learn from experience the use of a title will work just as well as a letter with a name. How? The powerful query letter you send overrides the missing name factor.

7. Do not make statements in your query letter to the effect, *"This script is perfect for director, James Cameron, actress, Jennifer Saunders, and Kate Winslet."* You'll blow it! The agent and producer will know you know nothing about how the industry works when you write statements like that. Unless you are writing to a packaging agency and they request such advisory don't recommend actors! Stay clear of casting suggestions.

8. Never fib about your qualifications. Some have tried this and it does not work. And if it does? You'll be found out and liars are punished, eventually, with abandonment due to a bad reputation. Don't fabricate education, industry relationships, film credits, contest wins, production deals, etc. Many writers do this and it may get the script requested, but at some point in the process it will be uncovered and the deal sunk. Why? Dishonest people usually are thieves and no production company will trust the script for originality even if it is copyrighted and registered. Trust is important in the business. Hollywood is full of lies, but you, as a writer, can't play the game. Be honest to all and to yourself.

9. The log line is still King in this business. A well-written short log line will always beat a long, boring query letter. What are all the agents and producers saying in the screenwriting magazines? "Send a brief log line." "Send a concise synopsis." But writers keep sending agents pages of information! Essentially, to market one script, only two short 6-line paragraph are needed. One for the short synopsis, and the second for a brief bio, in that order. If you have no bio? Just one paragraph will do. A full-page is okay if it is telling the story in an "entertaining" way and is not "explanatory" in nature. "Show don't tell" applies in the query letter synopsis!

10. Many agents and producers want to know the beginning, middle and ending of a story submitted in a synopsis. A trend is developing not to tell the ending of the story. I'd still option to go with the old method as it leaves no surprises. Trends can be just that, trends that don't last.

11. Know the difference between a cover letter, a query letter, a synopsis and a treatment. Each serves a specific purpose.

12. Want to know how to generate a bit more heat in your query letter? Look at your mail. Copywriters know what they are doing and they are masters in psychology. Selling scripts is a direct mail business! Read the mail and look deeply for the psychological buttons they are pushing to market the product. Notice how they tickle the emotions. Insurance companies sell "fear." Prosperity books sell "security" and "power." Incorporate direct-sales writing styles into your query letters to add punch to them. Of course, leave out the statement, *"Order your copy, today!"* But do insert a line where the reader feels obligated to respond, *"Looking forward to hearing from you soon."* or *"You better call or you'll lose a million bucks"* - only kidding.

13. Do not get cute in your query letters, *"I just know we will work well together!"* How do you know? The agent may be Bongo Bozo's son for all you know and you'll get what you asked for! In the agent's POV? You may be Majestic Captain Boney of the shipwreck, Asylum!

Rule of thumb: Always stay on the business track avoiding any personal intonations. As a writer you must understand you are despised in this industry right from the start. A screenwriter is often referred to as "A psycho with a script." Why? Because many desperate men and women are writing scripts and trying like mad to break in. Many of these writers have no business sense whatsoever. They make serious errors, not realizing they are seriously breaking the rules of the game. This marketing manual is designed to set you on a straight-line path to professionalism in your marketing endeavors. Think professional, be professional, write professionally. Control your emotions. Do not permit desperation to overrule common sense. Learn patience!

Cover Letter - A brief introductory greeting with very few facts on the page. It is used mostly when submitting a script to clarify a few things that are not in the query or synopsis or to just say, *"Enclosed is screenplay, Mystic Forest. Thank you. Enjoy the read."* You may want to include a line like *"Mystic Forest ranked first place in the Academy Awards Blockbuster Screenplay contest."*

Query Letter - A brief introductory to the storyline you are submitting and a bio. It's a teaser to get the reader to request your script. It does not sell the script! It sells excitement about the script/story. You don't need a biography if you don't have one related to writing credentials or education, so leave it out. Don't send a resume unless the agent requests it, or it's a killer resume loaded with screen credits!

Synopsis - A one-page version of the query where the essential elements of the story are conveyed in an entertaining manner. Don't "talk about" or "explain" the story in a dull manner. The reader should be lifted out of his/her chair and transported into the story. Write the synopsis in an action mode so the feel of the story can be realized.

Treatment - New writers should not waste time writing a treatment. You need a completed script! Treatments are for established writers who are known to be able to deliver quality scripts who are trying to sell the idea of the story in order to be hired to write the script. Once you have a script, a treatment is no longer needed. Write the script and bypass the treatment. There are many successful writers who have never written a treatment. This advice has just saved you weeks of hard work!

All you need to do now is write your script, draft a good query letter, a polite cover letter and a synopsis for each script you have. Each is only one page long, single-sided, with lots of white space on the page. See the illustrations for samples.

14. Yes, you can send a synopsis with your query letter to an agent. No, you cannot do this with a producer or prodco unless you submit a release form. You can send a cover letter to all, but it may not be necessary. Cover letters are usually used when submitting the script.

SAMPLE QUERY LETTER TO AGENT
I've been told, and you've likely read, not to submit multiple projects (shopping list) on one letter or mailing. It has long been advised to submit only one script query such as in Fig. 1-16, 1-17, 1-18, 1-27 and 1-25. With hundreds of rejections and the hundreds of dollars in postage and mailing supplies, etc., I became impatient and reasoned multiple submissions would work if only brief log lines were used. Good news, folks. It works just fine with agents, producers and production companies.

Here's a sample of what I used with success. See Fig. 1-8. Notice how I put a simple checklist at the bottom. This makes it very easy for the agent to respond. Always include a #10 S.A.S.E. (**S**elf-**A**ddressed, **S**tamped, standard business-size **E**nvelope.) Some writer's use postcards to save a few cents. Envelopes give privacy. You don't want the world to see your rejections, so don't use the postcard method in your query letters. The query letter response postcard is not the same as you would use as a return receipt for a script submission as illustrated in Fig. 1-14.

Postcards tend to get chewed up in the mail machinery and become lost. Letters withstand the rigors of transit. A query postcard balances on the edge of unprofessionalism. Opinions vary. The only postcard that should be used is for a return receipt when submitting your script. It is inserted in your submission package.

The query letter must be brief. Imagine the recipient walking into the office and seeing the typical fifty or more letters to read. You have ten seconds, maybe twenty on a good day, to grab attention. You don't have to follow the format of the letters I've written as demonstrations.

You can be more creative and open with a line like,

"My face is red. Why? Because grannies are tracking me down and have taken over my city. I'm the honorable mayor of Lost Angus and..." Letting your character tell the story. Or *"Imagine what would happen if little ol' grannies armed themselves with military might and took over (name the city agent lives in)? You would be out of business and in jail! The bad news is, they are coming!"* Or *"Freeze! Keep your hands where I can see them. You're under arrest for literary hijacking of screenplays. My name is Detective Columbus, Columbo's renounced brother, and my mission is to grab your attention!"*

Just being <u>different</u> than all the typical letters the agent will likely read today may get you a much better response. Why? Because it shows you have a new twist and are very creative. If it gets too corny or cute, it backfires with a rejection. Oh, well. You tried. No hard feelings. Keep trying alternatives until you find a formula that works for you.

Don't buy fancy-dancy stationery with cute drifting clouds, psychedelic borders circling the entire page, etc. Just plain old business grade stationery is fine. You don't need personalized imprinted stationery with matching envelopes. You may use off-the-shelf soft color cotton paper with an ordinary K-Mart #10 envelope with results equal to expensive stationery. First impressions count, but content is what sells.

No spelling errors! Keep it brief, just a few paragraphs. The query letter is to not sell, but to tease. The script does the selling. Plain and simple is the key in this business. Too much flash is the advertisement of an amateur.

Remember, never, ever, send your script to anyone unless they have specifically requested it. Many people still send scripts to agents, prodcos, directors, actors, producers by blind chance. This overloads the system and it always hurts the person who mails unsolicited scripts with a big rejection. Some rules can be stretched, but not this, due to legal consequences to your recipients. It's a game you should not play. If you persist, your name will get around and nothing you send will be responded to. Be professional and play by the rules on this one. Trust me.

Looking at Fig. 1-8 this is an authentic letter to a fictitious firm advertising some of the author's scripts. Note the statement "Referred by the *Hollywood Scriptwriter*." Use this <u>only</u> when you find a request for script submissions in the *Hollywood Scriptwriter* magazine (or substitute name of another magazine or book listing).

Often, a producer or prodco will request that you send the script when listed in the market section of the *Hollywood Scriptwriter*. Not a good idea unless you are certain the firm is reputable. Always send a query letter first with a S.A.S.E. When you receive a response, then mail the script.

Note: In Fig. 1-8 after the title of the script, immediately tell the reader the genre. State whether the script is a screen play or stage play or MOW. See item #5 and #6. At the top, mention all are feature film log lines. TV script and stage play otherwise noted. Let the reader know if it's a feature or a sitcom. Why? Agents also handle book authors. Is the log line a book? A play? A feature? It's precisely spelled out in this sample letter.

Also inform the reader if the script has a male or female leading role. Often, agents are looking for specifics. The log line is brief and to the point. Note #9 ranked high in a screenplay contest. It came in #6 out of 13,000 entries! (The first five were TV scripts so it actually ranked #1 in feature film). Explain this in the query letter or include a copy of the award with the query. Do not staple. You may use a paperclip, but that too is unnecessary.

MULTIPLE SUBMISSION LOG LINE QUERY

Fig. 1-8 is a sample of a multiple submission query letter. Some may disagree with this approach and that's okay. All I can say is the vehicle works very well. My reasoning? It says more without having to say, *"Dear Story Editor, I have written six screenplays and I've included six synopsis for your consideration."* Now that will tweak any agent's wire if you send a huge package like that. The log line listing sure beats having to mail six individual letters and cuts the cost of postage, supplies and time way down (see Fig. 1-24).

Note: You hear it time and time again, agents are looking for people who can demonstrate they have more than one script. Well, here it is, right in the agent's face and with each log line listed as a brief teaser. It works. I've had numerous prodcos and agents request scripts with this letter. Many have complimented the form. Enough said.

When you query agents give them the chance to be removed from your mailing list. See Fig. 1-18 (last line in letter text). Some agents slip into the marketing loop then later decide to permanently close doors to outside submissions and operate on referrals only. Believe it or not, very, very, few will check this line. You may receive two out of six-hundred who request removal.

RESPONSE TIME - LEARN PATIENCE, PLEASE!

When you send a script or query letter to an agent, prodco, producer, actor, etc., don't pester them with phone calls. It's a mistake to do so. On query letters, wait sixty days, then follow up with a polite letter asking the status of their response. When sending a script, treatment or synopsis, wait thirty days then write a letter asking if a decision has been made. Do not call!

Consider this business a mail-order adventure, because that's exactly what it is. If you do call, be very brief and extremely polite. The phone should only be used for "important" business. Soliciting your script may be important to you but may not be to the recipient. Use the mail to build a relationship then later phone calls may be permissible. Ask first.

There are writers who call agents and producers who talk forever, complain when they get rejected, or become rude and offensive. These people ruin it for everyone. There is a saying in this industry, *"Screenwriters are psychos with a script."*

If you play by the rules and take rejection with professional flair, it will keep lines of communication open for your future projects. This is a very tough business to tackle. It's uncaring and full of hype. Over time, repeated rejections can work on your nerves. Join the club. We all get rejections... dozens to hundreds, and more. Learn patience.

HOW TO FIND PRODUCTION COMPANIES

A good source is the *Hollywood Reporter*, *Hollywood Scriptwriter*, and the *New York Screenwriter* magazines. You can use the Weekly Edition of the *Hollywood Reporter*. A daily series is available, but it costs more and is not necessary for our purposes.

Hollywood Creative Directory, Dept. C, 3000 W. Olympic Blvd., Suite 2525, Santa Monica, CA 90404 (310)315-4815, (800)815-0503, lists over

7,000 producers, studio, network and development executives, including TV show staff.

New York Screenwriter publishes the Annual Screenwriter's Guide listing prodcos, agents, etc.

Hollywood Scriptwriter publishes the Annual Agency Review. See address listed herein under, "How Do I Find Agents?" And see paragraph #9 on querying producers and prodcos.

Another source: Ross Reports Film Guide Publications, Dept. A-3, 1515 Broadway, NY, NY 10036 (212) 536-5294 cost approximately $50 per year. Also by the same firm, Ross Reports Television and Film, Dept. A-3, P.O. Box 5018, Brentwood, TN 37024 (800-817-3273) lists talent agents, casting directors, network prime time programs, daytime serials, TV and network producers and packagers, syndicated cable and TV programs, literary agencies with interviews with industry professionals and more.

SAMPLE QUERY LETTER TO PRODUCTION COMPANY
1. Send the request to submit letter. See Fig. 1-9 or
2. Just send log lines with a General Release. See Fig. 1-8 and 1-3.

Always send the release whenever you mention the title, theme, premise, log line, or a synopsis of your story to a production company, director, producer, actor's manager. You don't have to send a release to literary agents, unless they specifically request a release when advertising in one of the screenwriting magazines. It will never hurt you to send a release, but it will if you don't when you should have. You'll get a quick response from the legal department officer rejecting your query. One exception. It's a good idea to send a release when submitting to an agent or manager that represents an actor you are trying to make contact with. I'd start with item #1 above as the best way to initiate contact. If you get no response, then try step #2.

A word: Do not send synopsis, detailed queries or log lines to the major studios: Sony Pictures, Disney, MGM, etc. It's a dead-end. Policy excludes any submissions unless a WGA signatory agent submits the script. You can, however, send the request to submit letter as in Fig. 1-9. If they write back saying, *"We are open to look at your material if your WGA signatory agent forwards them to us."* Then contact your agent to send your material. If you don't have an agent? Don't write to the major studios, period. It's a waste of your time and money.

GENERAL RELEASE FORM FOR PRODCO/PRODUCER/ACTOR'S MANAGER
Fig. 1-3 is a single page release. Use this when you submit your log lines, queries and/or script. You don't need to use this form when contacting literary agents. You don't need to use this release if prodcos or producers send you their own release forms.

Use the release whenever you reveal any details about the story or characters. See Fig. 1-10 for a sample query letter. Fig. 1-11 is an example of a unprofessional query you should not send to anyone.

RELEASE FORM TO AGENT
Generally, you do not need to send a release form to literary agents when you query them. You do not need to send a release when you mail an agent a script they have requested, but it doesn't hurt to do so. Fig.

1-3 is a sample of a release form.

HOW DO I FIND PRODUCERS, STUDIOS AND DIRECTORS?

Easy. Write to Lone Eagle Publishing Company, Dept. A, 2337 Roscomare Road, Suite Nine, Los Angeles, CA 90077-1851 (310)471-8066. Ask for their *Entertainment Industry* catalog. Here you will find books listing addresses. Contact Directors Guild of America 7920 Sunset Blvd., Los Angeles, CA 90046 (310)289-2035 for information on how to contact a specific director.

To contact a specific producer; Producers Guild of America, 400 Beverly Drive, Ste 211, Beverly Hills, CA 90212 (310)557-0807. Also, The Writer's Network, Dept. Z-1, 289 S. Robertson Blvd., Suite 465, Beverly Hills, CA 90211 (800)646-3896 can help. There are other methods, but these will get you rolling.

SAMPLE QUERY LETTER TO PRODUCER

Sometimes producers/directors advertise for scripts in the trade magazines, most do not. The best way to reach them is from a mailing list or from a book listing. Never, ever, never send them anything unsolicited. You should simply write a query asking permission to submit your script for consideration. See Fig. 1-9. You can use this letter to contact producers, directors, studio prodcos or an actor's manager.

HOW TO OBTAIN A LITERARY AGENT

Keep trying is the word. You can purchase a mailing list or develop your own from book and trade magazine listings. Persistence is the key, along with having a good sense of marketing your product, and having a script the agent believes is marketable. All of the information in this manual will help you find and obtain an agent.

Many of the large agencies are unavailable unless you are an established writer. It's no big deal. Many professionals confirm the large agencies are not the way to go as you get lost in the shuffle. Contacts are better, but you still can be left behind. I'll let the screenplay books handle that subject.

Getting an agent is a most difficult venture. You can only obtain an agent through sheer determination, persistence, good material, or by referral from another writer, producer or agent. Just keep on plugging away. Keep the query letters in the mail. For some it takes months, for others, years and hundreds of rejections. It's a numbers game and a test of patience. See Fig. 2-3 for a sample letter you can send to a writer.

Agents may say "No" today -- "Yes" next year. You just keep marketing your products, including producers and prodcos. When you make a sale you'll have your agent with a quick phone call.

If your query letter obtains a low response, try rewriting the query to generate sizzle. If the query grabs attention it will generate a request to see the script, that is, if the agency is currently in the market for such genre at the time you mailed the query. That's another reason why I like the multiple submission log line approach.

Bear in mind, most agents will send a rejection letter. You're looking for the agent who will say, "*Yes, send the script.*" It often requires a ton of mailings to find them. Novelists, salespersons, job seekers and all screenwriters experience the same denouncing rejection process, too. You are not alone.

LOCATING A MOVIE STAR TO READ YOUR SCRIPT

You have a completed script perfect for a specific actor or actress. (We all do). First, some advice.

1. You saw an actor in a (fictitious) action adventure movie "Sky High" that was a big box office hit. You have an action adventure movie similar to "Sky High," so you want to send it to the actor. The actor is not interested. Why? Because s/he already played a part like that before. So why would s/he want to do it again? It's not the genre, it's "similar" that is a turn off. Keep in mind the actor may want to do something else.

2. Don't write a script with a specific actor in mind, because if you do and the actor is not interested, you've dramatically limited your market It's a big mistake beginning writers make. Avoid it. Anyway, actors don't want characters and genre scripts that fit their image, they want stories that will boost their career. So just write a dynamite part and let the actors fight for the honors. Easier said than done.

3. Don't write a script with two star actors in it. Actors do not like competition, most of the time. They usually want to be the #1 character, most often the hero, of course.

4. Actors are constantly looking for great scripts. In fact, they are crying for them. They receive most of their scripts to examine from their agent or manager.

5. Do not send the agent or manager a detailed synopsis or script. You send them a basic query letter. Log lines of your scripts (Fig. 1-8) are okay to send. Include a release form like in Fig. 1-3. Be professional. Actors are concerned about being sued just as the producers and prodcos are. Follow the same rules. Use a query in Fig. 1-21-A or Fig. 1-22 to initiate communication. A simple "request to submit" letter with S.A.S.E. will inform the actor's manager you are professional and will not harass them with unprofessional hype, phone calls, etc. This also filters your letter from the fan mail, a good reason why you should not write to the actor or actress.

Write to the manager, agency, producer, director or prodco who has worked with the star. If your letter is ignored, wait a couple months and try again. Don't write to all at the same time. First query the manager or agent, then later try the producer, then the director and prodco. Wait six months and repeat the process again. See Fig. 1-22 B and Fig. 1-23.

6. Here's some good advice. When you finish your first, second, or third script you may be tempted to send the script to actors and actresses. Hold on! This could be a mistake. Why? You may not have the full experience yet that you need to write well enough to approach these professionals. Wait until you have at least six scripts under your belt. By this time, you'll likely have a good script to send. If you can't wait (most writer's can't), then go for it and hope for the best. As long as you are courteous, professional and do not pester or whine, it won't ruin your chances for future submissions.

7. If you send unpolished scripts to actors, you may ruin future opportunities for yourself (though not always). If your script ranks high in a screenplay contest, send a query to actor's agent you feel fits the character role. If you receive a great review from a script analyst, go for it. Get the drift? Generally, don't send script to actors' agents until you are ready to do so.

8. Agents and prodcos, if they like your script, will package the script with actors anyway. That's what they do. But if you have a hot script, it certainly will be advantageous to query actors. You don't have to focus marketing efforts on actors to sell scripts. Many writers don't bother taking this avenue. But it is a viable option to pursue if you want to explore this scenic road to sell your script. Why? There are actors who can "green light" projects by simply saying *"Yes."*

9. If you wish to contact a star's agent or manager: Screen Actors Guild, 5757 Wilshire Blvd., Los Angeles, CA 90036 (213) 954-1600. Be informed they, as most guilds, do not give out addresses. You can mail them a letter requesting they forward it to the star or manager. They are not a mail forwarding service so you may or may not obtain a result. Use the agent and manager directory listings in published books. They are listed in this manual. See Fig. 1-21 or 1-22 for sample letter. If you call the SAG (guild) they can tell you who is the star's agent or manager.

10. You can also find celebrity contacts in the Hollywood Reporter's *"Blu-Book."* It includes: TV and film production companies, studio executives, producers, directors, actors and celebrities talent, business managers, and literary agencies. Also, *Academy Players Directory*, Dept. 4-A, 8449 Wilshire Blvd., Beverly Hills, CA 90211

CHAPTER 8

S.A.S.E. IT'S MORE THAN WHAT YOU THINK IT IS

Always include the S.A.S.E. in a query letter, even if a few are not returned to you. It's just the cost of doing business. If you don't, the agency will absolutely not deal with you and you're simply wasting time and money and asking to be ignored.

Believe it or not, many agents persistently complain they are receiving queries without the S.A.S.E. It's amazing so many writers ignore this established marketing rule and wonder why they can't get anyone to read their scripts. Use the S.A.S.E. on each and every mailing! See Fig. 1-12, 1-13, 1-14. It's frustrating and expensive but those are the rules. Do or die.

MAILING SCRIPTS - FOLLOW THE RULES

When you send a script, you don't have to pay 1st class postage. Use "Special Standard Mail" (Used to be Special 4th-Class Mail, also known as book rate.) As of 1999, the Postal Service has changed the Special 4th classification to "Special Standard Mail." Your script is a "playscript" so it qualifies for the reduced rate.

You can purchase a "Special Standard Mail" stamp at any office supply outlet or you can allow the postal service to stamp the envelope (however, they perform a sloppy job that makes the mailing look cheesy). Use large type and red ink, same size and color postal service uses.

Some postal employees will question the contents to verify if the item qualifies for the special rate. Most have told me screenplays qualify under the "manuscript" section of the postal rules. I've had some tell me scripts do not qualify and told me I had to mail it at the expensive rate.

Who's right? DMM Issue 46, 7-1-93 Postal Eligibility Regulations E416 (1.2, f) clearly states playscripts qualify (which is what a screenplay is). Paragraph (e and i)... or scripts prepared solely for use with such recordings (or media). Insist on using the Special Standard Mail [old 4th-class rate book rate]. Ask for a supervisor (or higher authority) if you get flustered by a novice postal employee.

A screenplay is not a book as it is not permanently bound (pages glued to spine). However, it is a "manuscript" for all intent and purposes, for it is delivered to a literary agent, producer or prodco, and treated exactly like a book manuscript -- read and photocopied for distribution to potential buyers just as all book "manuscripts" are. The term in Merriam-Webster dictionary; *"A written or typewritten composition or document."*

The confusion lies in the terminology, "Book Rate" commonly used by postal employees. If it's not a perfect-bound book, postal employees may say the script doesn't qualify for Special Standard Mail. Considerable confusion. It seems postal employees make their own rules as they self-interpret the postal rule book on this issue. You'll get a different answer from each employee. Am I confused or what? If your post office insists scripts go 1st Class, then do so, but appeal for a resolution. Postal rules can change, so ask for the latest copy.

Example: First Class postage at the time of this printing is $3.00 and Special Standard Mail is about 4th is $1.74 to mail a script. You need not include a S.A.S.E. with the script if you don't want the script returned. Just make sure you mention this in your query letter, *"In the event you pass on True Bums, no need to return the script."* See Fig. 1-15. You do include a #10 S.A.S.E. as shown in Fig. 1-14. This will save postage money. It adds up fast!

It's cheaper to print a new script on your laser printer, and the next reader obtains a fresh clean copy. Plus, if you're like me, I often do small rewrites on my scripts each time they are rejected, so the old script is outdated and useless to have returned. You can send your script 1st class mail and the S.A.S.E. Special Standard Mail class. Unless someone is screaming, *"Send the script now!"* use Special Standard class mail.

In this business it's, *"Hurry up and wait."* So why bother with the expense of 1st class mail? You'll soon see how much postage costs add up when you have been shipping scripts and query letters for a few years. And it likely will take years to sell your first script. It's not unheard of to take a decade. You'll learn the meaning of patience in this business.

When you mail a script, use a bubble-type mailer so the script doesn't get all banged up in transit. The Tyvek brand bubble-type mailer cost more but works well and looks clean. The Tyvek non-bubble type is great for a S.A.S.E. as it is reusable since stamps and tape easily peel off to be used again if the stamps have not been cancelled. A good source of mailing supplies: Browncor International, 770 South 70th Street, P.O. Box 14770, Milwaukee, WI 53214-0770 (800)-327-2278.

You most certainly can use a standard paper bubble envelope if you wish. They are durable and won't tear in the mail. I only mention Tyvek brand as the envelope is the best you can buy. Your submission will be professional using any "plain" manila or white standard bubble-type mailer as long as it does not contain any "Air Mail," "Two-Day Delivery" or other useless insignia. "First Class Mail" or "Priority" imprinting or labels are fine as long as you ship it that way.

A fancy shipping envelope will not gain you any advantage over other scripts, so don't waste your money.

If you want your script returned, insert a non-bubble Tyvec mailer so it lies flat in your bubble-type mailer. Put the firm's return address on the upper left corner, your address in center, and affix postage. See Fig. 1-13. If you don't put the firm's return address you may not know who returned it if no rejection/response letter is attached to the script. Never mark the script with codes or other identifying tracking notations.

Very Important: On the outside of the envelope you must put the following at the lower left, "Requested Screenplay / Release Enclosed" or "Requested Manuscript / Release Enclosed." This is so the prodco, producer, or agent knows the script was requested and they know it is safe to open the envelope because it has a release inside. Otherwise, your script may be returned unopened or tossed in the trash. Why? Because people send unsolicited scripts and then later try to sue the firms for stealing their ideas. Remember, they are more gun shy of lawsuits than you may believe. Is this what is happening to you? Someone requests your script and you never hear from them again?

When making a mailing label I use the "ACT!" program, creating a mail merge template of bold font fields at 16-point of the address, return address, and **"Requested Screenplay / Release Enclosed"** labels. Once printed, I cut it out and affix to envelope with clear tape. This saves time from handwriting addresses and purchasing shipping labels and it looks professional. The same is used for the S.A.S.E. to return the script.

Critically noteworthy: I rarely use the S.A.S.E. as I hardly ever ask for my scripts to be returned. It's not worth the expense in postage! Also, I keep making small rewrites, so why bother with an old script? You can save money by not returning the script. Make certain you clearly mention you do not want the script returned on your cover letter, otherwise you will appear unprofessional for not inserting the S.A.S.E. Of course, you still send a #10 size S.A.S.E. envelope with the submission even if you don't send the S.A.S.E. to return the script. See Fig. 1-9.

A HUGE MISTAKE TO AVOID WHEN MAILING YOUR SCRIPT

Many writers are paranoid and they worry about two things: **1)** Did my script arrive? **2)** I need proof I sent these people my script just in case they steal it!

The solution is easy. Enclose a S.A.S.P. (Self-Addressed Stamped Postcard) the recipient can return to you. Write on the reverse side, "True Bums Script Received." Problem solved.

Now, here's what not to do. Never send a script using mailing services where the recipient must sign for delivery: Certified mail is one example. Fed-Ex, UPS and other special mailings where signatures are required for delivery are to be avoided, unless you are specifically requested to do so, do not use these services.

Agents and producers are tired of dealing with amateurs who are filled with multiple levels of paranoia. It's a turn off to receive scripts that must be signed for. It imposes a feeling of distrust right off the bat. It's the same reason why you don't put the copyright symbol on your script! So, reveal your professional state of mind by simply mailing your script with no return receipt or signature required. Use a S.A.S.P. for a return receipt.

For added speed, you may use the U.S. Postal Service "Priority" mail, but it really doesn't speed anything up, it just costs you more money, that's all. Your script has to sit and wait its turn to be read anyway, so don't bother with it. Use Special Standard or First Class mail.

Your method of mailing can determine your mental status and attitude. Simply looking at the submission envelope, the recipient can tell your mode of professionalism. If you are desperate? You will ship quickly because you are hungry for a sale and we know this industry fears desperate people! Priority mail and other overnight delivery packages reveals how desperate you are. Slow down, be calm, and send the script without fanfare. This transmits a much better impression of you. This is now a good time to review your query letters for any indication of desperation that may be revealed.

POSTAGE STAMPS - A DEAD GIVEAWAY OF AN AMATEUR SUBMISSION

Believe it or not, the type of postage stamps you use on all your mailings, especially query letters, has a strong impact on your presentation revealing your professional status. Business requires the use of business stamps. That means, American flag, Statue of Liberty, whatever business is using at the time. No stamps of flowers, images of persons, holidays, etc. When agents see unbusiness-like stamps, it reveals immediately they are dealing with a person who is immature in the business world.

WORD OF WARNING - SCAMS

There are unscrupulous businesses out there who want to critique and edit your script for a price. Some are plain out-and-out rip-offs. They will take your money and have some unknowledgeable editor literally trash your script beyond recognition and you'll gain nothing but a thinner wallet. On the other hand, there are mighty good services that can really make you shine.

Ask writers for referrals to the better firms before you part with your money. It is the author's personal opinion, agencies that perform total rewriting services for huge fees are in a conflict of interest business situation. If they can't represent you, they will take hundreds of dollars to rewrite your script and still not represent you. Put two and two together. An evaluation fee is one thing, but other services for large fees are quite another, so beware.

Here's a common scam. It's legal but designed to part you and your money... quite a bit of it at that. Some agent, producer or director is advertising for scripts. You send yours and you receive a phone call, *"We like it, but it needs work. I know somebody who can fix it for one-thousand dollars."* Or *"We have access to script doctors and evaluation services. If you decide to use these services we may (or will) represent your script."*

Advice? Use another independent firm that is not associated or referred by any agent or producer. Kick-back schemes (questionable referral fees) are commonplace in this business.

Some referrals are legitimate and not part of any scheme, but it's very difficult to decipher which are and which are not. It is true many agents will take on a script once it has been fixed of errors. However, only you should decide who shall fix the errors.

My advice would be to have a professional working or retired screenwriter do the fixing. Joe Fixitup in a dim-lit back-room office shouldn't be hired to do the job. There are other scams the screenwriting magazines can inform you about.

Screenwriting contests are booming big time. Submit to the well-known established big name promoters. Who knows what is really going on with all the others? There is no real auditing or verification taking place with many contest operations.

If you win a screenplay contest, or rank high in the first ten places with some unknown firm the film industry does not recognize as being worthy, they will not be knocking on your door to buy the script. It can, however, be a marketing tool to help you get your scripts requested when you mention the high rank in your log line or query. Competition is often of lesser caliber in the smaller contests and such contests are viable marketing enhancements for the novice screenwriter.

The author has mixed feelings about agents and production companies conducting screenwriting contests. They have taken a "creative approach" to soliciting scripts and getting paid for it! In my opinion it's a conflict of interest. Certainly, if you win you'll receive some prize money, representation and even an option on the script. That's the "lure" to get you to part with your money. They are working on the writer's dreams. Yet some are very legit while others are questionable.

Assume the firm makes $150,000 net on the contest entry fees and you win. They option your script for $10,000 and it sits in a closet somewhere for two or more years. They still made a great profit of $140,000! Can you see conflict of interest here? It is a great filtering device where a production company or agent can make money at the same time finding those rare gems. It's intelligent marketing for sure!

You will spend a small fortune entering every screenwriting contest to obtain recognition, prize money, options and representation. But when you add up the numbers, the contests are still not the way to go for most writers, only those who win. Everyone else loses. The best method still is old fashion marketing of your work through personal networking and query letters. The sales of spec scripts prove it! The traditional system will always work. It's not glamorous, but it's still the way Hollywood really works. Let's talk a bit on the bright side of screenplay contest as they do serve a very good purpose.

SCREENWRITING CONTESTS

Join the fun. Screenwriting magazines will keep you informed of the many contests, entrance fees and deadlines. It helps if you rank high in these contests, when expounding the fact in your query letters. It immediately shows the agent or prodco story editor this script has something going for it. I recommend you participate in the contests. Even ranking in the top 100 in some respectable contests can open doors for you. If you rank in the quarter-finalist stage that's good news.

Certainly, winning it will do wonders, but don't sell yourself short if you rank low. The same script could win next year, as judges are usually changed year-to-year. *Writer's Digest* has screenwriting, TV, and stage play competitions. Writer's Digest Screenplay Competition, 1507 Dana Ave., Cincinnati, OH 45207 (513)531-8250. You only need the first 15 pages for this competition, so you may want to submit your unfinished script (submission rules can change so check with Writer's Digest before submitting your script). The entry fee is a reasonable $15 or so.

Some contests charge as much as $50 to $75 to enter. Most hover in the $35 range. For stage plays, contests can be found in the Dramatist Guild quarterly and monthly newsletter.

A fairly good rule of thumb for selecting a contest is to determine who will be judging the scripts. They should be top names in the business, but also currently active players in production circles who have juice to green-light projects. What happened to the winners of the contest? Are they now working writers in the industry? The contest ad materials promise many things but are they realistic and actually achievable?

Many successful screenwriters don't use contests and some don't believe in them. I believe they can assist you in the marketing process to the extent of giving you recognition in your query letter even if you don't win but rank in the top one-hundred. Consider contests as a marketing tool. There are too many contests to list here. Here's a few to consider.

--Scriptwriter's Network, Dept. SS, 11684 Ventura Blvd., #508, Studio City, CA 91604. (323)848-9477.
--Southwest Writers Workshop. Address is in firms mentioned section.
--Writer's Digest Magazine. Address is in firms mentioned section.

SCREENWRITING MAGAZINES & SCRIPT RESOURCES

The *Hollywood Scriptwriter* and the *New York Screenwriter* magazines are already mentioned. *Creative Screenwriting*, *Script* and *Written By:*

magazines are certainly not to be ignored.

Discounts: You should inquire if discounts are available for readers of this book. Some have agreed to offer discounts, many will if you ask. If you see a percentage or dollar figure in the listing, a discount has been confirmed.

-- *Creative Screenwriting Magazine* contains at length interviews, etc. The cost is approximately $25 per year. Write to; Creative Screenwriting, 6615 Franklin Avenue, S4, Los Angeles, CA 90028-9723.

-- The WGA publishes a magazine titled: *Written By:* Contact; WGA, Written By: Magazine, Dept. J, 7000 West Third Street, Los Angeles, CA 90048-4329 (888)974-8629. Price is approximately $40 per year. Lots of professional guidance here and a great tool for writers to submit scripts to the television industry.

-- Here's another magazine: *Fade In:* Dept. T-1, 289 S. Robertson Boulevard, Suite 465, Beverly Hills, CA 90211 (800)646-3896.

-- A major source of feature film and TV shooting scripts: *Hollywood Collectables*, Dept. A-3, 120 South San Fernando Blvd., Suite 446, Burbank, CA 91502 (818)845-5422.

-- Here's a source to purchase film and TV scripts, The Script Shop, Dept. 5-E, 2221 Peachtree Road NE, Suite D-452, Atlanta, GA 30309.

-- A magazine that may be of interest to you is: *Editor & Writer*, Dept. 4-A, 526 Boston Post Rd., Wayland, MA 01778. Mostly on editing, but some articles are applicable to screenwriting.

-- *Sight & Sound Magazine*, Dept. B-7, 2323 Randolph Ave, Avenel, NJ 07001 is another film magazine you may want to read.

-- *Horizons Magazine* is a collection of literature intended for the film and television industry. It's designed as an opportunity for unknown writers looking for industry exposure. W.M. Publishing, Dept. J, 1130 North Broadway, North Massapequa, N.Y. 11758 (516)783-8428.

You need a support system to maintain your sanity. There will likely be months and years of rejection (no kidding). Subscribing to the *Hollywood Scriptwriter*, *New York Screenwriter*, *Creative Screenwriting*, *Written By:* and other magazines will help keep you plugged-in with the rest of the screenwriter's world. The interviews are uplifting or on occasion not so promising, but they will maintain your focus while awaiting fulfilment of your goal. There are few dedicated screenwriting support groups, except in major cities and on the Internet.

The cost, as you can see, to subscribe to all the magazines will run you over $150 yearly. The price is well worth the admission. If your budget limits you to only a few magazines, here's what to do. Write each magazine and simply ask for a sample issue. Most all will send you one to evaluate at no charge.

"Gentlemen: Please send me a sample issue of (name the magazine here) so I may evaluate it prior to submitting my subscription. Thank you."

Note: Reading about scriptwriting is important, but don't get caught up in a reading mode. You should be in a writing mode!

THE INTERNET'S WORLDWIDE WEB

The Web can be a spider's trap, where everyone is too busy surfing or chatting when they should be writing. The traditional print magazines I believe, are the most effective and productive in all areas encompassing the psychological and marketing aspects of the business you are likely to face. You need to have something to hold on to with your hands and the Internet can't do that for you. Sure, you can print out web pages, but it will never replace the personal touch of a print subscription (unless we run out of trees).

The Web is fine, just don't let it steal your time. You may meet some people who can help you. People who know people in the industry. Then again, you may meet some wonderfully talented con-artists to assist you in your financial affairs. Remember, Hollywood does not have a reputation for honesty. I advise not to post any of your story log lines on the Web until you register your scripts with the WGA and U.S. Copyright Office.

Is e-mail, heavily used by the Web, more effective than the U.S. Postal service's snail mail? No. Business mail is still the standard means of doing business in the entertainment field. Advertising your scripts on the Web could catch a prodco or producer's attention, so you may not want to rule it out as a last-ditch effort to sell a script that just isn't going anywhere.

The danger of advertising is "professional" writers could see your concept and write the script on the idea (ideas are not copyright protected) and you'll be holding the bag. This also holds true for producers. The Web is still too new to do business with absolute safety. I'm not saying the grand majority of writers and producers are dishonest, it's just that it could happen with one or two unscrupulous people out there, so why take that chance? There is no way to prove they stole your plot or characters. You never sent them a query letter!

Consider this: the industry is secretive and highly protective. When prodcos buy a script they want to keep the sale quiet (unless they are trying to attract talent and raise money for the project). For this reason it's probably not a fabulous idea to splash your log lines for the WORLD to see. On the other hand, it's becoming more and more acceptable as time evolves.

In any case, never display your entire script on the Web if it is open to other writers or just anyone who browses. If the website is secure, meaning proprietary people only have access, then this could be an avenue to pursue, still... with caution.

It is not advised to list the entire script's contents in electronic form for anyone to simply download. High security access with accurate tracking of these downloads is required by the service, or no deal. Time may change this point of view. For now, stick with the mail as it is the traditional, acceptable, professional method and you get to keep all the aces.

If a script is a dead horse, then the Internet may have a purpose, or the script should be buried with the horse or rewritten. You can list log lines on your own web page. Copyright your website's home page with a copyright symbol and everything is basically protected (but still individually register your scripts with the WGA and Copyright Office).

As you know, scripts can be sold from the Internet. Be leery of jumping on this bandwagon to riches, fame and glory. The risk of losing your work is high. It would be best to simply purchase ad space and advertise yourself as a writer with multiple scripts available, or explain your story in abstract ways so your idea can't be duplicated. Sell yourself, not the scripts.

When you receive responses via e-mail, it would then be relatively safe to do business. I advise you send a query to verify the credibility of the contact before sending the script. Yes, you could publish yourself with your own home page on the Web and it could be a waste of time and money. The great bulk of scripts bought and sold are acquired through the U.S. postal mail.

There are many website homepages pertaining to screenwriting. The WGA lists signatory agents on their site (www.wga.org). Bear in mind many of these agents may not want you to solicit scripts. Just because they are listed does not roll out the red carpet. I say try, but you may have better results obtaining your list of agents from the mentioned magazines in this book, who publish agencies and prodcos requesting scripts in each issue and in annual agency listings who are "open" to new material and writers.

Many of these listed agencies are in the Southern California area and have the best connections for selling scripts. New York agencies are listed which also have good association with Hollywood / Los Angeles or buy a mailing list.

E-MAIL QUERIES

Writers make the mistake believing e-mail queries do not need to follow proper protocol. For some reason, they feel the query can be a short blurb or a boring long treatment. For this reason, agencies are blocking out their e-mail address on many website listings. Can't blame them as they can not possibly read all the unprofessional mail and it simply clogs up their in-box absorbing too much time filtering the e-mail. Plus, they have the postal mail to filter, tons of it!

If you send an e-mail query, it should mimic as close as possible the illustration examples given in this book. Doing so will enhance your professionalism and likely obtain a positive response from the agency.

This advice may seem elementary, but we still receive many amateur e-mail queries in our book publishing business. It is amazing just how many people out there simply do not understand how to write queries, cover letters and the synopsis. The same is true with screenwriters and playwrights. If you make mistakes in the query letter phase of the marketing process, you will certainly be a duck lined up to be shot with a rejection letter.

The very first phase of the filtering system is looking at the query letter. We can tell, as agents can too, what is professional and worth requesting the material for review from the writer. Conversely, we know at a quick glance who to reject in ten seconds or less!

There must be a frame of mind when you draft your query letter. The first draft or two you concentrate on the message and the storyline and other basic elements that must be presented in a query.

The second phase frame of mind -- imagine you receive 1,000 queries per week. Your in-box is loaded to the size of a refrigerator stacked with letters. As you open them, one by one, what would you be looking for out of the masses?

1. You would recognize a professional by the type of stamp used on the envelope. All the fancy stamped envelopes revealing flowers and celebrities are discarded or sent to another employee for disposal or rejection. This includes all stationery envelopes loaded with cute cartoon characters, sunsets, clouds or other designs.

2. The envelopes you open are examined. You can tell right away by the fancy stationery to toss it aside. You may find proper stationery but the message is too heavy to read, just too much text. Or you don't see the S.A.S.E. so it's tossed right away.

3. You find good brief queries and you read them, but most all are simply boring to read. So you scream "*Somebody, entertain me, please! Give me something different!*" This is the mindset you need to please in your query letter, so it has to be very short and to the point and professional!

Good advice? Read books on how to generate query letters. Read examples. Magazines sometimes run special articles revealing winning query letters that made the writer happy with the results.

It takes a lot of hard work to write a good query. Keep rewriting it until it shines, sells the sizzle not the steak and makes the reader entertained. If not entertaining, it should at least be different than all the rest.

The purpose of the query is to motivate the reader to request your material for further review. It's just a teaser to stimulate action. That's all it does, but it's the most difficult marketing phase to perform.

Many writers simply do not even consider the above factors and write the query any such way they please. It's no wonder they receive so many rejections. The bottom line is this; professionals submit professional queries! These are the queries that make things happen.

See the illustrations in this book for sample query letters. They are effective and they work! Of course, you could do better, but the point is these letters are powerful tools, as is. If you follow the simple format and the style you will see an increase in agents and prodcos requesting your scripts for evaluation.

Keep in mind, these query examples are only effective for the screenwriting and theatrical industry. Do not try to convert them to the magazine or book markets. They will not work.

CHAPTER 9

STALE TITLES

The working title of your script should be brief and high-concept like a log line. It's an old marketing ploy when a script just isn't selling after a couple years to change the title. It's done all the time to hoodwink the prodco computers (or paper file) that has the script's title in the database from a past reader's coverage. Consider this option. It is best to rewrite the script to create a new version, but this is not always required.

MOVIE OF THE WEEK

MOW's are always in demand especially if a true story. The best stories are not always current national news disasters. Insiders bid for these paying lots of money for the rights. The stories you can find are in your own home town where competition is nil. You could even place an ad in the newspaper, *"Screenwriter needs true story for movie of the week. If you have an unusual life experience worth sharing, call:..."* The story should have wide audience appeal.

Examples: Government scandal and corruption, multiple tragedies in a person's life, survival in the wilderness, destruction of a neighborhood by a bad neighbor, etc. Another good source is the local courthouse. Ask the District Attorney about strange cases he's seen. You can review the legal files at the court clerk's office that sequences the case. Church priest, rabbi or pastor may lead you to interesting characters. Old newspapers at the library often turn up gold dust. Use your imagination.

Try to obtain the rights to write a true story on a female because generally, women are the MOW market. If you take a story idea from a API news release, odds are other writers and producers have made their moves already. Newspapers from a small town may have a sympathetic story of someone in the community. And don't forget the people you already know who have had difficult life experiences. It only cost $1 to obtain the rights.

If the movie runs, you can expect to receive approximately $30,000 gross ($15,000 for you; $15,000 for the story owner, less if agent commissions apply). Much more money will be earned if you employ an agent and tag yourself on as associate producer, and an agent will help you obtain international rights, residual payments on reruns, home performance (video) sales, etc., so hire an agent if you make a production deal.

But the first step is to find a story. People who have had a hard time in life, then ask if they would be interested in selling the rights to their story for a movie of the week. (They all say yes!). You sign a contractual agreement to split proceeds 50%-50%.

If you want a sample copy of a comprehensive multi-page story rights collaboration agreement, write the publisher of this book for a copy. The cost is low than having a lawyer draft one for you. Attorneys charge $300 to $500 or more. This sample contract offers protection to you (the writer) if sued, and gives you maximum opportunity to earn rewrite pay and promotions without compensating the story owner. You are only buying the story, not selling your life earnings or career.

The contract also protects from a lawsuit, by limiting disputes to arbitration applicable to the laws of California where entertainment law is well established (you may substitute California with your own state to prevent travel expenses in the event of legal disputes). No contract is perfect, but this one is good enough to get the job done, barring strange and unforeseen difficulties. Of course, you have the option of hiring your own attorney to draft the agreement.

You market the movie of the week to producers who specialize in MOW's or literary agents who handle the TV market. Keep in mind, MOW's can be easily converted to feature films. How? Just add hype to the story. True stories are "Based on a true story." It means you can fudge and put in dramatic elements that never happened, and that includes the actual MOW itself. As long as the storyline is basically correct, it's a true story. Strange, but true. So keep this in mind when writing your MOW, everything need not be absolutely true. A man stranded on a raft at sea may never see a shark, but in the MOW there will be plenty of hungry sharks, circling, snapping huge chunks of the raft. Get the idea?

Advice: Change the names of the original characters and the locations. You don't want a libel suit. There is always a bad guy or corporation involved in people's hard-luck stories, so it's smart to protect identities. A good law book you should read is: *The Writer's Legal Companion* published by Addison-Wesley Publishing Co. Writer's Digest Book Club may sell the book. Any bookstore can special order it for you in the R.R. Bowker's *Books in Print* directory. This is where you'll find every published book in the U.S.A.

The good news is the MOW has the best chances of selling a script for the new writer and seeing the movie on the screen. You can make a good living on MOW's, so consider this opportunity, too.

COLLABORATION RIGHTS

Novice screenwriters make the same mistakes over and over again, due to lack of knowledge of how the business functions and how laws operate. You can't plagiarize - stealing another's creative work -- so don't waste your time mimicking a story created by someone else. Too many new writers think they can write a better story than the established version, make a few changes, and sell it. Nope, you'll be sued unless you have a collaboration agreement with the lawful owners of the copyright and performance rights.

You can write what you want, but you may not have a legitimate copyright if you take the theme, plot, scenes, characters, etc., from another work. You play with fire if you alter a copyrighted or WGA registered script. Obtain permission first, then do it. Plagiarism will get you into deep trouble.

Now, you can write a speculation script (called a spec) based on established characters, if the plot and story is totally new and unrecognizable from a previously copyrighted version. However, you don't own the "character rights" and you must acknowledge this fact when marketing the script at some point. Here, you are taking a chance that the prodco or legal owner of the characters will be interested in doing your movie or play. It's like TV work. The characters have already been established and you're just writing a new story for them to play in.

You're best bet? For feature film, MOW's and stage plays, create your own work based on nobody's characters or story. Now you are the sole owner and you need no permission to market the product and you won't be sued for stealing. Why do novices do these things?

1. They have no creativity to conjure a character, or are lazy.

2. They believe the industry will be receptive to their idea.

3. They fail to comply with entertainment-related law.

4. They don't know better.

5. They don't understand how to market a script.

6. They believe that redoing a successful movie is performed by amateurs. Sequels are always developed in-house by professionals who own the rights to the copyrighted material.

7. Amateurs think that if directors can change scripts, they can too. Wrong. Directors are under contract and are legally authorized to alter the work.

8. Amateurs don't consider themselves as thieves because they do not understand the industry and laws. Once they do see the light, most will stay away from changing any copyrighted material. Those who are blind? A lawsuit will make them see fast.

That "director" I spoke of earlier? He was in process of ripping off scripts by altering the contents of successful scripts and trying to pass them on as his! Desperate men do desperate things.

MARKETING THE STAGE PLAY
Be prepared for a ton of rejection just as in film and TV. Here's a way to break down firewalls.

1. Write the script and contact the local performing arts theater in your town. Ask if any actors would be willing to perform an informal reading. You'll likely have success here. If you've never worked with actors, you're in for a great learning experience. Some are very fickle and will complain, etc. Just ride through it. Be flexible. If your play is rejected by the theater board? Ask around for a local director you can chum-up with or an actor and see if you can do a reading that way. You likely will obtain good results here and the actors will push for the play to be produced, somewhere, if they like it.

2. Once the play is read you'll receive input from your own observations of the script's strength and weaknesses. Actors, producer/director will give input. Make changes, if needed.

3. The actors may want to do the show and push for it at the board meetings. If so, invite a newspaper reporter to do a critique on the show. If the clip is good, attach it to your query letter and mail it to agents.

4. Let's assume all the above failed. You can try another theater. You can just send a query letter and mail it to agents. Yes, you can query the theaters.

5. After you've written your first stage play, join the Dramatist Guild, Dept. A-2, 1501 Broadway, Suite 701, New York, NY 10036. They will give you valuable information to market your stage play. Everything from contracts, theaters seeking scripts, agents, publishers, to good advice.

6. Produce your own show. Idea: Actors work for free in small theaters. Offer to pay them gas and food money. Contact Chamber of Commerce to contact charitable organizations and offer to give a show to raise money for the event. Say, $3 ticket at the door. Ask if the cast can have $1 of this $3 ticket fee. Now you'll have actors being paid, and yourself. You also have a show produced to your credit. Don't forget to invite the news reporter. Nightclubs need entertainment and are viable markets to explore.

7. Word of mouth spreads and if your show had a good audience response the local performing arts theater may want to run it, or a nearby town. Here you get the standard royalty fee per show. Could be from $50 to $1,300. Or you can base it on 10% of ticket sales so there are no up front costs to the theater. Make your own market.

8. Once the show is proven to be successful you can rent a theater, post advertising and produce your own shows. You can rent a movie theater or other large building and offer the owner 10% of gross ticket sales. These are just ideas that can work for you. Consider the possibilities. If your show is successful, you can sell the script direct to performing arts theaters for royalty payments. There is no reason why your play cannot be performed. You can <u>make</u> it happen.

9. Mail queries to the theaters. Dramatist Guild can supply addresses. I've bypassed the queries with small city theaters by mailing the script with a cover letter inviting them to run the play. You can't do this with TV or screenplay scripts, so don't even try it, as it's a different market with unique legalities. Queries, of course, are more economical.

10. Market Insight, Dept. S, P.O. Box 8598, Kansas City, MO 64114-0598 (800)985-4720, has a market report newsletter listing buyers of stageplays. Cost is approximately $40/yr for 12 monthly issues, $25 for 6 issues.

11. Get a copy of the *Writer's Market* book. It has many useful listings for the playwright. It's available on our website.

BASIC TIPS ON WRITING A STAGE PLAY

1. No dead time. Make certain each actor has some purpose while on stage or have him/her exit.

2. Dialog must be heavy, (very heavy compared to screenwriting) along with action. Dialog and action all of the time. The characters must be moving, doing something, saying something. What they say must reveal character and/or push the story forward. Just like film, but more of it. Ten seconds of silence is an eternity to a live performance audience.

3. If there are any clothing changes in a scene, make sure actors have the time to change clothes before they enter the stage again.

4. The story must be compelling. Leading characters must want something and want it badly, desperately, and let the audience know through lots of dialog and action.

5. Use sound effects (SFX). Actor stamps foot to floor, BOOM! Stomps to exit THUMP! THUMP! The characters yell, cry, laugh, whistle, blow a horn, etc. Lots of noise when noise is required. Audiences respond to sounds. Thunder, door bells, phone rings, object drops to floor, lights flicker, etc. Make it all so real. Silence is also a dramatic element, just don't overdo it. Music is important and touches the audience's soul.

6. Think of the potential audience response when you write. Will they laugh? Cry? Boo? Cheer? Or will they sit, listen, and get bored? Don't keep them waiting for something to happen too long. Excessive suspense can be lethargic. People have come to be entertained. Do it.

7. Comedy is not just telling jokes, it's ordinary things people do that are funny. Poking eye with finger, falling down, confusion, insults, embarrassment, pie in face, being slapped or pulled by the nose or ear, surprised, rejected, etc. Watch the Three Stooges and sitcoms for ideas, but don't get too slap-happy or too messy with pie throwing. You can buy books on how to write comedy to learn how it's done, but it generally requires a degree of natural talent to write comically.

8. Let the actors perform. Give them room to breathe and create. No need to tell them every move they have to make. So keep stage description concise like in a screenplay, but ever more brief. Nevertheless, don't be afraid to use directions to assist the director in blocking (where characters stand, look, step, sit, exit, enter, etc.) small theaters with amateur actors will need this input.

9. Read books on how to write stage plays, and go see a few plays. Better yet, ask if you can attend rehearsals. It's a good experience.

10. Don't forget to include drawings of your stage sets along with character and prop lists. Examining a published version of a play will give you details, but don't follow the published version format when writing the play script for submission purposes.

11. The nice part of marketing a stage play is that producers are so easily available. Simply enter the theater, ask for the producer and hand over your script. Another method? Give your script to actors. They often produce and direct at the theater.

For books on playwriting contact Playwrights' Ink, 414 W. 121st. Street, Suite 55, Dept. 1-A, New York, NY 10027 (212)666-4470.

MORE USEFUL INFORMATION FOR THE WRITER

Scenario Magazine publishes complete screenplays in a magazine format. Each magazine has intensive interviews with the screenwriter with approximately six to eight screenplays per issue. Lots of reading here. The screenplays are not formatted in standard script format to conserve space, so don't mimic the form. The author didn't see any marketing advice or agency/prodco listings. Things could change by the time you read this. Ask for a sample issue. There is a lot of intelligent writing in this magazine. Scenario Magazine, Dept. B, 3200 Tower Oaks Blvd., Rockville. MD 20852 (301)770-2900.

When you scan the pages of your script make sure there are no "T" pages -- a line of description at the top of the page and a column of unbroken dialog between characters that runs all the way down the page. This is termed "Talking Heads" as the actors just talk and bore the audience. The film "Contact" is a talking-head film (though it did well in box office sales). It's lots of talk in the first hour or so but the ending is incredible. Don't write a spec script with talking heads as it'll likely go nowhere, fast. Always break up dialog with action in the background (b.g.) or foreground (f.g.) or have the characters do something while talking. You can include sounds off screen (o.s.).

A WORD ON TREATMENTS

Writing a treatment is, in the author's opinion, a waste of time for writing a feature screenplay. For television they certainly have a purpose to break down the story beats to fit the half - to one hour - film/show. Everyone has their own opinion and many writers don't use them.

Since I have used Dramatica Pro and Blockbuster you could say the treatment is already done before the script is written. But there are many times I just have to let the energy flow from the brain to the keys, not knowing where the story is going. It's a mysterious process. Just tap into the universe of knowledge and let it rip. Writing a traditional treatment, for me, shuts down creativity. I can't seem to make it work, or I don't know how to make it work for feature films. I can do better with treatments with sitcoms, to a degree. I admit I have my weaknesses.

More feature film scripts are bought than feature film treatments by a wide margin. I tend to run out of enthusiasm if I write a 30-page treatment. So, my products rely on the completed script, a single page synopsis and the query and cover letter. That's all you need to market each script. If treatments help you, then by all means do them.

It is rare to be asked if you have a treatment. Most everyone is looking for a synopsis and a completed script. If you believe you have to write a treatment for each project, you don't. The treatment can come in handy to sell a concept with the promise to write the script once a step-deal is offered. In this case, it's a time saving device.

You could write three to four treatments in the time it would take to write an entire script. It is a viable marketing tool, and it could expand your inventory of potential sales. I wouldn't do this until you have a few completed scripts under your belt. You'll need to demonstrate you can complete a marketable script before anyone will buy a treatment. Usually, established writers sell treatments. The novice, and most all writers, must still write the screenplay, MOW, TV script to a finished product state.

MOVIES YOU MUST SEE

Here are five movies with unique artistic value that will help you in your screenwriting. They certainly helped me. Techniques you've never read before in any book unfold before your eyes. You may have a difficult time finding them at the video rental store. They do air on TV periodically. You could write to the major networks and ask when they will air again. I believe #1 and #2 were filmed by British prodcos. Check these out.

1. "*The Cormorant*" -- You will learn just how powerful a story can be told visually with very little dialog and the camera off the actors. How they made this film knocked my socks off when I saw it. I discovered a thousand errors in my writing. It's a mystery of a cormorant (a diving sea bird) and the relationship with his new human friend. (This isn't Jonathan Livingston Seagull, folks). It's a powerful story told <u>visually</u>.

2. "*England Made Me*" -- A story of an English businessman in Nazi Germany whose greed creates incredible destruction in his own home. Powerful characters and very strong acting. Low budget film. When Kate's brother is murdered you'll see and feel intense drama. This film helped me understand the power of three character conflicts.

3. "*It's A Wonderful Life*" -- Amazingly, many people have yet to see this movie with Jimmy Stewart and Donna Reed. It's available at all video stores. If you can write a better story than this, or just equal it... you are going to become very rich! This film is so perfect you couldn't change a word of dialog or alter a scene. Talk about perfect structure!

4. "*Terminator I and II*" -- If you saw them both, watch them again with a screenwriter's point of view. James Cameron is a genius with a camera and he wrote the script with a co-writer. The book, "*The Making of Terminator II*" is educational. These two movies can show you how to build tension and keep the action flowing. Every scene has a strong purpose with characters driving the story in a powerful way, wanting something badly.

5. "*The Last Shout*" -- by Jennifer Saunders. The true Queen of British comedy! Her TV sitcom, "*Absolutely Fabulous*" is truly funny and she can teach you much about identification with the character, comical dialog and character expression by watching her in action. She writes and performs her own sitcom and movie. Incredibly talented! The movie isn't a feature-type by American standards, but it's a great sitcom movie with lots of costume changes and sketch tactics. Jennifer Saunders is truly funny and that's why she ranks on my list. Roseanne Barr tried to bring Jennifer to American primetime, *"But her show is too funny*!" That's what the Network Executives said! It's a shame that America's citizens can't have fun watching Jennifer Saunders. You can buy her videotape sitcom series and her movie on the Internet and other sources with contacts with the BBC. Absolutely worth the price of admission!

There are many other movies to recommend and screenwriting books and magazines will point you in that direction, but one must realize it would require more than a lifetime to see all of the movies. You don't have to watch thousands of movies before writing your screenplay. Many writers are too caught up watching movies and not writing.

THOSE WHO MAKE IT

Those who make it in this business make it happen. Everybody gets rejection in this line of work, everybody. Expect it and learn to thrive on the challenge. Keep writing your dream. Never say quit even when you want to. We all reach points, many times, that we just want to give up and say, "*I quit. I've had enough rejection. This is a hopeless situation. Everybody else has success except me.*" If you're a writer, you'll be compelled to write again. This is good and it can be bad. If you fail for eight or ten years in screenplays then maybe your talent is with stage plays, magazine articles or books.

What I've done is write them all, screenplays, stage plays, sitcoms, MOW, etc. I've published books and you can too. Self-help books can reach niche markets. I've written technical and sports books. Consider the alternatives while you're waiting for the big opportunities to arrive. Why limit yourself? There is money and satisfaction in all writing endeavors, from comic books to magazine articles. Open up your horizons, but keep on writing your screenplays and mailing queries. You only need one to say, "Yes" and that's all you need. Those who persevere eventually win. Like in sports, "*The more you fail the more you win.*"

ADVERTISE YOURSELF

Once you finish your first script, you are a writer. Tell people you are. This doesn't mean your relatives, co-workers, or neighbors, but strangers you meet in the course of conversation. You can go as far as wearing a T-shirt, "*Screenwriters say, go see a movie*" or buying the hat the New York Screenwriter and Written By: magazine sells. These are extremes, but if you're in the major entertainment cities, you could be approached by a producer, manager, agent or another writer with good contacts in the industry. Then again, you could be harassed or meet a carjacker. It's a dangerous world.

Ultimately, the best advertising is just keeping your mail flow outgoing. Send your query letters relentlessly. You don't have to send a hundred a week if you can't afford it. Five per week gives you 260 queries in the yearly pipeline.

CHAPTER 10

HOT-SHEET FOR SCREENWRITERS

Currently, *Scr(i)pt Magazine* has a Hot Sheet page. Screenwriters who have an accomplished resume who have not yet sold or optioned a script may submit their information. Send a resume, photo and approximately 16-line paragraph about your accomplishments or a brief log line of scripts you've written. Best to see the magazine first before submitting so you can get an feel for writing up your slot. Scr(i)pt Magazine Hot Sheet, Dept. S, 5638 Sweet Air Road, Baldwin, MD 21013 (888)287-0932 (410)592-3466.

STREAMLINE YOUR MARKETING

It's okay to begin marketing with a mass mailing to generate initial contacts, but many writers fail for numerous reasons. Here are a few.

1) The mailing list is too broad (most are) and does not break down the agencies and prodcos to specific genres. If you have a comedy script and an action/adventure script, you will hit many that do not handle those genres. Luckily, many agencies accept all genre scripts.

2) You may only have one or two or three scripts to market. Nothing wrong with that if they are good scripts, but the rule is that it takes six to eight scripts to gain the experience to write a marketable script. Most screenwriters are not submitting their "best" scripts. Everyone is too excited and over anxious to rush into the marketplace. I was guilty of it, too, so I won't cast the first stone. You won't wait, so no use trying to convince you otherwise. Anyway, you could get lucky. My first three scripts were taken by an agent(after eight rewrites each).

3) Some people query agents and don't even have a completed script. They believe they can sell an "idea" and make a deal. It happens, but usually with producers and established writers who's work is respected and can deliver the goods.

4) Many scripts have gross errors: poor grammar, typos, misspelled words, poor structure, plot holes, unbelievable characters, the list goes on.

5) Writers will not rewrite their scripts. Sounds easy, but reality is it is difficult to rewrite. Running out of ideas creates a problem for making the script better. Time solves these problems.

6) Many pitch every script they have, sending a stack of synopsis/queries. Everyone in the industry will tell you not to do this. You shouldn't. I have found a loophole and that is multiple log lines have been deemed acceptable. But the single approach is, ultimately, a good way to go -- if you can afford it. It's expensive. There is no harm in trying both approaches.

7) Many new writers query the big guns. (I don't want to list the agent names, they will kill me if I do). Forget them. It is rarer than rare they will take a peek at what you have. You'll need a referral to gain access. But if you want to try, go right ahead, it's not illegal. You could be lucky. But why do it and waste your time and ruffle the agencies' feathers? Get a referral and do it the right way. If you have a script sale, then definitely do call. See Fig. 2-3 for a sample letter you can send to a writer requesting a referral.

The most effective way to query agents is debatable, but most agents prefer a query and one page synopsis pertaining to one script. What I did was mass mail multiple log lines to build up a list of responsive agents and prodcos. They requested scripts, rejected them, but left the door open with an invitation to submit other projects. From here on out I use the single query/synopsis approach with these firms.

But there is more. The ACT! program allows me to log-in the specific genres these firms are interested in. This tightens the market to a fine-point focus. You will be able to do this right away reading the screenwriting magazines as agents and prodcos list the genres they handle.

Keep your eyes open for a new agency. Here you stand a good chance of hopping on board as they need product to market. They are more willing to take on new writers. Problem -- many (not all) new agencies go out of business in a year or so. The *Hollywood Agents & Managers Directory* (approximately $50) lists agents but they also identify new agents in the listing. You can purchase it from the Hollywood Creative Directory, Dept. C, 3000 Olympic Blvd., Ste 2413, Santa Monica, CA 90404 (310)315-4815.

When you write to a large agency with multiple agents don't slam-bang each agent in the house. Write to one agent and just take it on the chin if you are rejected. Wait six months, then try another agent with another script. Don't try it with the same script. It turns them off. Okay?

Once you develop your own mailing lists of agents and prodcos you can identify each for the genre they specialize in. But keep in mind, I've seen agents and prodcos advertise comedy only, then later see an ad, "Now accepting all genre scripts." Things keep changing in this business.

ETIQUETTE - DEALING WITH THE DEALERS

Good manners -- a method of artistic social conduct execution. In all your dealings be polite, considerate and complimenting. Some will tell you to send a query letter then call the agent if you have not heard from them. This can be a catch-22. If the agent lost your address and wanted the script, a call would be nice to save the day. It's okay to call, but keep conversation very brief and to the point.

Taking up the agent's time is uncouth. I never call agents or prodcos unless it is related to an important business transaction that cannot be handled by the mail. Realize that phone calls are usually reserved for "critical" business. A follow up letter is recommended over the phone call. It can be considered disrespectful to call on the phone.

If an agent, producer, manager, or prodco does not return your S.A.S.E. a couple times, strike the address from the mailing list. Don't pester them with query letters. Don't take the rejection personal and deliver a nasty letter or phone call. It will only give you a bad name. The person you were rude to today may be a V.P. of Productions tomorrow. There is much upward (and downward) mobility in this business.

When responding to magazine agency surveys, try your best to follow the guidelines each agency requests for submissions. If the agency is currently closed for new material, leave them alone. Wait four to six months, then try. If the agency says they want a query and synopsis give them what they want. If you have many scripts, and the agent handles all genres, you can send log line listings, then let them decide which synopsis to request.

Reminder: Don't send multiple synopsis letters in one package. Some agencies request you just send the script. Generally, you should still send a log line list or a query letter first. What are you going to do? Send the agent ten scripts? You could, but it's your printing and postage bill.

This is a rough business. You have to grow tough skin to survive. There will be days (many days) of extreme frustration and anger. As you become more acclimated to this zany business, you'll learn patience and perseverance. Put your ego in your pocket and just be a nice guy or gal. Your attitude will determine the level of success you deserve. If you fear fire, don't be a fireman. If you fear rejection, don't be a writer. If you want an easy life, try playing slot machines for a living. You may lose your money, but have fun doing so. You chose to enter this business, so maintain proper etiquette and be satisfied you are making progress no matter how slow it crawls along. Stay calm.

Don't pester movie stars, directors and producers. Pester means being overbearing and constantly writing them when they don't respond to you. They receive thousands of these letters. It must be horrible to open the mail and see so many desperate people pleading for help or making grandeur promises of fame and wealth. What a relief it is to see a professionally written query. Once you send your script, don't hound them. Wait a couple months, or longer, then follow with an inquiry letter. See Fig. 1-21 B and Fig. 1-23.

I rarely use follow up letters. Sometimes nothing happens for six months. I'll still wait. Why? Because I'm too busy writing my next script and actively marketing others. In six months time, I'll send them another query anyway on the new script. At this time I may remind them of the previously delivered script. Keep busy and you'll have no time to fret about lagging responses.

If you want to follow up, go ahead. It's acceptable. Once a script is submitted it's okay to call. It's sort of like having a passport giving you permission to call. What gets writers in trouble is cold-calling when no script has been requested. **Reminder:** This is a mail order business. Use the mail. Save calls for important matters and keep them very brief.

Now let's suppose you call or you are called by an agent. Who is doing all the talking? Let the agent talk, but try to cut the conversation time by saying, *"Look, this long distance call is on your nickel. Would you like that I send you the details by mail?"* What this does is take you off the hook of blame for tying up the person on the phone. That's how they think, *"I'm not calling that writer back. Took up my time and I missed important things I had to do today."* Many of these people love to talk too much for their own good sometimes, and your own good, too! Keep conversations brief and business-like.

Never appear happy and excited when you receive a call, *"Wow! ABCD Productions? You liked my script? Great!"* Better to respond with a monotone voice, *"Okay, so what's the deal?"* Once you get excited, they lose interest. This is not a pitch session where you are pitching your storylines and you need to be enthused and show it too. Phone calls are impersonal by their very nature and injecting joyful exclamations is usually not taking care of business properly.

HOW TO OBTAIN A REFERRAL - OPEN DOORS TO OPPORTUNITY

Friends in the business and writer's clubs are valid routes. Another route is to contact a working writer and simply ask permission to submit a script for a read and referral to the agency that represents the writer. Keep the letter very brief and make sure you mention that no strings are attached, that you won't pester the writer if the outcome is unfavorable. Write something like: *"Be assured, if my writing does not meet your standards for referral, I will respect your decision with no further correspondence on the matter."*

Rule #1. Don't do this if you only have one to three scripts. Try this after you have <u>six or more</u> scripts under your belt. A professional writer is not going to want to read a new writer's material for referral reasons.

Rule #2. Enter the script in screenplay contests. If it ranks in the top fifty, then the script may be of quality for consideration.

Rule #3. Don't tell anybody I told you to do this. You did not read this here.

Rule #4. If you tell the writer you will respect his/her decision, you had better do so, even if the response is unpleasant. Take any constructive advice, rewrite the script and move on to another writer. If you upset or harass a writer, the word will get out and no one will read your scripts. Writers are terribly busy, struggling hard just like you, and if they are willing to read your script - believe me - they are doing you a great favor.

Rule #5. You could post an advertisement at a bulletin board where writers hang out. The less you say, the higher the odds of a favorable response due to professionalism. Don't beg, plead, offer money or gifts. A business card size ad works best, "Writer needs recommendation for representation. If you can help, please call...."

Rule # 6. See Fig. 2-3 for a sample letter you can send to a writer to obtain a referral.

FINDING A WRITER TO OBTAIN A REFERRAL

Writers can be found on the Web. You can also write your request for referral letter in care of the WGA. They won't give you the writer's address, but they may forward your letter to the writer's agent. Inquire first with the WGA to verify the forwarding policy still applies.

You need a writer that is actively working in the trade. A retired writer is essentially retired and out of the loop, in most instances, but they can still make a recommendation for you. In fact, a writer that is currently out of favor may gain an advantage to refer another writer to a major agency or production company, as it gives the writer an opportunity to pitch a few ideas. See Rule #6 above.

Be aware, that getting a referral is not easy. Why? One of the big reasons is; why should the working writer give you a referral to his/her agent only to increase competition? Now the agent is selling your scripts! See the angle? Another reason is reputation. The writer puts his reputaion on the line when making referrals so the script and the writer must be of good character. There is another way around these obstacles. See subchapter, *How To Use Coverage Reports*.

As you can see already, there are many angles of attack a screenwriter must handle in the marketing process; queries to agents, prodcos, producers, directors, stars, writers, using script doctors, reading books, entering contests, getting coverage reports and the list goes on. It's work! What you need to do is slow down and just handle each task with a sense of calm and ease, one step at a time. Do not rush, no matter how desperate you may be. Just relax and realize it takes time to market scripts. This is a tough business. Be tough, kind and patient.

MORE VALUABLE TIPS FOR MARKETING SCRIPTS

1. When you query the agent or prodco and receive a "pass" always keep in mind that in six months the agent that passes may be replaced. It happens a lot, and the new agent may request your script. So query again. At some point in time, you may want to consider dropping the agent from your database. I erase agents from the database when S.A.S.E's are not returned. If the agency is again listed in a survey requesting scripts, I'll try again. If again the S.A.S.E. is not returned, I'll drop the agent and consider it a lost cause for at least another year or two. Some agents will inform in advance not to send a S.A.S.E. This is different.

2. Agents and prodcos often list the genre they are handling in magazine ads. This often is not static. Preferences change. You'll see this in the annual surveys. Keep your database updated and record these changes. I have found that more than a few agents who say they specialize in comedy do, in fact, accept most all genre, except horror, as a general rule. Your best bet, of course, is to submit comedy scripts to comedy agents.

3. Never fax a script, synopsis, log line, etc., unless the agent specifically asks you to do so. Try to follow all submission instructions agents or prodcos give in an advertisement to the letter. However, don't forget that the multiple submission log line is a good alternative when you have more than one script to market. It may not match the advertised requirements, but it still works. It's brief, to the point, and cost effective.

4. Do develop a mailing list of agents, producers, and prodcos. How else are you to sell your scripts? Buying mailing lists is fine to jump-start the process, but the personalized lists you have developed over time will give you the best results in the long term. Often all it takes is one or two mass mailings to find the agents and prodcos willing to read your material. After this, you keep pounding away adding more agent/prodco listings as they appear in screenwriting magazines and directories. Don't forget to purge your database of undeliverable mail.

5. There are a lot of scripts out there, untold thousands entering the filtering system. Estimates run higher than 160,000 each year! That's a daunting figure, for sure. However, most are trash scripts (not my opinion, but the opinions of agents and readers). Oil rises to the surface, in time. The key word is, time. Keep your script(s) floating out there.

6. You will rarely, if ever, receive a coverage report. The only way to find out how your script measures up to standards is to pay a fee to have the script analyzed. Another method is to enter screenplay contests and see how the script ranks. Another is to have it read by a professional or writer's club at a reading. Family and friends won't cut it. They don't know what to look for, so they are little help to you unless they are accomplished screenwriters.

7. You are entering a no-fun-zone when you traverse into the marketing arena. Writing can be lots of fun, but the marketing endeavor is where the heart is broken, over-and-over, again-and-again. They say you must have tough skin to survive the rejections. I say you need armor and a stubborn, unrelenting, absolutely determined drive to succeed against all odds. This ability to continue on, despite hundreds of rejections year-after-year, does not come naturally, it has to sprout, grow roots and blossom over a period of time. It never stops hurting, but you survive it and push onward. You may feel at times you are doing the wrong thing and may need a psychiatrist. Gee, you must be a writer then! This is no conventional business. It isn't normal.

8. There is no absolute right or wrong way to sell a script. Whatever works, works. Sometimes rules must be broken a tiny bit to get the job done. That's okay, but there are some basic rules you must follow. Be honest. Be professional. Don't violate the major rules listed in this manual. It's okay to try innovative query letters as an attention-grabbing approach, to be different than the rest. It's not the way the package is presented, it's the gift inside that counts. Dull writing on fine stationery is as useless as an outhouse without T-paper. Be creative. Keep rewriting your query letters until they shine, or at least get your scripts requested.

9. Avoid dating your script with wordings that reveal years (1999 or whatever) that go stale, popular or public entities such as presidents who will be replaced by another. If you do, update your script to reflect the present state of affairs before shipping the script. That is, if your story isn't a period piece set in the past.

Here's a firm that may help you market your screenplays; Script Link, Dept. 1, P.O. Box 1750, Hollywood, CA 90078 (888)-801-1750 or (818)-990-1491.

HOW TO MEET PEOPLE IN THE INDUSTRY

Ask around. You can visit local TV stations, attend film festivals as a spectator or vender to market your scripts, meet the cast of the local performing arts theater group as somebody always knows somebody who knows someone in the industry. Go where entertainment people congregate. Attend readings, seminars, writer's club meetings, seminars, trade shows, film festivals, literary groups, guilds, performing arts classes, or start your own writer's club and invite industry people to a reading of your script, etc. If you can't attend major entertainment city events, use the mail and the internet to market your scripts.

I discovered if you let people know you're a screenwriter in the entertainment industry, other people introduce you to people they met. I've met a few at major trapshooting competition events (clay target shooting the uninformed call skeet). See the introduction to the sport near the end of this manual and writing opportunities this sport can give you.

Screenplay books can tell you more about meeting people. I'm certain everything has been tried, from disguising oneself as a grip to crashing a post-production party. You could join the Scriptwriter's Network to help you get work with their Producers Outreach Program -- The Writer's Network, Dept. Z-1, 289 South Robertson Blvd., Beverly Hills, CA 90211 (213)-848-9477. If your script passes muster it will be introduced to story editors, development executives, etc.

Here's a valuable tip to consider. You have a choice to attend a seminar in the Los Angeles area and one in, say, Las Vegas. You want to attend the seminar in LA because this is where all the film industry powers to be are and the guest speakers to appear will likely be just those people. This also holds true with film festivals.

You can spend time on the Internet to gain a ton of knowledge and advice, so much it may overwhelm you. Keep track of your time spent on line as it will steal your time away from writing. The people you meet on the Net may be legit or frauds, so pick your friends wisely. Yes, you can reach theaters to sell your stage play on the Internet.

Try the website; New Dramatist or Yahoo's search engine for performing arts/theater companies or Screenwriters' and Playwrights homepage. See subchapter, *Addresses of Firms Listed In This Manual*. There are too many to list here. Due to unresolved copyright issues, do not publish your play on the Web. If anyone asks for an electronic version of your play, I wouldn't do it, as the script can be copied to disk all too easily. Send the script on physical paper in the mail.

TRADE SHOWS & MEETING PRODUCERS

Keep in mind, if you attend any trade show, don't leave without obtaining business cards or your attendance is a waste of your time. This means you shouldn't be shy and lurk in the shadows, just be yourself and talk to people. Don't appear desperate, but do feel and act calmly confident and relaxed. Confidence attracts people and leaves good impressions so this means if you deliver a script, including writing a query letter, never apologize saying, *"Well, it's not yet perfect, but it will be by next month."*

If you downplay the script it dissolves enthusiasm for the producer or agent to read it. Say this, *"The script still impresses me even after reading and rewriting it ten times. I believe you will find the read enjoyable. I'd like to chat longer, but I have an appointment to speak to a director."* That may spark the fire that you are deemed an important person and will raise interest in your script. Be cheerful and add some clean humor to conversation as it's hard to reject a person who makes you smile.

Here are a few trade shows. Write for a program.
-- CMJ Music FilmFest Sound & Vision, 11 Middle Neck Road, Suite 400, Great Neck, NY 11021 (516)489-3114.
-- Independent Producers Pavilion NATPE 24,25 Olympic Blvd., Suite 550E, Dept. D, Santa Monica, CA 90404 (310)4534440.
-- Hollywood Film Festival, Dept. BK, 433 N. Camden Drive, Suite 600, Beverly Hills, CA 90210 (310)288-1882.

If you subscribe to the *Hollywood Reporter*, the major festivals and awards ceremonies, etc., will be advertised. There are too many to list here.

There are pros and cons to everything. Some writers do not like attending trade shows or festivals since they do not meet the "right people." The other side of the coin, writers do get results. Common sense prevails here on one major point. Go to a trade show or festival that is close to Hollywood as this is where the power players are.

SCRIPTS AVAILABLE

If you would like to learn more about the visual, punchy style of writing the author uses, you can purchase one of his scripts. See order form Fig. 2-1, visit Internet book sites: Amazon.com, BarnesAndNoble.com or visit our Website You can order James Russell's scripts from any major bookstore. Visit our website for a complete listing.

Punchy writing is not beautiful writing, but it is very effective for screenwriting. Combining your style with a tad of visual punch should enhance your script. What makes the author's scripts different from others you can buy?

1. It will be an author's script without camera angles and scene numbering, exactly how it should be presented to agents and prodcos.

2. You'll learn how to write visually.

3. You'll see the entire format of how a script is presented, page numbering and the pacing of the script.

4. You won't see "continued" on the pages or "cut to" and other directions that only serve to distract and upset the reader.

5. If you're new to screenwriting, seeing and reading the entire script will get you on the right track with your own scripts.

6. If you already have a few scripts under your belt, you'll see how to streamline your writing and avoid the deadly words that cause script rejection.

7. You can't buy many author scripts. So, this is how you can learn to write one.

8. If you mimic the format and style of the script presentation, you can be assured the script will be written well and presented professionally.

9. You may even like the story. See our Website if you wish to order a script.

Legal Notice: Keep this in mind. The scripts are not "sold" but are "loaned" for educational purposes. This does not mean you must return the script upon a specific time, it's just that you do not own the script outright or in any form. The copyright remains with the author, just as it would if you purchased a screenwriting book. And, you may not market the script to anyone whatsoever or circulate the script in any form or manner to friends, relatives, agents prodcos, actors, etc., for the purpose of generating a sale for financial gain. Purchasing the script does not authorize production rights, they are still reserved for the author. If you wish to circulate, you must request written permission from the author. This is to protect the script from entering the public domain and to maintain the integrity of the script for future option and sale.

MAILING LISTS AND SAVING $ MONEY $

Building a mailing list is an awful task. It requires years to type in all the company name and address listings and many hours of work to maintain the list. If you think mailing lists are expensive, read this entire subchapter and see for yourself the thousands of dollars you'll save. Using mailing lists is the fastest way to launch your screenwriting marketing adventure. The cost of mailing lists is tax deductible.

Note: Keep in mind you do not need to purchase a mailing list. Simply cull the names and addresses from the magazines listed in this book and build your list on a weekly basis. Mailing two query letters per week will reach 104 agents each year, and we know you can do better than that! Mailing lists are convenient for those who are too busy to generate listings and need to reach hundreds of agents, production companies and producers quickly in one mailing.

For those who can't afford to purchase a mailing list with preaddress self-stick labels, you can purchase a print-out directory of agents, prodcos, and some producers. Approximately 600 agents and prodcos. The cost is very low, as addresses are not on peel & stick mailing labels. The best feature of this list is the genre, submission requirements and identity is given, when known.

Example: "Wants comedy and drama, handles features and TV, script and synopsis required, independent production house." If you use the ACT! database? We can send the database file on disk (PC compatible not Mac), so you can simply load it and go to work. Same price. See order form Fig. 2-1.

For example, if you have a comedy script, you can find the firms that are aggressively seeking comedy. The list identifies (when known) if the firm handles features, TV or both. If you scour the internet you will find database firms that also offer mailing lists. Smart Girls Productions, Dept. S, P.O. Box 1896, Hollywood, CA 90078 (323-850-5778) offer a complete mailing service for those who simply do not have the time to be generating mailing lists and stuffing and mailing envelopes.

You can develop your own mailing list when you subscribe to the screenwriter's magazines, or *Writer's Digest Writers Market* book of literary agents and publishers and other sources listed in this book. It will take you months to type in 300+ addresses (never mind 600+) so you may want to consider the feasibility of purchasing mailing lists to jump-start the process. When magazines do present listings, they only list a handful of agents, producers and prodcos looking for scripts.

Bear in mind, there will only be a half-dozen listed and you'll have to compete with thousands of other screenwriters who saw the same ad or listing! This is where the mailing list comes in ahead of the pack, as you hit the agents and prodcos before they are listed in the ads. You effectively eliminate the masses from competing with you, generally speaking.

It's not a sure-fire bet, but it's an edge that will give you plenty of requests to see your script(s). Remember, this business of screenwriting is a mail order business, and all mail order businesses purchase or develop mailing lists. You must have a computerized database of addresses to market your scripts, so buy the "ACT!" program and get to work inserting one address at a time. The list will grow.

Now the bad news. As in any mail-oriented business, you may mail out 100 letters and only receive 5 or 10 requests for your scripts (5% to 10% response). That's the nature of the beast, and believe me, that is a good response rate! Mail order firms are lucky to obtain a 2% response. And, it's a fact, many writers get 0% response requests to submit their scripts!

If you follow the rules and instructions given in this manual, you should see a similar 5% to 10% result, or higher, because your marketing efforts will present your query and log lines professionally, and your mailing list will accurately reach the right people. It's simply penetrating the market and outpacing the competition. You can expect 50% will return your query with a "pass" and maybe 40% will not even return your S.A.S.E. Again, that's the nature of the business we are in and the frustrations that come with it.

If you can mail out 100 queries and get just one script (a 1% response) into the hands of an agent or production company, you broke a firewall. It only take one script to make the money. Unfortunately, it also takes money to make money. You have to think of your expenses as "start-up" costs of a new business. How many thousands of dollars would it cost you to start any business? A gas station? Restaurant? Gift shop? There are no guarantees these businesses will be profitable, either.

When an agent or prodco "passes" on your script or query letter, that doesn't mean it's a pass forever. The same agency or prodco may take on your script six-months from now or next year. So hold on to your mailing list entries you've developed over the years. You will always need them to market your next script for resubmissions.

Now you can see the economics of mailing multiple-submission query letters as shown in Fig. 1-8. Imagine the postal costs alone to mail all eight of these query letters individually to 600+ agents and prodcos at thirty-two cents, times two equals sixty-four cents per mailed envelope. About $384 per script! And these costs rise as First Class postage increases. Each letter requires double postage (the S.A.S.E. remember?) and that's not counting the stationery and envelope costs.

The expenses easily jump to $400 per script. The good news is, you can market eight scripts that would have cost you $3,200 to do individually for only $400! This method more than pays for the mailing label costs and marketing your scripts for the next five years or more! Do the math. You are actually in the black financially in comparison. If you obtain a 5% to 10% response you are way ahead of the competition.

No matter who says not to perform multiple-submission logline queries, you must consider the value of the advice versus the costs you will incur, and ultimately, the effectiveness of the response you receive. I was told not to do it by authors of screenwriting books and magazine interviews with agents, but I received a higher response by doing it! Who was right? The multiple-submission snagged me the agent I needed. Who was right? It broke down firewalls and delivered my scripts with major prodcos even without my agent's assistance or even mentioning having an agent in my query letter. Who's right?

I'm not saying it's my way or hit the highway. I'm simply stating the facts. It works! Whatever works, works. Don't argue with success.

Some agents frown on mailing multiple submission shopping lists, others don't seem to care. Producers and prodcos are very receptive to these shopping lists. I believe what matters most is the brevity of the log line approach and the interesting subject matter presented (the pitch of the story.) If the letter arrives and strikes a chord, it just happens.

Now once you've performed a multiple-submission mailing you can follow later with the individual query with the agents or prodcos that responded (returned your S.A.S.E.) Again, financially, you are way ahead as you weeded out those who have no interest in even responding to a new (or established) writer. Now you have agents and prodcos that are "open to you" to submit future projects.

Concentrate your efforts on these contacts reverting to the one page query letter on your next screenplay/play project. See Fig. 1-4, 1-11, 1-16, 1-17, 1-18.

Frankly, on a pure marketing basis, this method of multiple submission of log lines does work. Financially? It'll keep you out of the poor house. One major reason writers give up is a perpetual bombardment of rejection. Another reason is the cost is so high to do business. The instructions herein will not eliminate, but will reduce rejection and expenses to positively enhance your ability to stay in the game.

TIPS FOR PLAYWRIGHTS
These are only suggestions, not rules.

1. Write a play to interest women. Why? Because women comprise the majority of the stage play audience, and they tell their husbands and boyfriends which play they want to see.

2. The audience ranges between the age of eighteen to forty-five. You may want to consider what these age groups are highly interested in seeing when you write your play.

3. You definitely do not need an agent to sell your stage play. The agent may be more helpful to you in managing contract deals than marketing your work. And even then, you should contact the Dramatist Guild to insure the contract protects your rights by adhering to Guild guidelines.

4. When you write your query letter (see Fig. 1-27) you don't use story editor as a title, you use Literary Manager or Artistic Director. You could also mention you are a member of the Dramatist Guild.

5. You may have to wait six-months or longer for a response from a theater if you sent a script. You can contact the Guild to help you retrieve the script if you have been ignored for some reason. A theater can receive 150 to 1,000 scripts per year. So it takes time.

6. Unlike screenplay readers that only skim a script with dialog, your stage play will be read word-for-word by the literary staff. So no spelling errors, or else.

7. Theaters and play agents are picky-picky, so observe and do adhere to the submission rules they lay down in any listings. If they say, *"Only 3-act comedies"* or *"1-act comedy not over 15-minutes"* then don't send them a drama or 2-act comedy. Be professional by following the rules. Agents and Literary Managers constantly complain that writers do not believe or honor their submission guidelines. Be professional!

8. The query letter rules still apply. Don't send a script and don't call agents or theaters unless they specifically request you do so.

9. When agent or theater asks for pages of dialog, send the scene that is not only the best, but the one that gives a gist of what the story is about. It can be any act or any scene of your choosing.

10. Again, don't sign contracts without first having the Dramatist Guild review it for you, even if you have an agent.

PLAYWRIGHT MENTOR

A playwright mentor is a professional who is willing to give you advice and guidance in writing and selling your stage play.

--Dave Brandl, Play Script Consulting, Dept. 1-A, P.O. Box 234, Denver, CO 80201. (303)333-7018. Dave has evaluated hundreds of play scripts for publishers, producers, contests and festivals. He's a theatrical reviewer for a Denver newspaper and correspondent for Theatre.com. His published adaptation play *Miracle on 34th Street* is well known and his plays are produced over 100 times in theaters worldwide. Dave is willing to give readers of this book special consideration and will give advice on playwriting and marketing stage plays free of charge. Please, do not call him on the phone; visit his web site and start a "new discussion" to submit questions. Mention in your discussion you saw his listing in this book so he will know who you are. Website address is listed in *Addresses of Firms Mentioned In This Book*.

Dave Brandl offers a very attractive low fee for playscript evaluations; $150 plus a 20% discount for readers of this book. See the listing in *Script Doctors*. Musicals on non-musical plays are followed up with a comprehensive evaluation (approximately 2,000 words). The evaluation includes elements of plot, dialog, character, theme, presentation, marketability, target audience and submission tips. Turnaround time is only 3 to 4 weeks.

HANDLING REJECTION

It comes with the territory, expect it. Most people have a story to tell, *"My life is so interesting I could write a book."* Now it's, *"I can write a movie and a stage play!"* So the deluge of scripts pour into Hollywood and Broadway and most of them are junk. It makes it ever more difficult, for the good writers' scripts get lost in the jumble. And when you consider the "reader" is not reading your script, just scanning it over and developing terrible coverage, it's frustrating. But that's reality.

So, you just keep on writing, send more queries, put the script in the envelope and mail it out. It's like trying to win the lottery. The odds in Hollywood are still better than winning a state lottery, but it's a rough road to walk with many losers and few winners. This is why if your efforts fail in screenwriting you should try playwriting, as the market is much larger and odds of success seeing your work performed is way better.

Every writer receives rejections, even the multi-millionaire established pros. Rejection is a writer's life and it hurts. Tears extinquish flames. Each rejection is a kick in the head, so go ahead and cry, then get back to work. Just remember, everyone gets rejected, everyone! Join the club. Learn to disassociate rejection of the script from yourself. It's nothing personal. You'll get good at it in time.

If you think you have it tough, just try being an actor, rejection is personal. Producers too receive tons of rejections. It's not unusual for a producer to be rejected fifty or one-hundred times or more and then fifty more times and... well, you get the idea.

Keep in mind that opinions of the reader's evaluation are subjective. Another agency or prodco may react favorably to the script in its present form. I've had a reader hate one of my scripts calling it nonsense while another praised it and recommend it for production. Some will see the magic while others only see the faults, and every script has faults because nothing can be perfect to all people. There are a lot of scripts out there, but oil floats to the surface.

This rejection process is where you discover the truth about yourself. Are you a true writer or just someone who's trying to make a dollar? Money is an incentive, but if you are a writer, a real writer, you will continue to write regardless of the number of rejections you receive. It's that "something" in your being which compels you to write, to keep on, never look back, always moving forward with hope. Astronauts never use rear view mirrors! You need to develop a philosophy to handle rejection so it won't destroy you. Everyone in this business suffers reverses. Persevere!

Producers and directors and actors experience the same rejections as stage and screenwriters, involving many years of multiple rewrites, disappointment, overwhelming frustration and sadness. You are not alone. We all struggle in this business. Now there is something you must never do, no matter how much you want to retaliate, don't do it. Writers are on a "Hollywood High" when a script is requested. They sit back and wait for the big check to arrive, then when a rejection letter arrives they hit the floor. Some - thankfully few -- of these rejections may be outright insulting.

Don't fume and steam and write a condemnation letter for revenge. It does more harm than good. You can write a nasty letter to release pressure, but don't mail it! You don't want anybody bad-mouthing you or, worse yet, sending your letter around town as a joke. You met a bad apple, you feel rotten, so don't bite into the bitter fruit of revenge.

KNOWING WHEN TO QUIT

This subject rarely appears in writing books, but since this is a marketing manual it should be discussed. Technically, you should never quit and you don't have to. If you have written a few scripts you can keep on marketing them even when you enter the nursing home. (I hope it doesn't take that long to sell a script!).

The reality is, many writers do quit writing scripts and move on to greener pastures in alternative markets and traditional jobs. So when do you quit? Not until you have given it your best effort, at least five years of effort, and have six or more scripts under your hat. Some will disagree, and that's okay, this is just theoretical.

Sometimes taking a nice long break can be considered a "quit" to catch your breath, heal the wounds of rejection and climb back into the rollercoaster to ride again. So, you don't need to quit writing scripts permanently, that is. When you get overwhelmed, depressed, sick of rejection and the sky looks black, just take a break, quit for a week, a month or two and rest your weary soul. It's a good time to reflect, sort out the mind, recharge the batteries and go for it again. If you need six-months or a year, let it be.

Now for the bright side, if you think you are getting a heavy dose of rejection just try being a producer! You'll be rejected by angels (investors), studios, agents, other producers, directors, actors and writers too! When a writer's work gets rejected it's the script/story being rejected, not you! An actor? It's personal... rejection for actors is equivalent to a slap in the face!

SHOULD YOU WRITE A BOOK OR STAGE PLAY FIRST?
Book? No. Spec scripts are still selling and they always will. Sometimes they slow down a bit, but overall more spec scripts are sold than the rights to novels. It's just that novels hit the mainstream news media and spec scripts do not. Studios want novels to be splashed in the news to build publicity and attract talent. It's all marketing. So you don't need to write a novel first, okay? If you want to, go right ahead. It won't hurt to have a good novel and a screenplay too! Use every marketing angle you can dream up. Here's a firm that specializes adapting scripts into novels. The price is approximately $5,000 (low cost, considering if the book sells). Readers of this book obtain a 10% discount.
--The Novelizer / Marin Noble, Dept. A, Abberbury Road, Iffley, Oxford, UK OX4 4ES. +44 (0)1865-773862. 10%

Stage play? Yes. A play in production can generate a lot of heat in Hollywood and options for the movie rights will arrive. Yes, Hollywood buys stage plays! If your feature script isn't doing very well, try adapting it to a play and get it published and produced. If your play shows well in the theatrical arena, you may find Hollywood knocking on your door! Surprisingly, many screenwriters do not know of this technique of breaking into the Hollywood market. Now you know!

PRODUCING YOUR OWN FILM
This is a viable marketing option and is only mentioned here for this purpose, marketing. The route is too involved for the theme of this book, but there are other books available to tell you how to do it. It's a time-consuming job with a lot of rejection but many writer's have become fed-up with being subjected to other people's whims and strike out on their own. You could be the next new production company on the block if you succeed. Now you're talking the big-time league that could put you in Beverly Hills, or in the poor house.

An alternative to this extremely risky feature film route is to write, produce and direct your own educational instructional videotape, MOW or documentary. You may be an accountant or auto mechanic, and a video tape for students could do the trick for a video. If you examine your knowledge base, you will find a market for what you know and others need to know. There will always be opportunity in instructional videos and the cost is relatively low to produce, manufacture and distribute.

BOOKS TO READ

Here is a book you <u>must</u> read. *"The Screenwriter's Bible"* by David Trottier published by Silman-James Press, Dept. SB, 1181 Angelo Drive, Beverly Hills, CA 90210. Everything is covered for the screenwriter. From formatting to easy to understand plotting and marketing advice. Don't miss this one! If you've read it, <u>read it again</u>!

The book is frequently updated -- more than any other screenwriting book I know of and the advice of formatting and structure is simply direct, accurate and effective. If you follow the instructions in this book you're going places! Just read what the screenwriting interviews with agents and producers complain about and you'll see -- if you simply go back to this book you won't be making those mistakes. Read it again!

Any book written by screenwriter Michael Hauge is well worth reading. He mentions certain levels of sell which gear your script to the marketing process. Those are inside secrets revealed. You won't hear many agents talking about levels of sell, but Michael's advice is accurate. He also has a cassette tape and book, *"How to Write and Sell Your Screenplay."* I recommend you purchase both.

Everybody knows Linda Seger. Check out her books at any bookstore. *How to Make A Good Script Great* is a fine book to read.

Another book is *Screenwriting From The Soul* by Richard William Krevolin. There are other books, of course, but these writers mentioned above have nailed it down quite well. You should first begin with their books, then move on to others. Our website lists many books on writing.

CHAPTER 11

BEWARE OF EXCESSIVE KNOWLEDGE - IT MAY RUIN YOUR WRITING!
There are other fine books on the market, but reading the few mentioned above will give you a great script! Remember, less is more in this business.

Example: How many professors do you know who are writing and selling blockbuster screenplays? The body count is few. Who are selling the scripts? A few of their students and those who have never been to film school.

Excessive knowledge can destroy the creative imaginative process or block it from the written page. How many English majors have best-selling books? A few do, but not many compared to the sheer volume of published authors; stroll through a bookstore for enlightenment. Knowledge is not the prevailing factor to success, it's pure determination and imagination and that can't be taught in school. Einstien taught imagination was greater than knowledge and knowlege is power only when applied. Film schools are useful, but it's not what

Hollywood craves. If it were, they would be buying scripts from every graduating student and this is not happening. Film schools intentionally do not suppress talent. It just happens when any group of individuals congregate a sense of one mind forms.

I have met, and I'm sure you have too, directors and producers who are highly educated who can't launch a project off the ground, or those that do result in total disaster. I've seen doctors who can't operate a telephone, adjust a wall thermostat or perform other simple tasks. Knowledge has a way of tunneling your mind into narrowly defined perspectives, and too much of that is simply dangerous to creativity.

You don't need to be a professor to write a great script. You don't have to go to film school, and, many professional screenwriters actually advise against it. Everyone who graduates comes out with the same mind and the same formulas at the same -- you get the drift. If you are in film school, make certain you keep or create a strong imagination and maintain a unique voice in your writing. Allow knowledge gained to revolve around your wildest imaginations and creativity!

Screenwriting is hard to learn, but it's not that hard! The film schools will flood your mind with so much data and so many theories your head will spin. Still, film school is a good thing as long as you don't take everything you learn as Gospel truth. Heaven knows how many straight-A film school graduates can't even rank a screenplay in the top 100 of a screenplay contest! This is not to say the teachers are bad, but the creative process truly can not be taught. It comes from experience, actually writing tons of pages to develop a voice and style.

So the *good news* is this. If you don't have a college degree in cinema and you don't have formal writing skills, you can learn these skills on your own. I flunked English badly in high school, but I have three best-selling books on the world-wide market. I'm still not good at composition and I'd fail an English exam if I had to take one, but it's the message sent that is of *real value* to the reader!

Learn all that you can about screenwriting, then toss it aside if it interferes with the creative process.

DANGER ON THE WEB! - BE CAREFUL!

If you search the Internet screenwriting sites, you will see many interesting things. For example, everybody will be talking about the latest Blockbuster movie, examining it. A bunch of critics wasting their time exchanging knowledge and trivia that amounts to beans, when they should be busy writing their own scripts! There are thousands of these amateur "critic professors" condemning everything they see. Nothing and nobody escapes their condemnation, accusation and dissatisfaction. These disgruntled writers are reflecting their own failures for the world to see, and fail to even realize it! Fact, many are film buffs are not writers and just like to play games.

You will also notice that advice given is often bad advice, or just some advice they read in some magazine article and is misinterpreted. You will find very little demonstrative creative talent from these writers who are giving advice. I'm not talking about the magazine editors, but rather those chat room discussion groups. It's not a good idea to take to heart advice you get from these people, as most all are novice writers without any sort of credibility or accomplishments. There is no way to verify who they really are!

Many of these writers are so amateur they are actually discussing the screenplay they are writing!

1) We know this is stupid, as others are now stealing their story idea, the very people they are communicating with!

2) We know this is dumb, as you can never talk about your script while writing it or it will run out of fuel, stall cold and die. That's why thy are asking questions how to fix the script or how they can break the writer's block! Never talk to anyone about your script until it is finished.

You will notice everybody is talking about the same old things, same topics, same, same, same. That "pattern" thing is showing up again. An identical mind collectively communicating nothingness to nobody. It can be dangerous to your creativity to remain in these chat rooms too long. What you see and read will influence you, and there often is not much good to influence you on many of these public chat rooms.

The same applies to newsgroups which are separate from screenwriting sites. Amazingly, you will find writers asking questions that are so elementary it defies reason. The very answers are often posted on the website by the editors! It is a certainty many have never even read a screenwriting book, period! Yet, many of these people are giving advice. A perfect example of the blind leading the blind into the pit.

Then you have the know-it-all whom demonstrates a wonderful ability to give advice (or criticize others works) with such absolute authority and flair you would think they were consultants to the stars. The Internet has an inherent talent of making nobody appear as somebody. It is this deception that is dangerous for the novice writer, as the advice can be harmful and lead to failure.

In fact, so much poor advice makes it believable some are passing bogus information intentionally to make others fail. Don't be their victim! But let's not be too quick to blame. Confusion exists because confusion persists in Hollywood. Rules and standards constantly change, outdated books still reign supreme on bookstore shelves. Under these conditions confusion is bound to remain.

Your best advice will always, in most all cases, come from professionally posted articles and interviews from the website's editors. This is where the true value is. So, by all means visit all the screenwriting sites, just be aware everything you read is not Gospel fact. Some articles are way off the track, especially when it comes to the mysterious marketing principles where so much misunderstanding and conflicting advice reigns supreme. This book sets the record straight in that department.

Another danger is spending way too much time on the Internet. You should be writing, not surfing. Visit the sites often in short time periods, then get back to writing. Many writers have stalled their writing due to excessive Internet use. How? Easy. The Internet will give you so much information you will certainly feel you are not yet good enough to write a script! It can make you feel inferior seeing all that knowledge out there that must be learned.

Well, it does not all have to be learned. The books mentioned in this manual will get you going real fast, and with a darn good marketable script to boot! So, don't get overwhelmed whatsoever. You will never learn it all, no matter how many years you study screenwriting, it will never happen. As in all art forms, it can't be nailed down. It can't be taught. It's all creativity from within and that universe is as large as the physical universe, nobody can claim dominance, except God.

Note: For website addresses see the subchapter *"Addresses of Firms Mentioned in This Book."*

DEVELOPING CREATIVITY - THE SECRET FORMULA FOR SUCCESS!

The creative process is more powerful than the technical process! I make my living writing, so the end results all come down to that, results! I don't sell magazine articles, but I do write a few and rent them to other publishers, giving them first-serial-rights to use them. I don't sell my writing outright as other writers do to pay the rent. I retain full-copyright and I rent the use of the articles, so I can keep on re-marketing them, perpetually!

I wrote books and published them myself, starting back in 1981 and now, of course, publish other writers books. Starting a publishing company is a long, hard, process requiring many years of grueling work. It's a lot tougher than writing and selling screenplays, by far! And to get your books listed as #1 best-seller status is terribly difficult, but I've done it three times; 1997, 1998, 2000, and it will continue again, but it required twenty years to learn the "creative process" to get to this point. Still, not bad for someone who flunked English in school. You can make things happen if you want them to!

So, if you are considering getting into writing for magazines, you may as well consider writing a series of articles on the same subject and turn it into a book! You can rent each article out to earn money as you complete each step, and soon enough, you have a marketable book that will earn you money your entire life. And if royalties are not to your liking? Publish it yourself! There are plenty of books on how to become a self-publisher. It is not easy, it's expensive with high risk and very demanding of skills and time... it's hard work!

There is big money in publishing (and big risk), so don't overlook success anyway it may come to you. If you ever do sign on with a publisher, make sure the publishing rights are returned to you in the event they put your book in the backlist or "out of print" status. If not, you may lose big time! No book, no sales, no royalties and no chance to have it republished. Get reversion rights clause in contract!

I rarely pay for advertising as other businesses do, though I do have to with some publications. I put together "deals you can't refuse" with magazine executives and they run the ads for me, free! Every month! Year-in and year-out, perpetually! And I do it all by mail! I've had not one face-to-face meeting to put these amazing packages together as of this writing. And I do it in foreign nations, too.

What I learned in writing screenplay query letters has paid off handsomely in other areas of life. There is *great power* in creative marketing! Magazine writers evaluate my books, they sell the article and I get tons of orders for my books... all without spending a dollar on my part. I'm not bragging. I'm just trying to tell you to open up your mind and be creative... nothing is chiselled in stone. There are alternatives to everything. Be brave enough to try a non-traditional route.

Using your own creativity and life-experience with determination gives great rewards. I've seen many other people with more education than I do less. So don't let the negative thought enter your mind that your lack of a formal education is the cause of your failure. The more you learn about marketing your scripts, the more success you will have. Marketing is the key to open locked doors. Simple marketing!

Here's a tip: Go buy some books on how to sell cars from professional car salesmen. The average car salesperson is a "high-pressure pusher" and offends many to most customers. But the guys and gals who became filthy rich use "low-pressure" sales tactics. The gentle approach filling the "needs" of the customer. By developing a basic understanding of how to make sales happen, you will find in your writing of query letters, and within the script itself, sales procedures that will satisfy the needs of the reader, producer, studio and the audience! It's like doing a pitch for a film and you ramble on and on about the movie, but you are not touching the "needs" of those listening to you. No matter what you are selling, you have to learn how to sell! And that is fulfilling the needs of the buyers.

How do you find these needs? They are printed in articles in screenwriting magazines with interviews of powerful people in the industry. They tell you what Hollywood is looking for, so just deliver it, as best you can to fill their needs.

There is a secret formula to success, *"Be different!" "Do something different!"* When you follow the pack you end up competing with everyone else, but if you deviate from the norm, your chances are greater to succeed. I started by writing books no other publisher had. Visiting the bookstores, I discovered books that should have been written, but were not.

I basically found them by asking a simple question, *"I wish I had a book to help me pass engineering exams."* That was my first book, a question and answer book containing over 1,600 multiple choice test questions and answers for power plant engineers. Then, I discovered a publisher had a book similar to it, so I then saw a gaping hole, they did not have explanations as to why the answer was correct. When I put the explanation in, the book sold back in 1981 and still sells to this day.

Another book was *Trap Shooting Secrets*. A technical book about the sport of shooting flying clay targets with a shotgun, sort of like skeet shooting. Again, there were books that "talked a lot" about the sport with sporadic advice, but no technical instructional manual to help me shoot targets with precision. So, I interviewed professional shooters, tested the advice (which many did not want to give winning advice away very easily) and wrote the book.

The book was "different" than others, as it was like having a shooting coach by your side telling you exactly what to do. No other book did this. I took the detailed instructional concept of those electrical and plumbing how-to books and put it into the trap shooting book. The book hit #1 status. I then wrote the follow-on book, *Precision Shooting - The Trapshooter's Bible* an even more advanced-level book and it too went #1. Why? Because no other books were like it. Both were different. So, now I had three books, all so different than others on the market.

That is how this screenwriting book came into existence. After reading every screen writing book on the market I was still confused. I spoke with professional writers and received conflicting advice, or did not know the answers to effective marketing of scripts! Most just "lucked-out" somewhere in the process and found it tough to give advice to the novice writer trying to break in.

Though there are many books on screenwriting, including "how-to sell your script" types, not one book was dedicated to the actual marketing procedure. I needed an instructional book to show me and tell me exactly what to do and there was none to be found! So, being a writer, after many years of writing screen and stage plays, it was time to write *Screen & Stage Marketing Secrets*.

The point here is this; where there is a need, and you satisfy the need, you will succeed. Hollywood wants a creative movie with something different, but still familiar to what was once was a success. Stroll through a video rental store and look for a movie (story) that has not yet been filmed (written)!

You can obtain a movie database program for your computer as a research tool. If you find that story that has never been told, and you write it, the odds of success rise. Believe me, thousands of writers are stealing "ideas" from other movies and every story analyst knows these scripts when it comes across their desk!

Everything about you is different than every other person. It's your character, personality, thought process, style, voice, whatever you want to call it. You are different. Too much knowledge can adversely affect the natural creative talent each individual has. So, it's not a factor to success to have all the cinema knowledge and theory imaginable, but to have the power to be different that really counts to sell products, your script.

You know lots of people who know way more than you do about cinema studies, but how many of them are making a living writing movies? Few, if any. If fifty students attend a film school, fifty scripts will tend to gel the same way when finished, with minor deviations, but all following a familiar pattern. It's the nature of the beast. Knowledge is power, but useless if it replaces creative talent. Art is not smart. Art is talent. Talent is creative!

It is this educationally taught "pattern" along with other "patterns" derived from novice writers reading screenwriting books and other screenplays that forms a general pattern that is seen in Hollywood script submissions day-in and day-out. Nothing new! Just deviations from other projects that have already been done. Same old plots, same structures, typical worn-out characters and familiar scenes, etc.

Every agent and producer is screaming, *"Show me something different!"* Well, nothing much different can arise if creative talent is being squashed with technicalities and overly excessive cinema theory and studies. Like a stamp mill, producing screenwriters with no unique voice by the tens of thousands. A mass production of untalented writers who have lost, or never found, their unique inner creativity.

Another secret to success is to simply discard almost everything you have learned and just produce the product as you "feel" best to do, your way! Do it the way you want to do it. Not to the extreme of forgetting basic screenwriting format and structure, but bend the rules a bit. Dare to go into unexplored areas, let the script's characters pull you along where they want to go. Let the creative process take over!

If I had copied other books on the market, my books would never have become best-sellers, ever! Because they are "creative" and "different" is the reason why they sell, because they are valuable to the readers. Your script should be valuable to the producer. Being different than others is the key.

Now, ask yourself how much hard work would it be to write a producer and simply ask, *"What sort of story have you always wanted to film, but never could find the script to get the job done?"* You will get feedback and from there you will have a basis to totally beat the competition spec-script market!

Write the script and you may find the doors to Hollywood open wide. Of course, this is not a work for hire project, it is still a spec script, so don't expect or ask for payment of any kind. However, if you are an experienced writer, you can do so and likely be hired and paid according to Guild pay schedules.

To sum it up. Now you know why so many writers criticize the work of other screenwriters on the Web. It's a cold fact there will always be better writers looking in and wondering, *"How did they buy that script? I can write better than that!"* It's because the writer knew how to market his script!

A SIMPLE MARKETING PLAN THAT WORKS!

You apply simple marketing to your script writing by fulfilling the basic need everyone has, *"What's in it for me?"*

Example: *"What's in it for me?"* applies to each character in your story to give them the <u>drive</u> to action. Do that and the reader and others in the food chain begin to see, *"What's in this script for me?"* Get the idea? Very simple. Simplicity is often the key to success.

When you write a query to an agent the "What's in it for me?" factor is present in the multiple-submission log line query letter. The agent thinks subconsciously, *"I have an assortment to pick here, and with so many of them, the writer must be good."* That's another reason why the system works. Some agents don't like it. Too bad. Many do! And believe me, the results of getting your scripts read are far better than sending out individual query letters per script.

Remember, you have a product. Think of your script as if it were a cleaning chemical you invented. It is your responsibility to give people a demonstration by dropping off a sample at their doorstep (query letter for script.) Then you put some on consignment in hardware stores, auto repair stores, gas stations, etc. (sending scripts to the market.) If the product is good, people buy it (prodcos.) It's really no mystery. Scripts are products and that's how the industry sees a script... it's just a product, not a work of art. The writing process and the marketing process are two separate entities.

You <u>advertise the product</u> in your query or log line and the <u>script sells itself</u>. You don't try to sell the script in the query. That's a big mistake because it requires a full-page or two in a query to sell a script and nobody is going to read more than a few paragraphs. So, when you obtain a lead to submit a script, you enclose the synopsis and that can be a full page to help further describe the story to sell the product, but the script really must do all of the actual selling.

This is where your script must conform to marketing principles: formatting, professional appearance, acceptable submission and mailing methods that crossed over to the visual writing process itself. None of these have anything to do with the story structure or writing process except for the visual aspect of writing. You can see how the marketing process will influence the writing process itself.

Smart writers also know how to insert name brand products into the script so the producer can tickle these firms for advertising money to help pay for the film. Here's an example:

                     JENNIFER
                (spills her Pepsi)
        Why did you say that?

                     NANETTE
        Because it is true. You have mad
        cow disease.

Jennifer gasps then reluctantly nods with approval.

                     JENNIFER
        You're not supposed to mention
        that word... cow, in this house.
        I'm not that fat. You could be
        more kind to me, you know? A
        little sympathy would help.

Jennifer sips her Pepsi, lights a Camel, nibbles on Russell Stover chewy gels. Nanette stares, exits with disgust.

                     KAREN
                (to Nanette)
        Get back here you little squirt.
        How dare you insult your mother?
                (to Jennifer)
        Mad cow disease?

> Jennifer's eyes filled with compassion. Karen's eyes bulge as Jennifer extends her can of Pepsi to Karen.
>
> > JENNIFER
> > Well its not catchy... unless
> > juices are exchanged or something
> > like that.
> > > (screams)
> > It won't kill you right away!

-- Okay, you get the idea. It's the expensive products that need to be considered for revision. If a character drives a new Dodge Ram 3500 truck, could an early model do? Must it be an expensive truck? Why not an economical car instead? Unless you are doing a James Bond Jr. film, you need to keep costs down to increase market potential.

This brings to mind revising your scripts to have another low budget version. The story doesn't change, only the costs are reduced, and it could even be funnier if James Bond Jr. rode around in an old rusty Volkswagon bug or a beat up Saturn in ill-fitted, second-hand suits and cheap costume jewelry to impress the ladies.

Now go back and read the dialog above again. Did you see the spelling error? The word <u>suppossed</u> should be <u>supposed</u>. Also, the word, <u>its</u> should be <u>it's</u>. A computer program spell-checker will not catch those it's! Spelling is critical to the marketing process because that's where errors will be caught and a rejection given. There is little to no mercy in this business.

COMMON IMPROPER WORD USAGE YOU MUST AVOID

There are many words you have to watch out for. It is true you can break grammatical rules in scripts, yet you have to be careful not to be too blatant about it. Many writers make these mistakes in scripts, and they stand out like sore thumbs. Here are a few basic ones to watch for:

-- It's means, it is. Its always simply points to an object showing possession. *"It's the only way it will function."*

-- Their is always pointing to someone possessing something or to the owners. They're means, they are. *"It's their problem and they're the ones who must deal with it."* The word, <u>thier</u>, is commonly misspelled. <u>Their</u> is correct. Spell-checkers catch <u>this</u>, but only if the program has not accepted the misspelled word as being correct. Check the database!

-- That is a bad word to use, so get rid of all of them if possible. *"So that is the way it's done."* Use: *"It is the only way to get it done."*

-- You're means, you are. Your, points to possessing something. *"That's your problem and you're gonna eat it."*

-- Useless words, *"You could be loving me."* Use, *"Love me."* Get rid of those words ending in, "ing" if possible and it cleans up the useless words just like getting rid of the word, that.

You get the idea.

DO YOU NEED A LAWYER?

Not until you have a producer or prodco interested in your script and who wants you to sign a contract. Even then, you should get an agent or manager first, unless your attorney is acting as a negotiating agent, not just contract review. Once you have a deal struck, getting an agent to represent your specific project will not be a problem. If for some strange reason you still can't get an agent? Hire an entertainment attorney.

Never use an attorney who is not a disciplined specialist in entertainment law. Any lawyer can be an entertainment attorney at the drop of a hat. But they will only take your money and give you poor representation in return. In some instances, they will burn you so bad you'll end up paying the producer money! The lawyer in your small town simply will not do the job properly, no matter what s/he promises and no matter how much they charge in fees. You need a specialist.

Believe it, incompetent lawyers are a dime a dozen and many are corrupt to the core and will cut any sort of side-deal you'll never know about. It happens! It's done all the time by dishonest lawyers to make extra money or to secure existing business relationships... burn the client to get a better deal from the opposing party! They know how to skirt the law. I had a lawyer cutting side-deals, but to prove it was impossible. All the circumventions were performed covertly and verbally, with no paper trail and no trends in the deals to expose and introduce as admissible evidence. Live and learn!

It is very easy for an attorney to misrepresent you for his/her own personal interest and financial gain. The Business & Professions Code and State Bar rules are so liberally construed that if an attorney, "Acts in a reasonable prudent manner...". Well, what is reasonable? What is unreasonable? It's very easy for an attorney to prove she/he acted prudently and they will lie to the Bar and to a Judge with honest eyes. Do sharks have legs? Only when they attend law school.

How do you find an incompetent attorney? Look in your newspaper and if you see them advertising for business? Stay clear. This holds true for doctors, dentists, plastic surgeons, and other medical and legal professionals. Many professionals do not have to advertise. The "best" always have plenty of business. You'll find the incompetent and dangerous professional placing slick ads to drum up business. It's just the way it is; otherwise, why would they be advertising? To pull in the gullible! It's all to make a quick buck.

I personally have been financially and medically injured by a professional who threw a smart marketing "come-on" ad. Never again! Certainly, not all advertisers are bad... but I will never respond to ads or take a "second chance" after what I've been through. There are professional con-artists with licenses practicing law, medicine, and accounting, hiding their shameful scheme under their "respectable identity."

Some will throw an ad in the paper, blatantly violate the ad promises, then lie to the state medical or bar governing boards to escape liability! There are professionals who know how to hurt you, create an injury to turn you into a client or patient and get away with it! Just a word of advice I wanted to share with you. Beware of those ads that seem too good to be true or offer such wonderful benefits. It's not true!

When you need a lawyer to clinch a deal, use an entertainment attorney, only! You can find entertainment attorneys in Los Angeles. They are often listed in screenplay magazines. The WGA can steer you in the right direction. Very easy. Get a personal referral to an attorney from other writers.

How to find a <u>competent</u> attorney? Visit, call or write a court where the professional resides and do a search on law suits. If you see the professional as a defendant you may have found the wrong lawyer. You can call the State Bar to see if any pending disciplinary actions are active. But inquire on dormant, past discipline action, too! With doctors you can do the same. Check the courts and medical board. You may be surprised to see just who is listed!

GOING BROKE

There are many people selling products to aspiring screenwriters. If you bought every book, every computer program, attended every seminar, etc., you'd have to declare bankruptcy. If your mailbox is like mine, it's jammed with never-ending offerings. In your first year or two of getting into this business, your adrenaline is high and you could be taken for a ride. Use discretion and buy slowly.

Many of the offers are very good and many are not necessary. Not all advertisements you see in the screenwriting magazines are endorsed by anything but the ad itself. The magazine does <u>not</u> endorse advertisements or advertisers.

Best advice? Do your shopping, and if possible, find writers who have attended certain seminars and recommend them, tried products and like them, etc. I've bought products that were quite useless and a monetary waste... even from big names in the entertainment education field, mostly due to outdated advice.

Usually, established screenwriters with a track record who give seminars will be a great value. This is not to say other seminars are of no value, not at all. Screenwriters who write books also give you a great deal of information. I have not read a book from a producer or director that is of any substantial value to the screenwriter, yet. They do better in seminars.

There are cassette and videotapes available and I've found most of them to be expensive and not of much use. Some may disagree with this, and that's okay, too. Some people won't like this book and that's okay, too. No one product can make success happen!

Everybody has the answer to your problem. All the solutions are available for a price. Life will be easy if you part with your money. The screenwriting market has gotten out of hand with more information but less usable data a screenwriter really needs to sell his/her product. This manual tries to bridge the gap and give you information you can apply right now! It's only part of the picture, a segment in the puzzle, a step in the right direction. Just watch where you step so you don't fall in with the sharks who will eat your money and give little back in exchange.

I have made recommendations in this marketing manual of certain products: books, magazines and computer programs. They are good products and well worth the money! Agents and other items and services listed are not recommendations or testimonials unless specifically stated. Of course, the opinion is mine, others may not agree, but that's okay.

SCRIPT TALK - KEEP THE ACTION FLOWING

Let's not forget that many scripts are rejected on appearance alone. Do follow the guidelines in this book so your presentation will be immediately judged professional. Do obtain a dedicated computer program to format your scripts. It will save you time and grief.

Read your script and make sure you can see your characters moving in time and space with lots of action taking place. Action does not need to be an explosion, it could simply be a smile.

All agents are open to read new material. All agents want to make money. All agents don't want to miss out on the hottest spec script of the year. But not all agents will allow you access to them. The big agencies will lock you out until you can obtain a recommendation or referral from another established writer, producer, actor, director or whatever. Go for the smaller agencies, especially in the Los Angeles area.

When you send a script to an agent, producer or director, your script will not be read by these principles. Your script will be read first by a reader. That's the firewall to penetrate. Read every magazine article and book written by a reader! You can read all the theory of writing books but you'll go nowhere fast if you can't satisfy the reader. Write what the reader needs to see! That doesn't mean a genre preference, it's a format and style thing. How the story is written is as important as the story itself.

Script length is shrinking and the text on page is less. That is a recent trend, but I bet you this will be the rule thirty-years from now! Shorten your scripts to the new standard. Those who do will get faster reads, better coverage and move up the food chain. Those who don't will be rejected at some high-level point in the process. It is a fact, most scripts are rejected due to the script being too long! And that was under the old rules! This is an instant firewall. Reader picks up script, looks at page number at back page, tosses it aside.

Talking about asides? Don't write notes in the script, typed or handwritten. You can get away with it with book manuscripts, but absolutely not in screen or stage plays. If you can't see it happening on the screen, you can't write it into the script. No statements, *"If possible, get a large car with no back seat."* No asides, *"Director should crane-shot the train."*

Even if you can see it, don't use it; "The ship fades as the actors walk away." Is this really important to the story? If not, leave it out. Now, if lovers were standing on the deck? That would be a different matter, as it's a story element. There is nothing worse a visual medium writer can do than write something that can't be seen or heard on the screen or stage! *"The spacecraft lands but we don't see it."* And the audience can't feel things in the theater, *"We can feel the cold wind on Christine's legs."*

Don't use words such as, *"We see the jet crash."* It really irritates readers to no end! Just say it, *"Jet crashes."*

Keep your description short. Long action paragraphs will not be read anyway. Split up the action into smaller segments. Four lines of action can be easily split into two lines. If the script looks heavy to readers they will pass on it.

The first ten pages of the script had better scream! The reader will read past page ten to the end, but here's the danger. If the reader gives the script a go, the producer and executive won't read past page ten! It's sickening, but it's true. They will read it, if the story is a page burner. Few are. So this means get rid of the multiple pages of back story. Learn to put back story elsewhere, not in the first 10-pages!

Titanic had lots of back story, but you are not James Cameron! Don't do it. If background must be inserted in the beginning, give it quickly. Action does not need to be car chases and death. It can simply be setting up your characters for a real fall or dilemma which "screams" tension without having them verbally shout.

No scene numbering in the script unless you are directing the script or writing the script under contract for a director. Otherwise, you write a simple author's script.

Don't follow the format in old screenplay books. **Example:** Using, CUT TO: after each action scene. Don't even use the word. The only transitions used in the author's script are, FADE IN: and FADE OUT:. Other cuts can be used such as, DISSOLVE TO: but do so very sparingly. Do not tell the director what to do. That's his job! Just tell the story.

It is dangerous to read "shooting scripts" as the beginner is told to do so in the magazines and books, *"Read all the scripts you can."* But the novice is not told, *"Do not mimic the format!"* Now you are being told. Write the author's script. If you send a shooting script to an agent or producer it will be discarded with an instant rejection.

Your script is laser-printed on three-hole punched 20 lb. white paper and bound by three hole punched 80 lb. white or neutral color covers. You use two or three brass #5-type, 1 1/4" brads. No fancy colors, no fancy binding. It looks boring, but that's the signature of the professional script!

STRANGE GOOD NEWS

Agents are crying for quality scripts but the real world fact is that quality does not always sell! Luck does. How? Because the script has captured the imagination of a buyer. This too is also a hard sell because there is little imagination in Hollywood when it comes to taking chances. Most buyer's careers are short-lived and to recommend a green light requires risk. If the venture fails the executive is blamed.

Everybody is looking for somebody else to make the recommendation so if the project fails they have someone to hang. So we have the agents pushing scripts and the readers and buyers all to willing to say, "No!" A "yes" may shorten or end a job and paycheck. Strange isn't it? So many good scripts are circulating and being rejected based on nobody wanting to stick their neck out to make the recommendation.

With this in mind, you can see why you will receive many rejections even if your script is great. And you can see why you have to just keep sending it out over and over again for many years until someone feels comfortable about the thing and goes for it. It is easier to develop and market your own consumer product than to sell a script, and that itself is hard enough to do. Eventually, you will sell one or more if you persist with a forever attitude. Just keep on sending your scripts out all of the time over the years and pray!

The other horrible truth is eventually you will get an agent, maybe sell a script and become a "hot" writer. The head-hunters will call from the big agencies and promise the sun, moon and stars. They can deliver, but abandonment is the future. Once you are no longer "hot" you'll be lucky to even have them return a phone call or answer a query letter... until you become "hot" again and that's a big "if" indeed.

So remember to save a bunch of money and don't spend it foolishly on new cars, new homes and stupid investments that require huge amounts of leveraged money. Why? The money will not last. Your success will be rags to riches to rags. Easy come, easy go. Don't ever forget that your fortune is not in your hands, it is at the whim of those who don't like taking chances. Some other "hot" writer will appear and you'll turn cold once again. It's like the music industry, very few musical groups last for the long haul. Used and abused.

So who is the most powerful in Hollywood? Directors? Agents? Actors? Studio executives? Producers? None of the above. The most powerful person is the script reader! If the reader "recommends" a script, then everybody has their scapegoat! The project can move forward knowing they have someone to blame if all goes bad at the box office... including the writer. If all goes well, everybody else takes the credit and the glory. Since it is hard to jingle the imagination of the executive buyer to risk a script they don't even read, then write for the reader who also does not read the script. Fun, isn't it?

There are no easy answers to marketing scripts and there are any number of ways a script can be sold. This manual's purpose is to give you the awareness of the realities, to give you that edge so your script will be professionally submitted, to make the reader and buyer say, "Yes" and take a chance with you. After all, if the script is terribly formatted and full of heavy wordage, it sinks.

Keep the script circulating in the mail and sooner or later it happens. Once you stop it's all over. Once you begin it never ends.

AUTHORITATIVE QUERY LETTERS - EXAMPLES YOU CAN USE

Don't make the mistake of writing weak pleading query letters with an attitude of humble submission. Take a look at the sample query letters in this book and you'll notice one thing... the subject matter gets down to business quickly. Most importantly, there are no pleading words or attitude of writing to a superior person. Agents and prodco executives are not divine (they only appear so). Here's an example of a pleading;

Dear Agent Bobby Cash:
I know you are very busy today. Please take the time to read this brief query. I know one thing. If you read the script, which is way better, you will certainly sell it. Give it a try, okay? Please contact me at your earliest convenance.

Very Sincerely Yours,

-- Can you see the problems above? Convenience is spelled wrong, the writer is begging, sounds desperate and excessively "buddy-buddy." Also, Bob or Bobby is improper, use Robert in the salutation. There are no friends in business! Business is simply business. Keep it that way. Now lets convert this to a more professional approach.

Dear Robert Cash:
(Start with your script log line here). *The script is available for evaluation. Mail the S.A.S.E. today requesting the screenplay. Thank you.*

Sincerely,

-- Of course query letters are naturally longer but the exercise here is to identify pleadings and authority. Keep your letter factual by nature with action words. Notice how the rewritten query has the elements of authority. Who is telling who what to do? This is exactly what agents and producers want to see, somebody in control, a sign of a professional! Read your query letter again and this time insert elements of authority to give yourself power (yet retain politeness).

Many screenwriting magazines and books publish sample query letters. Read them very carefully with the assumption you are the recipient and you have 100-letters to open on your desk. When you read a letter telling you do something (in a slick way not appearing arrogant) you immediately sense "professional" by the writer.

You can write a query anyway you wish. Just make sure it sticks to business and gets to the point. Industry pros are very busy people (very busy!) and you must communicate with power and authority or they will not respond. Or, they will respond only to toy with you, have you send the script only not to read or return it. They know who can be victimized simply by the lack of a "authoritative tone" in the query.

There are more than a few cruel people in this business who relish adding salt to wounds. Be professional and you'll see less abuse and way better results from your efforts!

Lesson to be learned is to never appear weak or submissive in your communications, in writing or verbally. Be polite but businesslike in all you say and do and you will certainly see positive results arise from the ashes of despair. Desperation, no matter how desperate you may be must never be revealed. If you do, it will be a major cause of rejection.

Everyone likes a powerful person. Be powerful! Write with power and authority. Make their heads spin in your direction! See the illustrations in this manual for query letter samples.

TURNING THE TIDE - BREAKING THE RULES - PACKAGING

The writer must never break the established rules and protocols. The industry expects writers to conform. Who is the industry? Agents, producers, prodcos, directors and stars. The good news is you don't have to break rules. What you want to do is get everybody else to break the rules! The industry's doors are closed tight. So it seems. They break the rules all of the time. All will take a script without agency representation despite the rules they proclaim to the public. How? Usually through recommendations.

You obtain these recommendations by many means, primarily from other writer's in the business, but you can "package" your query letter! Send your query to a specific actor, producer, director and inform them each is receiving the package deal. If your query is well-written, they will request the script and they will break the rules for you to get the movie made. If they want it bad enough, they will get it at all costs! They will even secure an agent for you to handle the deal to comply with their written policies. Studios may even start a bidding war to get your script!

The point here is you did something different than just submitting your query to agents. You packaged your script and tagged on the major elements yourself. Normally, packaging agencies handle these deals, but there is nothing stopping you from doing it yourself. It's just a smart way to go. Even if nothing happens on the first attempt, you have established contacts for future projects. Your script gets exposed to people in high places. That is one method to use to turn the tide of rejection into opportunity. See Fig. 2-4 for an example query letter to package a script with principals.

The packaging concept comes in very handy in sending a query to an agent. They need help in deciding to whom to send the script for the best possible results. You should have a list of principals handy, as it is only a matter of time you will be asked for it. But do not send any packaging information to an agent in the initial query letter. You may send it only when they request the script, but it is still not necessary. Some agents will send you instructions what to include in your submission package. Follow the advice precisely!

Before you try packaging, make certain your screenplay has ranked in the top 100, at the least. Top fifty is better! Even if the script has ranked lower, you can do it but you should hire a script consulting firm or professional to critique the script to help you rewrite it so it has star attraction power. Packaging is not for the new writer with sloppy scripts, you will only waste your time and money ending up with a huge series of rejection. Then again, even a good script gets rejected, so don't be dismayed. Keep trying.

Note: high ranks in screenplay contests and professionally submitting your script, query, cover letter materials, with a script that can deliver the goods, will get you where you want to go. Think of script evaluation and consulting costs as purchasing a combination code to open a safe. It's a lot easier to open that safe with the code than using an acetylene blow torch. See the list of Script Doctors.

SHOTGUN THE MARKET

Amazingly, many writers get stuck in a groove and find themselves on a single marketing path. This narrow marketing avenue is always submitting to agents, and nothing but agents. They believe that once they get representation they will have it made in the shade. Not so. You may as well get used to the idea you have to write to everybody in the business, even when you do have an agent!

The advice given here is to get your query letters custom-built: one for agents, one for directors, one for producers, one for stars, one for prodcos and do this for each script. Now what? Get them all circulating in the mail! You have to shotgun the market.

Don't worry about getting an agent and don't mention in your query letter you do not have an agent, just send the query and stay on the subject matter of the screenplay. The recipients don't give a hoot if you have an agent or not, they want a marketable product, that's all. They will get you an agent at the snap of their fingers, if needed, or you can take your pick once a purchase is eminent.

Point is, hit them all with your query letters! There are many writers who have sold scripts and later obtained agency representation by first writing directly to the principles; stars, producers, directors prodcos, studio executives, even secretaries who work for powerful people in the business.

NOBODY WANTS MY SCRIPT - NOT SO!

You would think with over 160,000+ scripts circulating in the system nobody in the industry would be foolish enough to spend $500 or more to place an advertisement in a magazine looking for scripts. All the production houses are flooded already with scripts from writers and agents, so there is no need to place advertising. Right?

Incredibly, ads are placed all of the time in many magazines! Most are from producers and production companies and this is where opportunity knocks loudly for the writer, represented or not.

It is a good investment, in fact, a writer's toolbox, so subscribe to as many scriptwriting/industry magazines and newsletters as you can afford. You should ask your library to subscribe to the expensive magazines and directories. Respond to the ads and you will see the doors of Hollywood are not so closed after all!

CHAPTER 12

WRITER SURVIVAL TIPS

There are many articles and chapters in screenwriting and theatrical books explaining how to survive in Hollywood and Broadway. Here's a few tips.

1. Agents and producers will lie to you with politeness. Get used to it! It begins with, "*You are a fabulous writer.*" or "*This script is* *great! We just love it!"* Then every promise in the book will be made to you. This generates the "Hollywood High" that the pros call "hype." It is easy to fall into the hype, but don't buy into it. Keep a level head, stay professional!

2. You have an agent, maybe a small agent, then you sell your script and the big prestigious agencies contact you to join them with juicy offers and promises of making ultimate high-levels of income. So, you fire your agent and move on into the big time.

This can be a serious mistake! Once you do this, it is revealed disloyalty by everyone in the business and you lose respect. Nobody will trust you. Firing a good and helpful agent (who also wants to make it big with you) reveals your arrogance and gullibility and sheer uncaring nature for others. Think about it. You fired the person that made you a star! And you did this for pure selfish reasons, greed!

3. Maintain honest relations with everyone because your future depends on it -- even if everyone else is lying to you! You must retain your integrity at all costs, so the "fibbers" will respect you. Hollywood is a very strange world, unlike any other industry. Lies perpetuate within every phase of the organizational chart. But once you, the writer, lie? It's over.

Hollywood is one big lie built upon another. The very foundation is a lie of which it is all built upon. There is little truth to be found, but loyalty and integrity is ultimately demanded from the writer. Be careful what you say to anyone. *"Gossip is like taking poison and hoping the other person will die!"* Stay clear, as it will certainly come back to bite you.

4. Reliability is of extreme importance. When you are commissioned to write a script, deliver it, on time! It is incredible how many new screenwriters sell a couple scripts and go hog-wild on the town, living it up to the max, taking drugs, sipping brew; life is a grand party! Then they soon discover the income has ceased. They reneged on the responsibility of the job.

Can't happen to you? Go to Reno or Las Vegas for 1-week and with nothing else to do but gamble, you'll soon see how fast you will part with your money! Same with Hollywood. It's a grand party! Stay off the drugs and alcohol and you'll survive. No problem!

5. Maintain your creative voice, for it is easy to lose it! When you get hired to write scripts you will be beat to a pulp in a matter of days. *"Your writing is horrible!" "This is pure junk!" "Write it this way! My way!"* Story editors and executives will tear you up and eventually break your spirit and you'll lose the style and voice you had that made you successful in the first place!

Most new screenwriters simply fall apart and leave Hollywood in less than two-years! Best advice? You have to obey your employer and write the way they want you to, so you must do so. But to retain your original creativity and voice, write your own spec screenplays. Simple advice, but it works. It's the only way to retain your creative writing and remain sane.

Remember, you are a unique individual and you do not need the approval of others to retain inner content and happiness. If you need help, see a psychologistist to keep you on keel. Get religion or keep your faith strong in God. Hollywood's glitter and glamour behind the scenes is really a deep pit of depression and hell. Those who make it are not so vain to believe that money and recognition buys happiness. It only buys misery for the gullible. Keep the faith! You'll need it.

6. Celebrity Status Danger: You will be the talk of the town. After all those years of being unknown and poor, you are now filthy rich and glamour arises. Hollywood's twinkling stars shine upon you! The danger for the screenwriter is to not follow the "Movie Stars" plight. Stars must look like stars, act like stars, dress and live like stars. It's how they stay employed. It is not expected the writer to be such a party animal. In fact, it's frowned upon! So, don't change your appearance trying to look like a movie star or you'll eventually be run out of town. Writer's are to remain low-key.

The moment you begin thinking like a "star" your personality and thought processes will change which will take you in another direction in life, adverse to your employers! You may become cocky, overly confident, rude, uncaring, participate in cruel gossip, look down upon other people, ego expands so large it drives those who like you far away. It can happen to you, easily! Best advice? Just stay humble and polite to all you meet and you will see greater things to come. You are a writer, not a star, so get back to writing and deliver your projects. That's why you are paid the big bucks.

7. Desperation Kills: Hollywood is filled with desperate men. Step onto a car dealers lot and you can smell it coming at you; a desperate salesman ready for the kill! You can see it in his face, his pace, his eyes, and his desperation turns you off, right? Same with screenwriters pitching scripts. Agents and executives can see your desperation and it turns them off, too! Take an acting class to learn how to control it. Yes, you should be enthused when pitching a story, but desperation should never be allowed to intrude, as it will produce an offensive odor. Strongly put words, but wise to hear.

The mortgage is overdue and you have to sell a story. The pressure is boiling inside of you ready to explode. *"I've got to sell this script! I have to or I'll lose my home!"* Get a job! Pay your mortgage, then come back and pitch your script without the internal pressure gnawing within you. Never reveal desperation, never! It makes people afraid of you. Desperate people do desperate things. You must remain professional in all your dealings. That being; cool, calm, thoughtful, caring, willing to listen, behaving with relaxed confidence. Write those words down on a piece of paper and recite them before you enter the pitch room.

8. The bottom line is to remain true to yourself and just be, you! Never gossip no matter who deserves it. That person has friends with power (or will have) and it will be your doom. There is nothing worse to have a fortune and lose it! Keep your lips pursed, unless you have something nice to say. You will see the retaliation come upon others as the years unfold, but it shall not touch you. You will be well-rewarded for being a "nice person" in Hollywood, despite what you see, otherwise that dishonest cut-throat people make it big. Their power and success usually fades away.

The turn-over rate is very high! Everyone is expendable! Nobody rules! Corporations operate Hollywood, not people on the larger scale. Relationships count for everything due to the turnover factor. The little guy is always moving up replacing the big guy, so don't trample on the little people! Be cordial and professional to everyone you meet and your career will be quite assured to last.

9. If you find yourself in a tight spot, realizing you have told a tiny lie by mistake or said a bad thing? Correct it right away. Apologize to the offended parties (believe me, they already know what you said ten minutes after it was voiced). The industry is full of setup con-artists. People, desperate people, who will set you up for a fall, so they can rise up in your place or gain favor with others in high places.

Honesty and integrity is respected, even among the dishonorable! You may be thinking, *"None of this advice has anything to do with screenwriting!"* Well, you won't be screen writing for long if you fall into these traps!

10. Extraordinary Politeness Fails - Have you ever met a person who is just too nice to believe? Of course you have, and it made you wonder of the person's sincerity is really valid or just a false front. It's a disease in Hollywood totally out of control infecting the gullible. It's where the "hype" and "Hollywood High" thrives. Don't be too polite! Be a businessperson! Know your role!

Agents and stars act differently because their jobs demand it, but as a writer you must be the "sensible one" in a world of insanity. The more professional and undisturbed you appear, the more respect and employment will come your way. Once you become "giddy" like the others, you lose respect and money. It is important to be "different" than the pack of wolves, so you don't become a hungry wolf yourself.

11. There are many nice people in power in Hollywood, too! It's just that the not-so-nice desperate people outnumber the honest on many levels. The cut-throating is extreme on the lower levels, and more professional on the upper levels (can I say this?). Well, it's supposed to be and in many instances it is.

The new screenwriter is in for a tumble when employed in Hollywood. You will be faced with incredible levels of workload (infused with big money) and faced with insults reaching to the core of your soul. In no time at all you'll feel like a failure! But if you just remember these little helpful tips of advice given in this book, you will survive the onslaughts and retain your integrity, honor and employment.

The important thing here is to learn. Keep your eyes and ears open and learn from other's mistakes. A writer who is willing to learn and maintains a good spirit of professionalism stays employed. A writer who snivels, rebels and complains is driven into the winds of despair.

WRITING SCHOOLS
We mentioned earlier some screenwriters advise against taking courses to learn how to write screenplays, generally meaning, it's the intensive study that can be harmful to the creative process, but knowledge is

still certainly required. Taking "light" courses can't hurt you! Also see subchapter *"Script Evaluations - Script Doctors."*

Discounts: You should inquire if discounts are available for readers of this book. Some have agreed to offer discounts, many will if you ask. If you see a percentage or dollar figure by the listing, a discount has been confirmed.

-- *Writer's Digest School*, Dept. J-5, 1507 Dana Avenue, Cincinnati, OH 45207 (800)759-0963, has a few writing courses you may want to consider: novels, short story, screenwriting, etc.

--Screenwriter's Online, Dept. W, 16752 Bollinger Dr., Pacific Palisades, CA 90272 (310)459-5278 5% This firm offers the online screenwriting class "Screenwriter's Online's Master Class On Screenwriting" hosted by top Hollywood professionals, academy award winning screenwriters, studio executives, agents and producers. They have a website run by professional screenwriters who get their scripts made into movies.

-- Cyber Film School, Internet Film Group, Dept. S, 124 Cumberland St., 3D Floor, Toronto, Ontario, Canada M5R 1A6 (416)928-0463

Every large city has a film school. Some evening classes are available at community colleges. They offer drama, acting and writing courses. However, not everyone can attend school, so that's where screenwriting technical books can come into play to help you. Plus, you'll need the books anyway regardless of what school you attend.

A list of schools are not given here as there are simply too many to list. You can find most all on the Internet and some advertise in the screenwriting magazines. See the Yellow Pages in the phone book.

COMPUTER BACKUP WARNING

All scripts today are written on computer programs. It is easy to become complacent and trust the computer will never fail. It has been so reliable, it won't fail, so you think! The day will come a major failure will occur to the disk or memory and will prevent access to your data. This means all your query letter and synopsis boilerplate templates will be lost. All contact addresses gone, and all your scripts burned up in smoke, forever lost! To prevent total disaster get a Jaz, Zip or CD-rewritable drive or any other external device where you can remove the media containing your files to safe locations.

Safe is not in the home, it is in your vehicle and a copy in a safe deposit box at your bank. Homes burn, earthquakes shake, hurricanes, tornadoes can be equally damaging.

Keep these backup files current. Do not use any backup program! Copy your files straight, uncompressed, to the disk. The backup program may not work when transferring to the new hard drive in your computer. Often, the backup program itself, and its coding algorithm, is destroyed in major hardware and software failures and can never be recovered (many people do not know this).

A disk recovery service can be employed, but be aware they will never get all of the data! Just one line of missing code will stop you from ever recovering your scripts or books or whatever is important to you.

When you back up your files, do not rely on the program's backup feature. They do work, but for absolute safety of your data, go to your file directory (Windows Explorer) and use the cut and paste copy method to copy the entire program along with all the subdirectories that contain your data to your backup drive. This way you preserve all of your program settings and data in one perfect package.

Simply copy the program and paste it onto your new hard drive and you are back in business. Do not trust any backup program and never use compression features as they will certainly fail. Remember, there are only two types of computer owners; those who have lost critical data files and those who will!

FIREWALL CHART
A marketing chart, Fig. 1-26, is provided to reveal the levels of firewalls a screenwriter must penetrate. The chart is only a basic example. There are other organizational chart configurations deviating from this theme.

Example: The agent may submit directly to a studio head, or to a director or movie star, bypassing producers and readers below in the chart. You can do the same. The idea is to understand how the submission system works, so you can ease your way past the firewalls. The flip side of the coin is, it will do you no good to penetrate these walls if your script is no good. This is subjective, as novice writers believe their scripts are fabulous; experienced writers know their script is likely not up to highest standards (no script is perfect). Submit the script anyway, as the reader just might like it.

If your script is being constantly rejected, have it evaluated to discover why. Get it into a screenplay contest and see how it ranks. But remember, good scripts are also rejected for many years. Some are kicked around Hollywood for over a decade before they get made into a movie. It's just timing. The time was right for the script. This is why you need to keep your scripts circulating.

TEST YOUR KNOWLEDGE
See Fig. 1-19 for a True or False test. See Fig. 1-20 for answers and explanations. When you need a quick solution to a problem when marketing your script, you can always resort to this test for answers.

INDUSTRY CONTACTS - USE THIS AGENT & PRODCO FORM
Fig 1-30 is a handy contact sheet you can use to keep track of your submissions. Sometimes, a computer just does not work as well as a hard copy file. If an agent or prodco calls, you'll have instant access to your file for reference, without having to wait to start a computer or have to call back later -- the agent/prodco may never answer the phone! Plus, if your computer's hard disk fails or database file becomes corrupted, so it it no longer readable by the computer, you will have a hard copy to continue on with your business.

CHECKLIST - SUBMISSION PACKAGE
Now that you are ready to submit your package to the agent, prodco, producer, director, etc., you'll need a checklist to insure the submission is complete. See Fig. 1-29. Do not rely on memory, use the

list! You may forget to include a critical item in the package and all your effort will be wasted due to an improper submission.

More scripts are rejected due to improper submissions than any other reason besides poor story structure and formatting. If you forget the release form or fail to apply the "Script Requested" notice on the mailing envelope, the script may be shredded or returned to you unopened.

Do not forget to sign your query letter and release form! No signature legally means, "No Authorization" and the materials will end up in the rejection heap. This list will help you maintain quality control in your submission procedure.

THE LAST WORD

This is the beginning of your journey and it all starts today. Most writers quit just when they are getting good at screenwriting. Don't let this happen to you. Yes, it can take two to eight years or more to reach the goal. As with any profession, it takes time to become proficient. Work at your goal slowly, but surely, ever pushing forward despite the odds (way better odds than hitting a state lottery, but it's still a gamble) and the unmerciful relentless rejections and let-downs.

One thing you can be certain of... marketing your scripts will no longer be the major cause of rejections. Now you can concentrate on polishing your screenwriting skills to make that first sale. Read as many screenwriting books as possible. Also, if you wish to succeed you must keep on writing. It's okay to take a long break so you can live a normal life again. Your writing will become more focused and relaxed.

Subscribe to the magazines, keep writing and the doors will open. I'm certain this information I have shared will be of great value to you. If you have any suggestions or comments about this manual, feel free to write me. (Yes, include a S.A.S.E. if you wish a reply). If the information has helped you in any way, I'd like to know that, too. Good luck to you and never give up the dream! -- *James Russell*

NO CHAPTER 13

When elevators stop on floor 13, then this chapter will be written. Until then,

CHAPTER 14

INTRODUCTION TO TRAP SHOOTING - YOU CAN MEET PEOPLE HERE

Scriptwriters are busy folks under tremendous psychological pressure and a relief valve is necessary to maintain a level of sanity. They also need money to pay bills and have some down to earth fun. I have found trapshooting to be a blessing in so many ways as a social diversion. If you are in Los Angeles, trapshoots are in; Chino, Newhall, El Monte, Edwards Air Force Base, Las Vegas, etc. What is trapshooting? Shooting flying clay targets with a shotgun in competition tournaments. Sort of like skeet shooting. There are over 6,000 registered tournament shoots annually in the USA. It's a hidden sport, but it's a huge one at that.

I've met movie industry people at these shoots. It's no secret some actors, directors and producers attend to get away from it all.

Contacts can be made, but primarily it's a recreation activity with an opportunity to win a few hundred to a few thousand dollars... for having fun. If you've never tried it, you are in for a thrill. To get started you can visit my website. See Title Page for the URL address or use a search engine to find James Russell Publishing or type in the words, trap shooting. I explain the sport in great detail and give free trap shooting lessons on line.

This trapshooting sport is serious business. There is big money at stake in these shoots, and you will shoot against the professionals. No other sport will give you that privilege. The social climate is the ultimate... you won't find a better bunch of people who will instantly accept you the way you are, as though you were a long lost friend on your first visit. It's truly a breath of fresh air for the writer who lives a frustrating life of rejection! The parties are huge and the food is fantastic.

To get you started Shotgun Sports Magazine will send you a complimentary copy. Call 800-676-8920 or 916-889-2220. Address is listed in back of book. You may be surprised to find opportunities for your writing in this sport as there are many magazines looking for trap shooting articles!

TRAP SHOOTING WRITING OPPORTUNITIES
Many trap shooters own huge businesses and need print, radio and television advertising copy scripts, video scripts, newsletter stories, product photos, etc. Shooting manufacturers are wide open for product reviews and you can sell articles to the magazines -- big names like, Winchester, Federal, Browning, and Remington are just some of the major firms supporting this sport.

Magazines need writers. *Shotgun Sports* and *Trap & Field* are major players in the USA. *Clay Shooting Magazine* and *Pull Magazine* are principles in the United Kingdom. If you write movies with gunfire in the scenes, it is to your advantage to shoot a few guns to get the feel of the action.

Ask for a complimentary issue of:
--*Trap & Field Magazine*, Dept. J-R1, 1000 Waterway Blvd., Indianapolis, IN 46202 (317)633-8802.

If you live in Europe ask for a complimentary issue of:
--*Clay Shooting Magazine* / Brunton Business Publications, Thruxton Down House, Thruxton Down, Andover, Hampshire, England SP11 SPR.

Contact:
-- Amateur Trapshooting Association (ATA) 601 W. National Road, Vandalia, OH 45377 (937)898-4638. The name is deceptive as there is nothing amateur about the ATA. They are the leading association of trap shooters in the USA and Canada and they hold the Grand International shoot in Ohio where over 100,000 shooters arrive to compete!

If you live in the Pacific Northwest or Western Canada you can contact the *Pacific International Trapshooting Association* to sign up for their registered shoots in Northern California, Oregon, Washington, Idaho, Utah, all the way up into Canada and Alaska. Pacific International Trapshooting Association (PITA). Address is listed in, *"Addresses of*

Fims Mentioned" in the back of this book.

Give it a shot!

IS YOUR BOOK PUBLISHED?
James Russell Publishing is open to new writers, but see our Submission Guidelines on our website before you submit. Have you considered writing a screen writing or performing arts book?

CHAPTER 15

AGENTS YOU MAY CONTACT - SPECIAL LISTING
The agencies listed below have agreed to give readers of this book special consideration. In other words, they are willing to take a chance with you and accept your query letter since you have read the book and will (hopefully) perform a professional submission with a marketable script! Some offer discounts on extra services.

This is a golden opportunity for you to make a great first impression and may even get your script sold. Please, finish reading this book first. Apply all that you possibly can to enhance your script and query letter before you contact the agencies. Remember, these agencies are opening the doors for you, so give them all the respect they deserve. You will be given one shot -- make your best aim by being professional in all aspects communicating with these agencies. Do not be tempted to rush the process. You have lots of time to contact the agencies and managers. Haste makes waste.

Rules & Instructions: Standard rules still apply. We are not listing phone numbers, so you can't be tempted to call the agent. Simply send your query letter with S.A.S.E., sit back and wait. You should mention in your query letter in the first line or paragraph, **"I am a reader of Screen & Stage Marketing Secrets and submitting in accordance with your special listing in the book."** These are agencies who can get your scripts sold, so be professional. See Fig. 2-5 for a query letter you should use to contact these agencies. **Note:** James Russell Publishing or the author receives no financial compensation from these agencies in the form of kickbacks or referral fees. All listings in this book that are not clearly display advertising in nature are listed without compensation and listed for the benefit of the screenwriter and playwright.

Advice: E-mail address and fax number is not listed, so you can't make the mistake of submitting an unprofessional submission. Never mail an e-mail or perform a fax submission, unless it complies perfectly to the illustrations shown in this book. Many writers make this big mistake of sending unprofessional e-mail and fax submissions ruining a perfectly good opportunity. Use the postal mail with S.A.S.E. included!

Agencies that do not list submission instructions? Send them a single page query letter and S.A.S.E. and a single page synopsis if you wish. Anything more and you are risking a rejection. These agents are very busy people and they have no time to read huge query submissions. Even the single page synopsis should be streamlined to 3/4 page, just to be safe. Since you are not shotgunning the market, do not send them a multiple submission logline list. Send just one query for one script. Certainly do mention that you have other scripts, then make a brief logline for each in the last paragraph of your query letter. This will let the agent know you have more in the wings and may request one or two to read.

WARNING: DO NOT RUSH! You should not fire off a query to these agents until your script has been fully evaluated by a script doctor and has ranked within the top-100 or better in a screenplay contest. Read this book again to make certain your scripts comply with industry rules, standards and requirements. Yes, even your query letter and synopsis should be evaluated by a script doctor. You may include a copy of your screenplay ranking certificate or an excellent script doctor evaluation. Get your ducks lined up first, then you will be ready to contact these agencies. Take your time! The faster you move does not mean the faster you'll make a sale. Remember that famous race between the tortoise and the hare?

AGENT & MANAGEMENT FIRM LISTING

An asterist(*) indicates agency is a WGA signatory agent. Agents that are not signatory most certainly can sell your scripts and may use sub-agents that are signatory to make the sale. Agents that are not signatory now, may be in the future! Some agents have indicated they are in process. A double asterist(**) indicates the firm is a management company. Management companies can not be signatories, but production can be. A listing indicating "film" means, feature film movies, not MOW's or documentaries.

Note: All agents and management firms below have agreed to give readers of this book *"special consideration."* Please use the cover letter format in Fig. 2-5 so they will know you are responding as a reader of this book -- otherwise, they can't give you special attention.

**--AEI-Atchity Editorial/Entertainment Intnl., Dept. SB, 9601 Wilshire Blvd., #1202, Beverly Hills, CA 90210 10% discount on editorial service. Novels/nonfiction books, screenplays, teleplays.
*--A Picture Of You Literary Agency/Lenny Minelli, Dept. SW, 1175 Elizabeth Drive, Hamilton, OH 45013. Film/TV.
--Cedar Grove Agency Entertainment, Samantha Powers/Story Editor, Dept. 09, P.O. Box 1692, Issaquah, WA 98027-0068. Film. Note: No horror, period pieces or erotic thrillers.
**--Feigen/Parrent Literary Management, Joanne Parrent, Dept. SB, 10158 Hollow Glen Circle, Bel Air, CA 90077. Film.
--Finesse Literary Agency, Karen E. Carr, Dept. KEC, 655 N First Street, Wood River, IL 62092. Stage Play/Film/TV.
--King Productions, Review Dept., 50 Reeves Bay Trail, Flanders, NY 11901. Film. Prefers sci-fi/fantasy, but accepts all genre.
*--Monteiro Rose Agency, Inc., Dept. 1, 17514 Ventura Blvd., #205, Encino, CA 91316. Film.
--Paul S. Levine Literary Agency/Law Office, Dept. A, 1054 Superba Avenue, Venice, CA 90291-3940. Film/TV/Books.
--Reynolds Companies/Tom Reynolds, Dept. A., 321 N. 46th Ave, W., Deluth, MN 55807. Film/TV Note: Working toward signatory status.
--Sedgeband Literary Associates/David Duperre, Dept 3., 7312 Martha Lane, Fort Worth, TX 76112. Film/TV all genre.
--Silver Screen Placements, William W. Levin, Dept. SB, 602 65th Street. Downers Grove, IL 60516-3020. Film/Novels. Note: Requests query, one page synopsis, two random script pages and S.A.S.E..
--Sligo Literary Agency, Eric Bollinger, Dept. SS, 45535 Pueblo Road,

Indian Wells, CA 92210. Film/TV.
**--Smith Entertainment, Dept Area 123, 2818 La Cienega Ave, 2nd Floor, Los Angeles, CA 90034. Film.
*--Stanton & Associates Literary Agency, 4413 Clemson Drive, Dept. TC, Garland, TX 75042. Film/TV. Offers 5% discount for readers of this book.
*--The Surratt Agency, Sher Surratt, Dept RJ, 5214 Hillside Road, Cleveland, OH 44131. Film/TV.
*--NY Creative Management/Jeff Schmidt, Dept JR-1, Drawer 1578, Stony Brook, NY 11790. Film.
*--Williams' Literary Agency, Sheri Homan, Dept 1-A, R1 Box 109, Kosciusko, MS, 39090. Film/TV Note: Mention you saw our listing in this book will guarantee a speedy reading and reply. No sex or gay/lesbian themes.
--Writer's Network/William K. Vogeler, Dept. SB, 7700 Irvine Center Drive, Suite 800, Irvine, CA 92618. Stage Plays/Film/TV. All genres.

SCRIPT EVALUATIONS - SCRIPT DOCTORS

Some agencies in this listing charge a reading fee and will include a written evaluation of your script for $30 to $125. Script analysis firms charge $90 to $500+.

When contacting the listed firms below, ask for a brochure. One plus is these(*)literary services firms are also agents/promoters and may take you on board, which may or may not do you any good. More agencies and script analysis evaluators are listed in screenwriting magazines. See subchapter "*Screenwriting Magazines and Script Resources*." See subchapter "*Writing Schools*" to learn how to write scripts.

Discounts: You should inquire if discounts are available for readers of this book. Some have agreed to offer discounts, many will if you ask. If you see a percentage or dollar figure by the listing, a discount has been confirmed for you, a reader of this book.

Websites: The firm's are listed below. Website URL addresses are in the subchapter, *Address of Firms Mentioned In This Manual.*

-- Bob Shayne Co., Dept. B, 29229 Heathcliff Road, #1, Dept. A, Malibu, CA 90265 (310)457-8098
-- Creative Script Services, Dept. D, 11738 Moorpark St. Suite F, Studio City, CA 91604 (818)754-4779 $50 discount. Note: *"We will read and if viable represent your material."*
--Dave Brandl, Play Script Consulting, Dept 1-A, P.O. Box 234, Denver, CO 80201. (303)333-7018. Stage Plays only - $150. 20%.
-- Dave Trottier's Screenwriting Center, Clearstream, Dept. SB, P.O. Box 520248, Salt Lake City, UT 841542-0248 (800)264-4900 www.clearstream.com
-- *Dennis E. Mullenix Literary Services, Dept. T, 4210 North University Ave, Peoria, IL 61614 ($40 first. No reading fees on future submissions).
--Guru-My-Screenplay, Dept S, P.O. Box 140977, Austin, TX 78714.
--Harry Preston, Dept. TC, 4413 Clemson Drive, Garland, TX 75042 (972)-276-5427. 5% discount. Author, Screenwriter, Ghostwriting, editing, rewriting of books and screenplays.
--Hollywood Screenplay Consultants Dept. B, 17216 Saticoy St., 303, Van Nuys, CA 91406 (818)994-5977 (also offer screenplay ghostwriting, classes, competition). 20% discount on consultations. 20% on course.
--*Lee Shore Agency, LTD., Dept. B, 440 Friday Road, Pittsburgh, PA 15209 (412)821-0440 (Approximately $65 reading fee includes telephone

consultation evaluating the merits and suggestions of your script).
--Michael Hauge Hilltop Productions, Dept. SB-1, P.O. Box 55728, Sherman Oaks, CA 91413 (800)477-1947.
--Muse of Fire. Screenplay evaluation service. $50 discount.
--Richwood Script Consultants, Dept A, 1801 Century Park East, Suite 2400, Los Angeles, CA 90067. (310)319-2075. 15%.
--Script Doctor, Dept. T-1, 3500 W. Orange Grove, Suite 12105, Tucson, AZ 85741 10%.
--Southwest Writers Workshop, Dept. 1, 8200 Mountain Rd., NE. Suite 106, Albuquerque, NM 87110. (505)265-9485.
--Star Literary Service, Dept. 2-A, 1540 North Louis Avenue, Tuscon, AZ 85712 ($30 is standard fee).
--Screenplay Consulting/The Screenwriter's Room, Dept. C-2, 12240 Venice Blvd., Suite 11, Los Angeles, CA 90066 (310)-397-2970
--The Complete Screenplay, Dept. 4-A, 14105 Castle Blvd., #204, Silver Spring, MD 20904 (301)847-1410. 10%.
--The Script Works, MGM Plaza, Dept. G-1, 2425 Colorado Avenue, Suite 265, Santa Monica, CA 90404 (800)806-4425.
--Universal Development, Dept. J-9, 12400 Ventura Blvd., #317, Studio City, CA 91604 ($95).

* Note: Some of the above agencies charge fees for rewriting services. The author is not endorsing any of the above except as otherwise noted. The agencies listed above may or may not be signatory to the WGA.

Recommendation: There are many fine script doctors. Dave Trottier and Michael Hauge have been fixing scripts for a very long time and are professional in all aspects.

OTHER SCREENWRITING RESOURCES

Here's more resources of interest to the writer.

-- Frederick Mensch Multimedia, Dept. B-3, 254 S. Greenwood, Ave., Paatine, IL 60067. (847)776-0747 This database indicates which types of screenplays have been recently purchased, the producer and executive who made the purchase and agents who made sales. You can target your queries to the individuals most likely to be receptive to the specific genre you have written. One year subscription is approximately $30. Some, but not all contact mailing addresses are given.

--Muse of Fire. Helpful advice for the screenwriter. Visit: www.loop.com/~musofire. Discount: Free! Also offers screenplay evaluation service with a $50 discount to readers of this book.

--Screenwriters & Playwrights Home Page 3550 SW Pomona St., Portland, OR 97219 (800)294-7176. Publishes a book *Screenwright: The Craft of Screenwriting*. $10 rebate for readers of this book.

-- See, *Story Engine* subchapter.

ADDRESSES OF FIRMS MENTIONED IN THIS MANUAL

We can't always stay current with changing phone numbers and addresses between print runs. If you can't find the firm listed, try using a search engine on the Web.

A

-- Academy Players Directory, Dept. 4-A, 8449 Wilshire Blvd., Beverly Hills, CA 90211.
--AEI-Atchity Editorial/Entertainment Intnl., Dept. SB, 9601 Wilshire Blvd., #1202, Beverly Hills, CA 90210 Web: www.aeionline.com
--A Picture Of You Literary Agency/Lenny Minelli, Dept. SW, 1175 Elizabeth Drive, Hamilton, OH 45013.
--Applause Theater & Cinema Books, Dept. O, 211 W. 71st St., NY, NY, 10023 (212)496- 7511.
--Ashley Software, 27758 Santa Margarita Pkwy #302, Mission Viejo, CA 92691. 800-229-6737.
--ATA Dept. B, 601 W. National Road, Vandalia, OH 45377 (937)898-4638.

B
--Ballistic Software. See Hollywood Screenplay Software.
--Bob Shayne Co., 29229 Heathcliff Road, #1, Malibu, CA 90265 (310)457-8098.
--Book City, Dept. T-7, 308 N. San Fernando Blvd., Burbank, CA 91502 (818)848-5615.
--Browncor International, 770 South 70th Street, P.O. Box 14770, Milwaukee, WI 53214-0770 (800)-327-2278.

C
--Cedar Grove Agency Entertainment, Samantha Powers/Story Editor, Dept. 09, P.O. Box 1692, Issaquah, WA 98027-0068. Web: www.freeyellow.com/members/cedargrove/index.html
--Cinovation, Inc., 1750 15th St., Boulder, CO 80302 (800)788-7090 (303)-786-7899. Web: http://scriptware.com
--Clay Shooting Magazine / Brunton Business Publications, Thruxton Down House, Thruxton Down, Andover, Hampshire, England SP11 SPR.
--Clearstream - See David Trottier
--Creative Screenwriting, 6615 Franklin Avenue, S4, Los Angeles, CA 90028-9723.Creative Screenwriting, 6615 Franklin Avenue, S4, Los Angeles, CA 90028-9723.
--Creative Script Services, Dept. D, 11738 Moorpark St. Suite F, Studio City, CA 91604 (818)754-4779 www.thescript.com
--CMJ Music FilmFest Sound & Vision, 11 Middle Neck Road, Suite 400, Great Neck, NY 11021 (516)489-3114.
--Collaborator, Dept. 1-J, 4335 Van Nuys Blvd., PMB#205, Sherman Oaks, CA 91403. Web:www.collaborator.com
--Cyber Film School, Internet Film Group, Dept. S, 124 Cumberland St., 3D Floor, Toronto, Ontario, Canada M5R 1A6(416)928-0463 Web:www.cyberfilmschool.com
--Cyber Film School / Impact Pictures, Dept. S, 30 Mountainview Ave., Toronto, Canada M6A 2L3 Web: www.cyberfilmschool.com/scriptmaker.htm

D
--Dave Brandl, Play Script Consulting, Dept 1-A, P.O. Box 234, Denver, CO 80201 (303)333-7018. Web:www.suite101.com/welcome.cfm/playwriting
--David Trottier, Clearstream, Dept. SB, P.O. Box 520248, Salt Lake City, UT 84152-0248 (800)2644900 (801)274-0110 www.clearstream.com
--Dennis E. Mullenix Literary Services, Dept. T, 4210 North University Ave, Peoria, IL 61614
--Directors Guild of America 7920 Sunset Blvd., Los Angeles, CA 90046 (310)289-2035
--Dramatist Guild, Dept, A-2, 1501 Broadway, Suite 701, New York, NY 10036 (212)398-9366

E
--Editor & Writer, Dept. 4-A, 526 Boston Post Rd., Wayland, MA 01778

F
--Fade In: Magazine Dept, T-1, 289 S. Robertson Boulevard, Suite 465,

Beverly Hills, CA 90211 (800)646-3896.
--Feigen/Parrent Literary Management, Joanne Parrent, Dept. SB, 10158 Hollow Glen Circle, Bel Air, CA 90077.
--Film Guide, Ross Reports Publications, Dept. A-3, 1515 Broadway, NY, NY 10036 (212)536-5294
--Final Draft, Inc. Dept. E, 16000 Ventura Blvd, Suite 800, Encino, CA 91436
(800)-231-4055 Web: www.finaldraft.com
--Finesse Literary Agency, Karen E. Carr, Dept. KEC, 655 N First Street, Wood River, IL 62092. Web: http://users.marz.com/~angel1
-- Frederick Mensch Multimedia, Dept. B-3, 254 S. Greenwood, Ave., Paatine, IL 60067. (847)776-0747 Web: www.moviebytes.com

G
--Guru-My-Screenplay, Dept S, P.O. Box 140977, Austin, TX 78714. Web: www.guru-my-screenplay.com

H
--Entertainment Employment Journal, Dept. 2-A, 5632 Van Nuys Blvd., #320, Van Nuys, CA 90036.
--Hollywood Reporter, Dept A, 5055 Wilshire Blvd., Los Angeles, CA 90036 (213)525-2000.
--Hollywood Creative Directory, Dept. C, 3000 Olympic Blvd., Ste 2525, Santa Monica, CA 90404 (310)315-4815, (800) 815-0503.
--Hollywood Collectables, Dept A-3, 120 S. San Fernando Blvd., Burbank, CA 91502 (818)845-5450.
--Hollywood Screenplay Software, Ballistic Computing, Dept. A, 8 Pima Court, Oakland, NJ 07436 (201)651-0746. Web: www.ballisticware.com
--Hollywood Scriptwriter, Dept. S, P.O.Box 10277, Burbank, CA 91510 (818)845-5525.
--Hollywood Film Festival Dept. BK, 433 N. Camden Drive, Suite 600, Beverly Hills, CA 90210 (310)288-1882.
--Hollywood Screenplay Consultants, Dept. B, 17216 Saticoy St., 303, Van Nuys, CA 91406 (818)994-5977 www.swiftsite.com/cine-vision2000
--W.M. Publishing, Dept. J, 1130 North Broadway, North Massapequa, N.Y. 11758 (516)783-8428. www.wmpublishing-horizons.com

I
--Independant Producers Pavilion NATPE 24,25 Olympic Blvd., Suite 550E, Dept. D, Santa Monica, CA 90404 (310)4534440.

K
--King Productions, Review Dept., 50 Reeves Bay Trail, Flanders, NY 11901. Web: Use search engine to locate.

L
--Lee Shore Agency, LTD., Dept. B, 440 Friday Road, Pittsburgh, PA 15209 (412)821-0440. Web: www.leeshore.com
--Lone Eagle Publishing, Dept. A, 2337 Roscomare Rd., Suite 9, Los Angeles, CA 90077 (800)345-6257. (310)471-8066. www.loneeagle.com
--Lou's Books, 5647 Atlantic Ave, Long Beach, CA 90805 (213)423-1403

M
--McFarland & Company, Dept. A, Box 611, Jefferson, NC 28640 (910)-246-4460.
--Market Insight, Dept. S, P.O. Box 8598, Kansas City, MO 64114-0598 (800)985- 4720.
--Monteiro Rose Agency, Inc., Dept. 1, 17514 Ventura Blvd., #205, Encino, CA 91316. Web: www.monteiro-rose.com
--Movie Magic Screenwriter, Screenplay Systems, Dept. A, 150 E. Olive Ave. #203, Burbank, CA 91502 (800)84-STORY Web: www.screenplay.com
--Muse of fire. E-mail:musofire@loop.com Web: www.loop.com/~musofire/

N

--NATPE, National Association of Telvision Program Executives. See, Independant Producers Pavilion.
--NY Creative Management/Jeff Schmidt, Dept JR-1, Drawer 1578, Stony Brook, NY 11790. Web: www.nycreative.com
--New York Screenwriter, Dept. S, 545 8th Avenue, Suite 401, New York, NY 10018 (800)418-5637.
-- Novelizer. See, The Novelizer.

O
--Opamp Technical Books, 1033 N. Sycamore Ave, Los Angeles, CA 90038 (800)468-4322.

P
--Paper Direct, Dept. A-6, 100 Plaza Drive, Secaucus, NJ 07094 (800)272-7377.
--Paul S. Levine Literary Agency/Law Office, Dept. A, 1054 Superba Avenue, Venice, CA 90291-3940. Web: http://pw1.netcom.com/~pslevine/lawliterary.html
--PITA has relocated and has not forwarded us an address. See, ATA
--Play Script Consulting, see Dave Brandl.
--Playwrights' Ink, 414 W. 121st. Street, Suite 55, Dept. 1-A, New York, NY 10027 (212)666-4470.
--Producers Guild of America, 400 Beverly Drive, Ste 211, Beverly Hills, CA 90212 (310)557- 0807.

Q
--QPB Book Club, Dept. S, Camp Hill, PA 17012-0001 (717)6976443.

R
--Register of Copyrights, Washington, D.C. 20559 (202)707-3000 or(800-688-9889).
--Reynolds Companies/Tom Reynolds, Dept. A., 321 N. 46th Ave, W., Deluth, MN 55807. Web: www.uslink.net/~reygen
--Richard Curtis, Box 11-J, 75 East End Avenue, New York, NY 10028.
--Richard William Krevolin, E-mail: krevolin@usc.edu, Web: www-rcf.usc.edu/~krevolin
--Richwood Script Consultants, Dept A, 1801 Century Park East, Suite 2400, Los Angeles, CA 90067. (310)319-2075. www.scriptnotes.com
--Ross Reports Film Guide Publications, Dept. A-3, 1515 Broadway, NY, NY 10036 (212) 536-5294
--Ross Reports Television and Film, Dept. A-3, P.O. Box 5018, Brentwood, TN 37024 (800-817- 3273).

S
--Samuel French Theater & Film, Dept. S, 7623 Sunset Blvd., Hollywood, CA 90046 (213)876-0570.
--Scenario Magazine, Dept. B, 3200 Tower Oaks Blvd., Rockville. MD 20852 (301)770- 2900.
--Screen Actors Guild, 5757 Wilshire Blvd., Los Angeles, CA 90036 (213) 954-1600.
--Screenplay Consulting/The Screenwriter's Room, Dept. C-2, 12240 Venice Blvd., Suite 11, Los Angeles, CA 90066 (310)-397-2970 Web:www.screenwritersroom.com
--Screenplay Systems, Dept, A, 150 East Olive Ave., Ste 203, Burbank, CA 91502(818)843-6557.
--ScreenStyle Software & Books, 3010 Hennepin Ave., #278, Minneapolis, MN 55408. (888)627-8812. Web: www.screenstyle.com
--Screenwriter's Online, Dept. W, 16752 Bollinger Dr., Pacific Palisades, CA 90272 (310)459-5278 5% www.insider@screenwriter.com
--Screenwriters & Playwrights Home Page, Dept. TX, 3550 SW Pomona St., Portland, OR 97219 (800)294-7176 Web: www.teleport.com/~cdeemer/book/index.html

--Script Doctor, Dept. T-1, 3500 W. Orange Grove, Suite 12105, Tucson, AZ 85741
www.scriptdoctor.com
--Scriptshop.com, Dept. B, P.O. Box 11742, Atlanta GA Orders Only Phone(770)234-4000. Web: www.scriptshop.com
--Scr(i)pt Magazine, Dept S, 5638 Sweet Air Road, Baldwin, MD 21013 (888)287-0932. (410)592-3466. www.scriptmag.com
--Script Link, Dept. 1, P.O. Box 1750, Hollywood, CA 90078 (888) 801-1750 or (818)-990-1491. Web: www.scriptlink.net
-- Script Thing, Script Perfection Entertainment, Dept. 1-J, 4901 Moreno, Blve, STE 105, San Diego, CA 92117 (800)450-9450 Web: www.scriptThing.com
--Scriptware - see Cinovation.
--Scriptwriter's Network, Dept. SS, 11684 Ventura Blvd., #508, Studio City, CA 91604. (323)848-9477. Web: http://scriptwritersnetwork.com
--Sedgeband Literary Associates/David Duperre, Dept 3., 7312 Martha Lane, Fort Worth, TX 76112. Web: http://members.home.net/sedgeband/
--Shotgun Sports Magazine, Dept. JR, P.O. Box 6810, Auburn, CA 95604 (800)676-8920. Web: www.shotgunsportsmag.com
--Sight & Sound Magazine, Dept. B-7, 2323 Randolph Ave, Avenel, NJ 07001.
--Silman-James Press, Dept. SB, 1181 Angelo Drive, Beverly Hills, CA 90210.
--Silver Screen Placements, William W. Levin, Dept. SB, 602 65th Street. Downers Grove, IL 60516-3020.
--Sligo Literary Agency, Eric Bollinger, Dept. SS, 45535 Pueblo Road, Indian Wells, CA 92210. Web: www.insomniac.com/sligolit/
--Smart Girls Productions, Dept. S, P.O. Box 1896, Hollywood, CA 90078 (323-850-5778).
--Smith Entertainment, Dept Area 123, 2818 La Cienega Ave, 2nd Floor, Los Angeles, CA 90034. Web: www.smithentertainment.com
--Southwest Writers Workshop, Dept. 1, 8200 Mountain Rd., NE. Suite 106, Albuquerque, NM 87110. (505)265-9485.
--Stage & Screen Book Club, Dept. S, 6550 East 30th St., P.O. Box 6309, Indianapolis, IN 46206. Web: www.southwestwriters.org
--Stanton & Associates Literary Agency, Dept. TC, 4413 Clemson Drive, Garland, TX 75042.
--Star Literary Service, Dept. 2-A, 1540 North Louis Avenue, Tuscon, AZ 85712
-- Surratt Agency, Attn: Sher Surratt, Dept RJ, 5214 Hillside Road, Cleveland, OH 44131
--Symantic, 10201, Torre Ave., Cupertino, CA 20559 (800)707-3000.
T
--The Complete Screenplay, Dept. 4-A, 14105 Castle Blvd., #204, Silver Spring, MD 20904 (301)847-1410. Web: www.thecompletescreenplay.com
--The Novelizer / Marin Noble, Dept. A, Abberbury Road, Iffley, Oxford, UK OX4 4ES. +44 (0)1865-773862. Web: www.geocities.com/hollywood/5289/ 10%
--The Screenwriter's Bible. See, David Trottier.
--The Screenwriters Room. See, Screenplay Consulting.
--The Script Shop, Dept. 5-E, 2221 Peachtree Road NE, Suite D-452, Atlanta, GA 30309.
--The Script Works, Dept. G-1, MGM Plaza, 2425 Colorado Avenue, Suite 265, Santa Monica, CA 90404 (800)806-4425.
--The Surratt Agency. See, Surratt Agency
--The Writer's Network, Dept. Z-1, 289 S. Robertson Blvd., Suite 465, Beverly Hills, CA 90211 (800)646-3896. Also see, Writer's Network.
--Trap & Field Magazine, Dept. J-R1, 1000 Waterway Blvd., Indianapolis,

IN 46202 (317)633-8802
--Truby's Writer's Studio, Dept. J-9, 751 Hartzell St., Pacific Palasades, CA 90272 (800)33-truby. (310)573-9630 www.truby.com

U
--Universal Development, Dept. J-9, 12400 Ventura Blvd., #317, Studio City, CA 91604

W
--Williams' Literary Agency, Sheri Homan, Dept. 1-A, R1 Box 109, Kosciusko, MS, 39090. Web: www.geocities.com/~williamsagency.
--Written By: Magazine, WGA, Dept. J, 7000 West Third Street, Los Angeles, CA 90048-4329 (888)974-8629.
--Writer's Computer Store, Dept. RU, 11317 Santa Monica Blvd., Los Angeles, CA 90025 (800)272-8927.
--Writer's Digest Book Club, Dept. J-5, P.O. Box 12948, 1507 Dana Ave., Cincinnati, OH 45207 (513)531-8250.
--Writer's Digest Magazine, Dept. J-5, 1507 Dana Ave., Cincinnati, OH 45207 (513)531-8250 [also address for the annual screenwriting competition].
--*Writer's Digest School*, Dept. J-5, 1507 Dana Avenue, Cincinnati, OH 45207 (800)759-0963.
--Writer's Guild of America, East, Dept. J, 555 W. Fifty-seventh St., New York, NY 10019
--Writer's Guild of America, West, Dept. J, 7000 W. Third St., Los Angeles, CA 90048-4329 (213)782-4520.
--Writer's Network. See, The Writer's Network.
--Writer's Network/William K. Vogeler, Dept. SB, 7700 Irvine Center Drive, Suite 800, Irvine, CA 92618. (Literary Agency) Web: www.absolute-sway.com/pfp

LISTING ERRORS
Things are changing all of the time and sometimes we just can't keep up. If you find a listing that no longer exists, or has relocated to a new address, please let us know so we may include an update in the next printing.

CONTACTING THE AUTHOR
You are welcome to contact the author to submit suggestions for future editions of this book. You may use e-mail or postal mail. Please enclose an S.A.S.E. or visit our website.

TESTIMONIALS
If this book has helped you, we would like to know! Please write to us and tell us what you liked about the book. We also encourage constructive criticism. We look forward to hearing from you!

FORTHCOMING TITLES
The Internet Address Book -- a handy book that not only logs all your favorite websites, but also records critical computer data so you can recover the data from computer hardware and software failure. Visit our website for details. It will be posted when the book is available.

CHAPTER 16

ILLUSTRATIONS - PERFORMING PROFESSIONAL SUBMISSIONS
Illustrations begin on the following pages. They are compiled in the last pages of this book, by design, for quick reference.

Some publishers use "belly-banding" compiling illustrations all into the center pages of the book. We use "back-end banding." Because the program we used to write this book, a dedicated scriptwriting program, is not designed to insert illustrations within text. Now you know why the illustrations are in the back of the book.

Note: In the illustrations, please ignore the upper right page numbering used for pagination of this book. If page numbers are required, such as on a script's page, they will be shown on the illustration itself such as - 2 - or - 3 -. Dashes are normally used to box page numbers in scripts.

FADE OUT:

Fig. 1-1

SCREENPLAY / SITCOM OR STAGE PLAY COVER

SCRIPT COVER FRONT AND REAR
Three Hole Punched

SIDE VIEW OF SCRIPT

Front of script faces round head of the brass brad.

Heavy 1 1/4" Brass Brads

Two brads used. One in top hole, one in bottom hole. Center hole not used.

The script cover, according to some inside sources, should have no title or wording, while others say it is okay to put the title of the script on the cover. I chose to keep the cover plain when mailing my scripts. The cover of the script is of a heavy 60# to 80# stock, which is approximately three times the thickness of the 20# paper in the script. Soft color covers are generally acceptable, but it would be wise to stick with just plain white or a soft cream tone or vellum. Despite what you may believe using bright or fancy colors will make your script stand out from the pack, this will only place your script at the bottom of the pile or in the round file (trash can). Either way, it'll be a pass (a nice word for rejection).

Notice the side view of the script; the pages in the spine are exposed. This is so the pages can be marked by the production company with a magic marker and easily viewed while stored on a shelf. If you only use two brass brads to bind your script, you still punch three holes in the cover and script pages.

A good paper punch for screenplays is the Acco 650. The cost is about $235, but it does work well. Small $30 three-hole paper punches are available and work fine, but they only take 30 sheets of #20 pound paper at a time. I've used the cheap punches for years. It's a good way to start.

Do not use any fancy fasteners. Use the standard #5 size, 1 1/4" heavy-gauge solid brass brad fastener. Acco makes the proper size and thickness. Stock #71505. You don't want the script to fall apart while the reader is reading the script, do you? It's these seemingly frivolous details that, if not adhered to, tip off the reader that the script is from an amateur. It's a strange business so don't try to fudge on these rules. Consider if you were a reader, wouldn't you pick the script from a pile that looks professionally packaged over others that are using gimmicks you know are unprofessional?

You can use three brads if you wish. I know the pages are easier to read with three, but believe it or not, using two brads enhances the professional appearance of the script. The same is true of placing no title on the front cover. Package your script as shown and your script will be picked up and read, and that's what we want. Some writers place a brass washer on the brad's blade-end and file the sharp points down. It's optional.

Screen & Stage Marketing Secrets   Fig. 1-2   Page 139

Title Page of Screenplay

Keep the title page simple as shown here. No need for copyright or WGA number. Some agents, prodcos and producers feel it is intimidating to put the copyright and/or WGA number on the script and is a sign of paranoia and amateurism. Opinions differ on this. As long as you do register the script, it is protected -- so the numbers are not needed. Hollywood has strange rules and perceptions. By the way, script pages are always 20# white. Don't use colored paper no matter how nice it looks. There is no page number on the title page. Some screenplay books may tell you otherwise, but this example is an acceptable format to use. If you have an agent representing you, put the agent's name, address and phone number in place of yours at lower right corner only as shown. You could write to WGA and ask for guidelines to format title pages.

```
                    JOEY

                     by

                James Russell
```

DO IT RIGHT THE FIRST TIME

Make certain your script is written in author format.

The scripts you buy are production shooting scripts and new writers often are led to believe these are the formats to use when submitting scripts.

Also, magazines publish scripts and they too have the wrong format. They do this to conserve page space. This book teaches you how to write the author's script.

```
James Russell
000 Writing Drive
Reno, NV 89512
(775)000-0000
```

Screen & Stage Marketing Secrets   **Fig. 1-3**   Page 140

RELEASE FOR LOG LINE QUERY

Monday, July 07, 2010

GENERAL RELEASE FORM

Log Line Titles and WGAw No.: "Mystic Forest" 548501, "Tempest" 588414, "Fabulous in America" 639338, "Joey" 665287, "Vortex" 669863, "Stage Play" 669773 , "Revenge of the Grannies" 530610, "True Bums" 552736 , "Tough Beat" 567972.

Submitted Hereunder:

To: ABC Agency
        Story Editor

   I am submitting to you certain program material, the title and / or theme of which is indicated above and enclosed herein a copy of loglines (which material is hereinafter referred to as the "program material"), upon the following express understanding and conditions.

1. I acknowledge that I have requested permission to disclose to you and carry on certain discussions and negotiations with you in connection with such program material.

2. I agree that I am voluntarily disclosing such program materials to you at my request. I understand that you shall have no obligation to me in any respect whatsoever with regard to such material until each of us has executed a written agreement which, by its terms and provisions, will be the only contract between us.

3. I agree that any discussions we may have with respect to such program material shall not constitute any agreement expressed or implied as to the purchase or use of any such program material which I am hereby disclosing to you either orally or in writing.

4. In the event that you have an independent legal right to use such material which is not derived from me, either because such material submitted hereunder is not new or novel, or was not originated by me, or has not been reduced to concrete form, or because other persons including your employees have submitted similar or identical material which you have the right to use, then I agree that you shall not be liable to me for your use of such material, and you shall not be obligated in any respect whatsoever to compensate me for such use by you.

Sincerely,

James Russell

James Russell
780 Diogenes Drive
Reno, NV 89512
775-348-8711

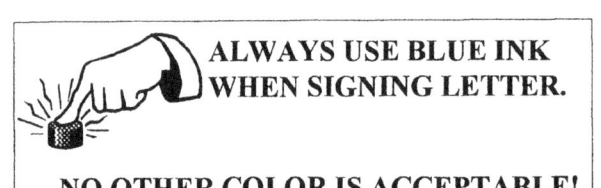

Note: If you don't want to use this form, you can design your own in the "ACT!" contact manager program. You can write to a production company or agent and ask for a copy. The screenwriting magazines can also obtain a release for you. Many production companies will accept this release (above) for the initial submission of log line or query, but will likely send you their own release when they want to read your script. Just sign it and get your script in the mail. A prodco that sends a release is highly unlikely to steal anything, so don't worry about it. **Always send a release when you query a producer, prodco, director, or actor's manager. Literary agents are the only ones you don't have to send a release to. Make sure you understand this. Don't forget to sign your name in blue ink before mailing.**

Screen & Stage Marketing Secrets   Fig. 1-4   Page 141
Sample of a Single Page Synopsis

SYNOPSIS - FEATURE FILM
TOUGH BEAT

Donald Bucks / Producer   October 1, 2012
ABC Film Productions

WGAw No. 567972

Premise - Correctional Officers struggle to survive the deadly games inmates play.

There's a new prison in town. A job boom for the community. CAROL BLAKE (25) joins the Department of Corrections, endures boot camp and is assigned to Wormwood Penitentiary, designed for California's most notorious convicts. Carol is thrown to the sharks. She falls in love with officer RUSS BENSON, despite her mother's firm warnings.

Carol's rudely awakened by the hostile working conditions and squeezed into the line of fire. Sophisticated convicts devise cunning setups, so well-schemed, the best-of-the-best custody officers are compromised, blackmailed to mule drugs and weapons, smuggle uniform for escape, perform sexual favors.

Carol grows teeth to survive, but the convicts relentlessly set her up behind the scene. Witnessing her fellow officers' careers destroyed, Carol believes the cons devised a means to compromise staff, though management refuses to listen as they themselves are silent conspirators.

Pressuring management, Carol wins a teaching assignment to educate officers and staff to the games convicts play. Retaliation strikes. Convicts spring the levers, move to expose Carol for serious rule violations then move in for the kill as she's escorted off the premises. Russ and other officers are shanked by convicts as the trap closes. All is hopelessly lost.

Ending, married to Russ in a new home, Carol receives notification from the State Personnel Board offering reinstatement. She tears the page in two. Free at last! Carol walked the toughest beat in the state.

Tough Beat is based on true psychological techniques inmates use to manipulate staff.

James Russell

James Russell
000 Easy Street
Road To Fame, Nevada 89512
707-000-0000

(The title of your screenplay should be typed in Italics.)

Note: Full name and address to recipient is not required. These are "fields" inserted by the "ACT!" contact manager program for mail merge mailings. Keep the synopsis short, telling the story briefly. You can fill up the entire page if you wish, but less is more. I kept this query low-key, not emphasizing the violence and heartache in the story and it still worked just fine. Personally, I find it harder to write a good synopsis than to write the entire script. I am never satisfied with the end result. I have multiple versions after rewriting tens of times and I hate them all. Ultimately, the script will sell the script no matter how great the synopsis is. **Hint:** You must always tell the ending. Never say, "The story ends with a surprise which you'll find in the script. May I send you *Tough Beat*?" This is not a sales pitch, it is a synopsis. Focus on the story. You can "sell" the script in your cover letter. **Plaese**, no <u>mispeled</u> words in the synopses, okay? You could likely write a better synopsis than shown here. I admit my weakness, as I have a difficult time writing them. It seems no matter what I write it all sounds wrong. However, it gets results as written so it works as is, for now.

Fig. 1-5
Stage Play Format

<u>ACT I</u>   1.

<u>SCENE 1</u>

SETTING: TWO BEDROOMS.   STAGE 2 CURTAINED.

<u>AT RISE:</u>

STAGE 1.

                          (SAMANTHA PETUNIA PANTHER (29) lies in
                          bed, snoring. Cigarette dangles from
                          lips. Hair and face a wreck. This gal
                          believes she's overweight, but isn't.)

STAGE 3.

                          (MARY BEE CANARY (29) wakes up, dials
                          phone. Her hair's electrified. She's
                          a well-built, dim-witted, incompetent
                          woman.)

                          (Phone rings. Samantha fumbles to
                          answer it.)

                      MARY
     (all smiles, on phone, slurred speech)
Rise and shine, Sam, you fat little turkey.

                          (Mary applies makeup as she talks.
                          She too is in bed.)

                    SAMANTHA
Uh? Oh? It's you, Mary. Why must you cast insults
upon the waking hour? It sets up my day rotten.

                          (Samantha removes wine bottle and ash
                          tray from under covers, has a hangover,
                          twirls finger in ashes.)

                    MARY
     (laughs, lights cigarette)
Because it's my way of being beautiful, honey, by
making others feel ugly.

                          (Samantha wipes ashes on eyebrows,
                          grabs mirror, sees smears.)

                    SAMANTHA
You know how I feel about my face in the morning.

Fig. 1-6
Screenplay Format

```
FADE IN:

EXT. VATICAN / ROME - DAY

TWO CARDINALS run through St. Peter's square, shove
tourists out of the way.

INT. RECTORY / LOS ANGELES - DAY

Priests JACOB(40) and SIMON(45) disrobe, put on Pope attire.

                    JACOB
          I don't think we should do this, Simon.

                    SIMON
          Will you shut up for once, Jacob?
          He'll never know.

ALTER BOY(10) hides under table, runs out.

                    JACOB
          He's going to rat on us.

                    SIMON
          So what?  The Pope's in Rome.  Look,
          you said you wanted the nuns to look
          up to you.  Believe me, they will do
          more than look.

                    JACOB
          Do everything I command?

                    SIMON
          Everything.

EXT. ST. PETER'S SQUARE / ROME - DAY

TWO CARDINALS race up steps, open door, enter,

INT. VATICAN / ROME - DAY

TWO CARDINALS hobble on knees to POPE GREGORY FINKELSTEIN (60)
who sits on his throne, clips fingernails.  NUNS fan him with
palm branches, massage his arms and shoulders.
```

Fig. 1-7
Sitcom Script

[Annotation: Of course you don't put this here.]

- 1 -

(teaser)

A

[Annotation: 1st page to tease audience to stay with the show prior to commercial.]

[Annotation: Each scene is lettered.]

FADE IN:

INT. JOEY'S LIVING ROOM - DAY
(ANGUS, MICHAEL)

ANGUS SITS AT DINING TABLE, READS BOOK. SFX. DOORBELL. SHE OPENS DOOR, SEES A SMILING PRIEST HOLDING A LEATHER BAG.

                  ANGUS
    Father Michael, I'm so glad you could

    make it, come in.

MICHAEL STEPS IN, FEELS BAD VIBES, TURNS TO LEAVE. ANGUS GRABS HIS WAIST, PULLS HIM INSIDE.

                  MICHAEL
    Let go of me. There is evil in this

    house beyond my capabilities. I can

    smell it in the air.

                  ANGUS
    It's my mom's incense. She can't sleep
    without it.

INT. JOEY'S BEDROOM - DAY
(MICHAEL, SHERRY, BONUS, ANGUS, JOEY)

ANGUS AND MICHAEL SNEAK IN. ANGUS HAS BOWL OF WATER IN HAND. PRIEST, A BLACK WHIP. A HUGE COVERED LUMP UNDER BLANKETS. INCENSE BURNERS FILL THE ROOM WITH THICK HEAVY SMOKE.

                  MICHAEL
    I command thee demons to come forth
    from, Joey.

WHIPLASHES BLANKET, SHERRY EXITS, MICHAEL'S TERRIFIED.

Screen & Stage Marketing Secrets   Fig. 1-8

SAMPLE OF A MULTIPLE SUBMISSION QUERY LETTER

ABC Agency
Story Editor
123 Glitter Gulch Ave.
Hollywood, CA 9000

Dear Story Editor: ← *A name is best, but if no name? Use Story Editor. It will be fine.*

I was referred by the *Hollywood Scriptwriter*. Listed are feature film log lines. TV script and stage play otherwise noted. All scripts WGA registered.

#1. "Mystic Forest" -- fantasy / quest. A boy saves a desperate family of raccoons in a magical redwood forest healing the wounds of a divided timber town. Male lead.

#2. "Tempest" -- action / thriller. Convicts take over maximum security prison. A duel of wits between the warden and convicts explodes with violent retaliation. Male lead.

#3. "Fabulous America" -- comedy. An extremely possessive mother pursues her daughter to return home to England. Every trick in the book is applied with hilarious results.

#4. "Joey" -- comedy. A sympathy-seeking mother and her rude movie star friend tear up the USA on their search for success, evading the Sister's of Mercy and FBI from a sinful life. "Joey" is available as a backdoor series; 2-hour feature film, 1-hour primetime pilot and 5 episodes to launch the sitcom.

#5. "Vortex" -- MOW / drama. Frightening true story. William Nolte fends off the full assault of a corrupt and violent prison administration when he blows the whistle.

#6. "Stage Play" -- comedy stage play. Two actresses chase two actors to marry them using every trick in the book. When all fails, they use a theatrical stage play to get the "I do."

#7. "Revenge of the Grannies" -- comedy. Militant grandmothers assault the city of Lost Angus.

#8. "True Bums" -- comedy. Three movie executives abandon their wives to live as bums on the railroad.

#9. "Tough Beat" -- drama. Female correctional officer fends off the deadly games criminals play. Ranked 6th place in the Writer's Digest screenplay competition.

Thank you for the opportunity to submit. I await your early reply.

Sincerely,

James Russell

James Russell
000 Big Heart Lane ← *Hand Sign each query, no computer printouts. Use blue ink.*
Lost Sands, CA 00000
712-000-000

____ Send script indicated above.   ____ Send synopsis
____ Additional instructions_____.
____ Pass at this time.
____ Please do not send us future mailings of log lines.

Not everyone agrees with this approach but you don't have much to lose by trying it, then again, you may even do very well. One thing is certain... you will save a lot of money and you will develop a database of responsive agents you can later send a more detailed query.

Fig. 1-9
Cover Letter Attached To Script
(Do Not Staple -- Use A Paper Clip)

ABC Film Productions
Donald Buck, Producer
123 Glitter Gulch Ave.
Hollywood, CA 9000

October 1, 2002

Dear Donald Buck:

Enclosed screenplay "*True Bums*" as requested with synopsis and general release. The script is WGA registered.

In the event you pass on this project, no need to return the script. Please return the S.A.S.E. to inform me of the decision.

Enjoy the read.

 There is no need to mention script is copyrighted. The date displayed will outdate your script!

Sincerely,

James Russell

James Russell
P.O. Box 0000
Eugene, OR 97440
707-000-0000

 Below, you will see an error: the titles of the screenplays are not in *italics*. While this alone may not create a rejection, it is a mark against you. Add a couple spelling errors and you are sunk!

You may want to use any of these alternative statements. Regardless, the cover letter you attach to the script should be very brief. No need to "sell" the script unless there is some important information not mentioned in the query you originally sent or in the synopsis you are enclosing with the script.

*Thank you for requesting my MOW teleplay "Vortex." I wish to stress this story is not only true, the system that created the hell for Mr. Nolte still thrives and continues to destroy unsuspecting employees. Synopsis and general release enclosed with S.A.S.E.

*The enclosed screenplay "Tempest" is based on a true story at a Texas prison. Although the story itself is original, the violent nature of the scenes actually occurred due to a corrupt warden. Inmate frustration could only result in a full-blown riot. "Tempest" tells it the way it was.

*"Revenge of the Grannies" appears to be timely due to the current acquisitions (or pre-production statistics) of farcical comedies in the Hollywood Reporter by the major studios I've enclosed a synopsis, general release and S.A.S.E.

*Thank you for your phone call. You mentioned you needed a screenplay at low budget to be shot in the Los Angeles area. "Tough Beat" can be entirely filmed at one location, the Los Angeles County Jail. This script also ranked #6 of 13,000 entries in the Writer's Digest Screenplay Contest. Actually #1 in feature film - the first five rankings were television serial and sitcom scripts. A general release, synopsis, and a S.A.S.E. is enclosed. Thank you for requesting "Tough Beat."

These are only a few examples. Notice the information given is very brief and supportive to the theme to induce the producer to send the script immediately for coverage without actually asking to do so. This is called generating heat, making your script hot and standing out from the rest of the pack. Generally, the less you say the more professional they believe you are.

Screen & Stage Marketing Secrets — Page 147

Fig. 1-10

RESPONDING TO PRODCO OR AGENT ADVERTISING

AD

SCRIPTS WANTED

We are seeking comedy feature scripts. All genre considered.
Please include single page synopsis along with your script. Mail to:

Big Deal Productions
1799 Silver Screen Hwy., Culver City, CA 90145

RESPONSE LETTER

Big Deal Productions   October 28, 2005
Story Editor
1799 Silver Screen Hwy.
Culver City, CA 90145

Re: Advertisement in Hollywood Scriptwriter.

Dear Story Editor:

Enclosed find a synopis of my comedy screenplay, *Grandpa Takes On The Mob*.
Please indicate below if you would like to read the script. I've enclosed a general release, and log line listing of alternative selections. All scripts WGA registered.

Thank you.

Sincerely,

James Russell

James Russell
P.O. Box 000
Eugene, OR 97440
701-000-000

____ Send "Grandpa Takes On The Mob" screenplay.
____ Additional instructions _____.
____ Pass at this time.

> **Always include an S.A.S.E.**

> **VERY IMPORTANT**
> When you send a script, include a release form and note this on the shipping envelope. See Fig. 1-13.
>
> This rule of sending a release also applies to mailing query letters to prodcos and producers. Don't break these rules.

Note: No name was given in the ad, so it's okay to address letter to the Story Editor. Though they asked for the script, it is best to send a query first. If you want to send the script, go ahead. Notice the letter is just a brief contact allowing the single page synopsis to be the salesman. Use nice stationery for this cover letter. If they like the synopsis, they will request the script. If you feel the script can do a better job than the synopsis you may want to just send the script instead especially if the agent or prodco is well known. The choice is yours. Many writers write long descriptive query and cover letters. This is generally a mistake. Consider the advertiser will receive hundreds of letters and will be swamped for time to read them all. The log line is a high concept pitch and informs the reader this submission letter is likely from a professional because it is so brief and to the point. No guarantee, but the less you say -- odds weigh in favor your script is requested.

Screen & Stage Marketing Secrets — **Fig. 1-11** — Page 148

SAMPLE OF QUERY LETTER *NOT* TO SEND

October 29, 2006

Comedy Productions
Dale Funny / Producer
321 Slapstick Street
New York, NY 0001

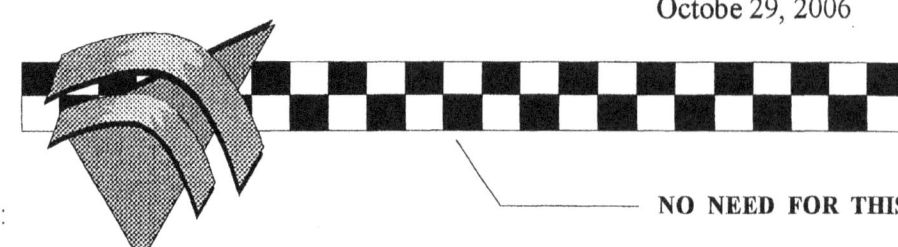 — NO NEED FOR THIS

Dear Dale Funny (or Story Editor):

I have a script, "*Jam Baby Jam*" that will rock your socks off. I'm talking **big money** here, better than "*The Lost World*" or "*Terminator*." Fact is, I need an agent or production company to take on this script. I'm a professional writer, as I only write for money.

"*Jam Baby Jam*" is a story about a flying elephant swooping down upon an unsuspecting town. The hero, BOB BAKER (60) is an ex-Marine with contacts with the underworld. It's his job to stop the ferocious elephant and he does so with bravery never before seen on the silver screen.

This elephant is no ordinary one. It has the teeth of a T-Rex and sprays acidic urine on all in its path, disolving people and things. I mean, this beast is mean street U.S.A. jammin' all the bad guys on the spot, then it takes over the city, the state of Texas and flies into Washington D.C. eating all the polititions you didn't vote for.

And there's more! Much more! Flying tigers arive to aid the elephant and they convince the ants to join up with them to take over the world. Bob hates ants, so he gets involved even after he said "no" to the President!! Now the fun begins as Bob strikes back, saving the world.

I want to send my script to you. I know it will make us both <u>wealthy</u> and sucessful!!!

Looking forward to you saying yes.

Sincerely,
Jake Bubbles
Jake Bubbles
P.O. Box 101`
Fallen Star, Pluto 97769
901-000-000

PS: I'll even give you 30% commission, double what you make now!

Note: The story is insane, but it could actually sell if it were written properly and presented professionally. This query letter is absurd, obviousely, but in reality, people do send such letters to agents and producers. Not only is the month spelled wrong, the writer is proclaiming bold statements of grandeur he obviously couldn't deliver. See if you can find additional errors in this query along with four more misspelled words.

The more you write, chances increase the reader will see unprofessionalism. So, keep your query letters brief and let your script do the talking for you. Writing a good query letter is hard to do. If it were easy, everyone would have their scripts requested and there would be fewer rejections. For starters, get rid of the exclamation points (!) **bold type** and <u>underlined</u> words. Never talk about making money or how profitable the movie will be at the box office. Never expose hype. This is about as bad as a query can get, but there has been worse. The stationery is too flashy and distractive. **Mispelled: dissolving, politicians, successful, arrive.**

Screen & Stage Marketing Secrets   **Fig. 1-12**   Page 149

SAMPLE OF #10 SIZE BUSINESS ENVELOPE FOR QUERY SUBMISSION

Fancy envelope is not required. Standard white 24 pound is fine.

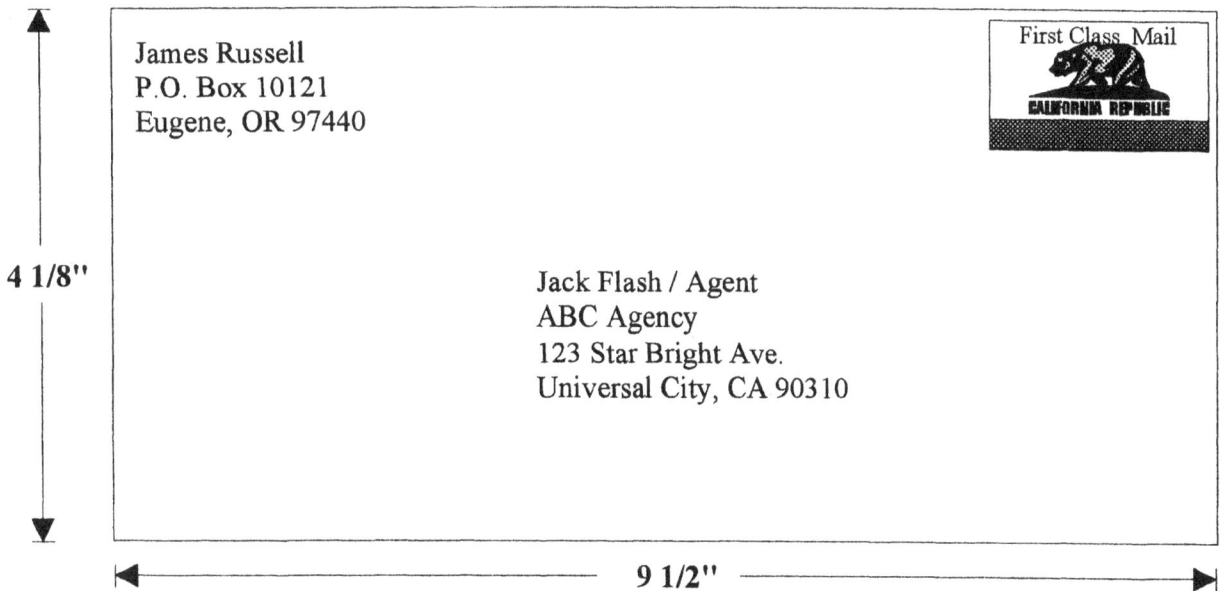

SAMPLL OF #10 SIZE BUSINESS ENVELOPE S.A.S.E. FOR QUERY SUBMISSION

(Insert the below S.A.S.E. envelope into the above mailing envelope along with your query letter)

You can leave this blank if query letter has a response checklist as shown in Fig. 1-8

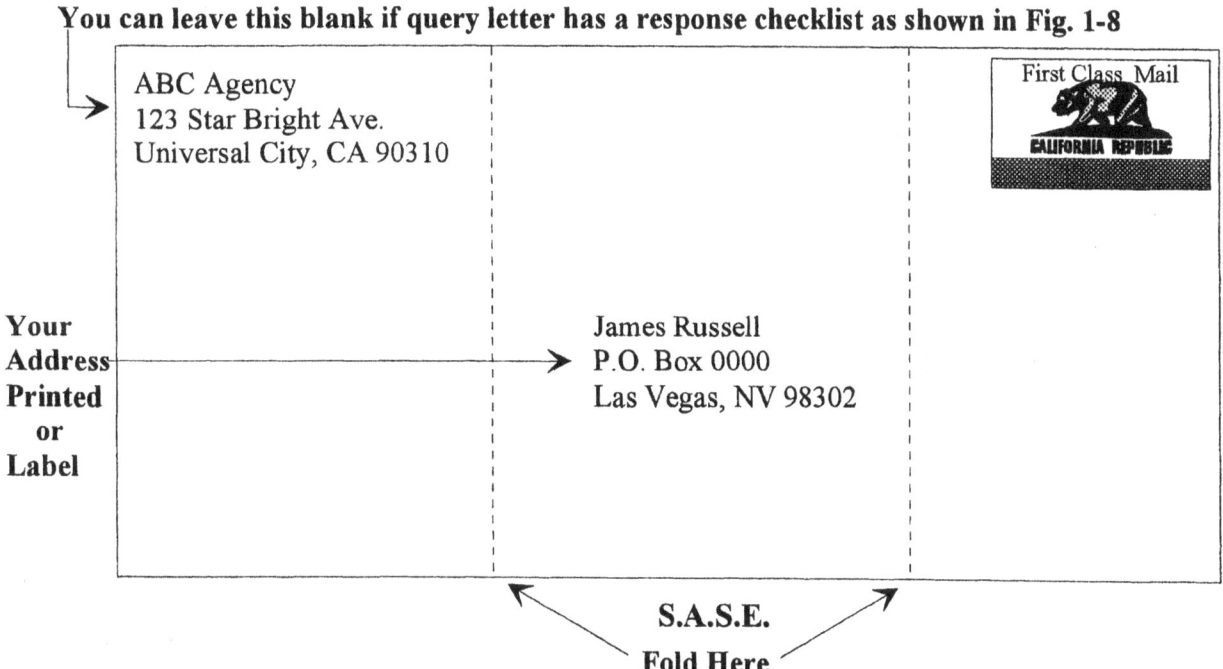

Simply fold the S.A.S.E. return envelope and insert it into the envelope above addressed to the agent along with the synopsis, log line listing or query letter. When you insert your letters, the open ends should be facing the upper flap so if an automatic letter opener is used, or other device, it will not snag on the folded crease area of your letters and slice them in two. Letters easily get lost when this happens. Place the S.A.S.E. into the open end of the folded letters. Why? So the agent can see right away there is a S.A.S.E and it is a professional submission. I always fold the S.A.S.E. so the postage stamp is exposed. I want the agent to see there is postage on the S.A.S.E. and it adds color to grab attention. The "ACT!" program can print crisp text envelopes for you, or you can use labels to fix to the envelope. Preprinted labels are faster and cheaper.

Screen & Stage Marketing Secrets

Fig. 1-13
ADDRESSING THE MAILING ENVELOPES
For Shipping The Script
Bubble-padded envelope 10x13 Size or Larger

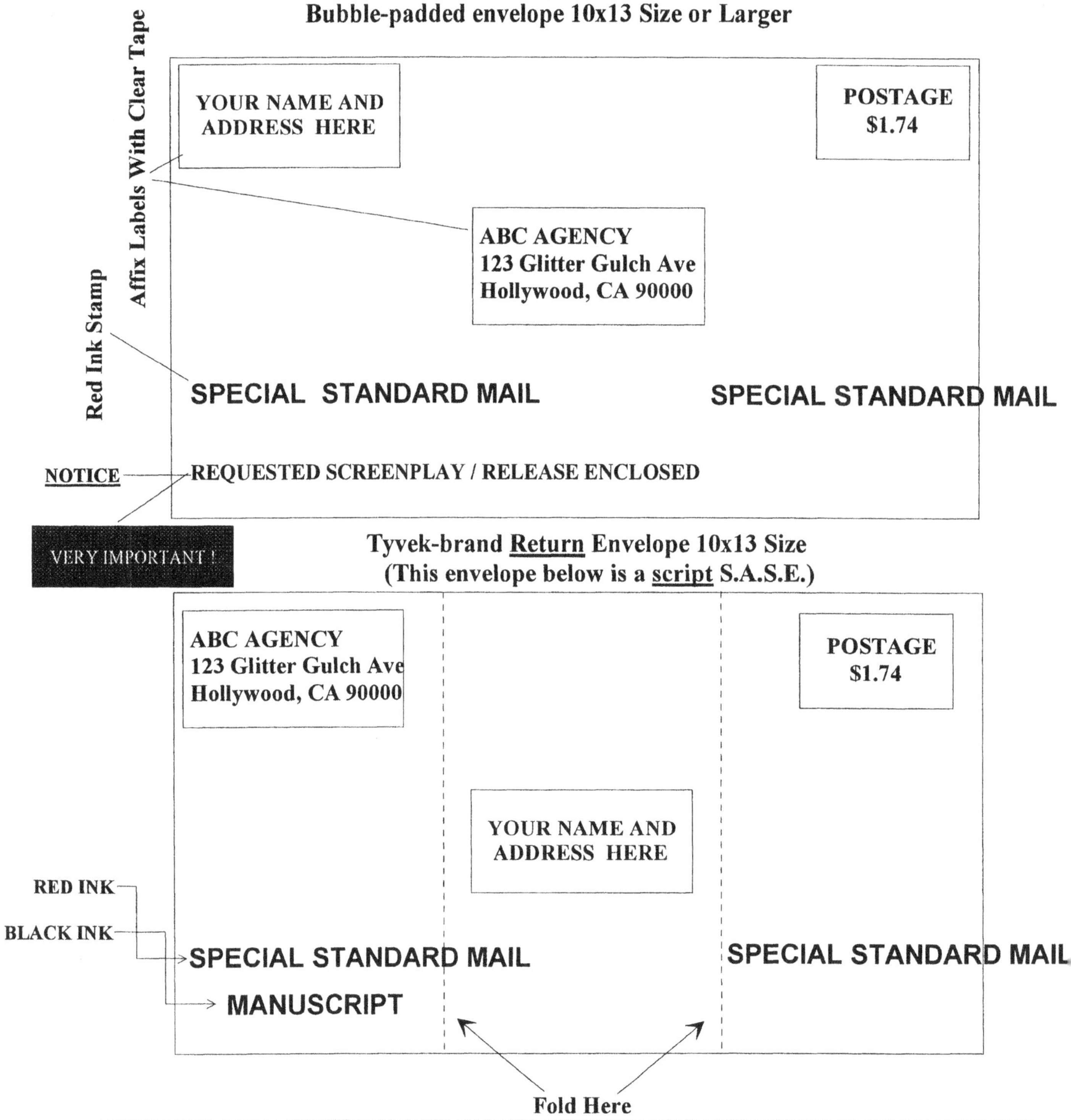

Affix Labels With Clear Tape

Red Ink Stamp

YOUR NAME AND ADDRESS HERE

POSTAGE $1.74

ABC AGENCY
123 Glitter Gulch Ave
Hollywood, CA 90000

SPECIAL STANDARD MAIL   SPECIAL STANDARD MAIL

NOTICE — REQUESTED SCREENPLAY / RELEASE ENCLOSED

VERY IMPORTANT !

Tyvek-brand Return Envelope 10x13 Size
(This envelope below is a script S.A.S.E.)

ABC AGENCY
123 Glitter Gulch Ave
Hollywood, CA 90000

POSTAGE $1.74

YOUR NAME AND ADDRESS HERE

RED INK
BLACK INK

→ SPECIAL STANDARD MAIL   SPECIAL STANDARD MAIL
→ MANUSCRIPT

Fold Here

A Tyvek envelope will easily fold for insertion in the padded envelope with your script, that is, if you want the script returned. Tyvek protects script from tearing in transit. Notice "Requested Screenplay / Release Enclosed" tells the receiver this is the script they requested. **Very important!** People still send unsolicited scripts to agents and prodcos and it's returned to the sender. Let them know your script was requested, if in fact it was (don't cheat, it won't work). "Special Standard" is stamped twice on each envelope, as shown. Affix postage and addresses and you'll have the look of a professional submission. Follow this mailing format and you'll have no problems. You can use manuscript mailing boxes, but envelopes are lower in cost. Postage may be higher than shown here, so ask the postal employee the current cost for Special Standard Mail for shipping manuscripts.

Screen & Stage Marketing Secrets **Fig. 1-14** Page 151

HOW TO PACKAGE A SCRIPT SUBMISSION

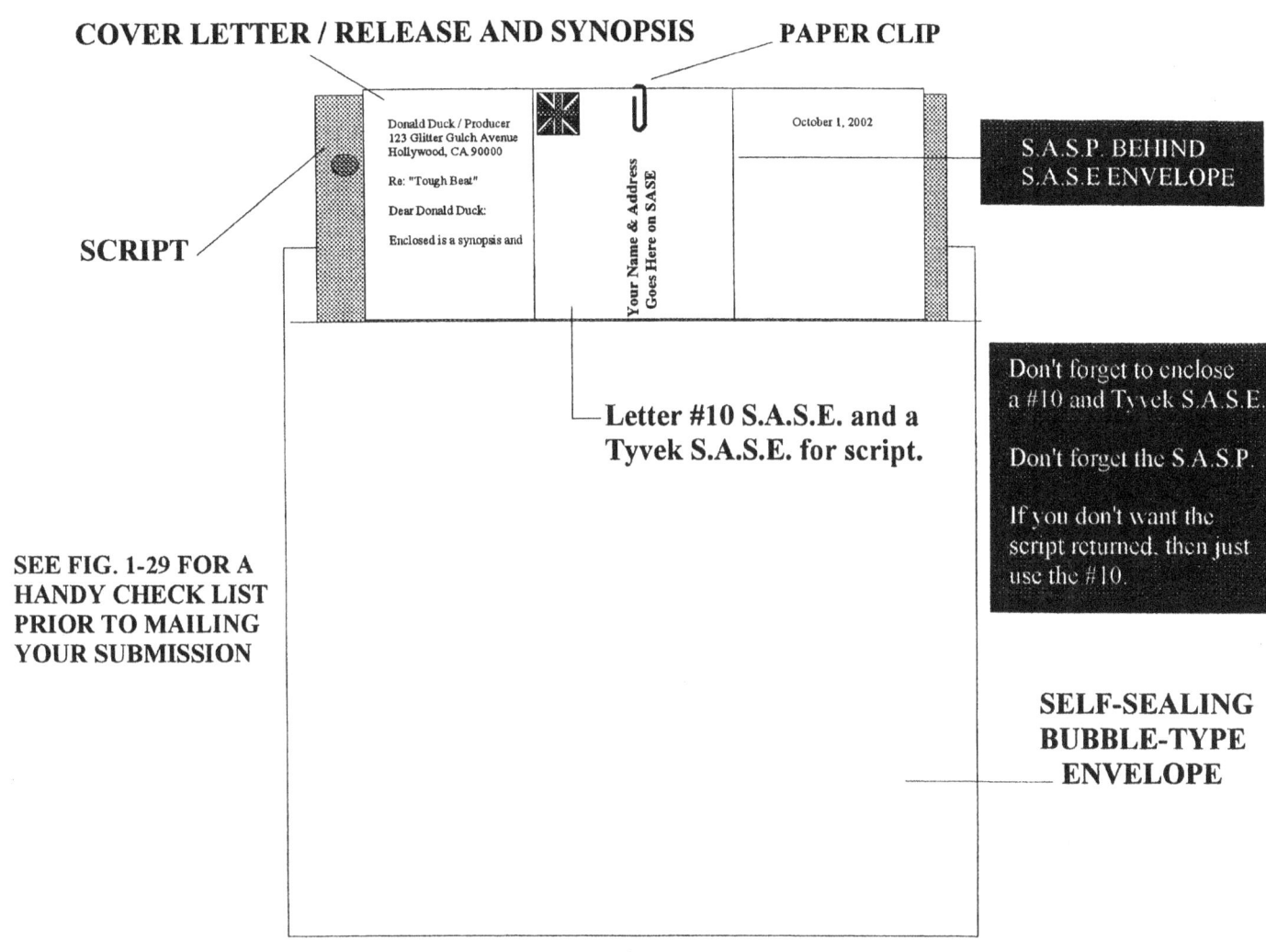

Note Use a self-sealing mailing envelope or seal it closed with tape. Never use staples. You don't want anyone to cut their fingers when handling your package. Never staple anything to the script, use a paper clip. If you don't want your script returned, you can use a standard #10 business-size envelope as shown. I usually put the S.A.S.E. behind the cover letter/synopsis, but it doesn't matter as long as you enclose one. Using the Tyvek brand non-tearable envelope for the S.A.S.E. to return a script is best as it easily folds and adds no bulk or weight to the mailing package. S.A.S.P noted above is a postcard return receipt.

➤ Cover letter should be on your best stationery, as this is a personal mailing and you need to maximize your impression. Synopsis can be printed on lavender paper. Release always on white paper only, as it is a legal document. See Fig. 1-15 for a sample of a cover letter.

Some writers use manuscript boxes to ship scripts. They are expensive and not necessary. See Fig. 1-13 (top drawing) on how the envelope is addressed and stamped. If you want to use the best shipping envelopes, then consider the Tyvek bubble mailer for shipping the entire package as shown above and use the Tyvek non-bubble type for the S.A.S.E. if you want your script returned. You can use the standard paper type bubble envelope to ship scripts as they work just fine too. If you run into any problems with postal employees on Special Standard Mail rates, refer them to Postal Regulation E416. Never send scripts via UPS, air mail, overnight, unless requested to do so. US mail is expected, so stay with the program.

Screen & Stage Marketing Secrets   **Fig. 1-15**   Page 152

SAMPLE OF A COLD CALL QUERY LETTER TO SITCOM

Comedy Productions					October 19, 2001
Dale Funny / Producer
321 Slapstick Street
New York, NY 0001

Dear Dale Funny (or Story Editor):

I am requesting permission to submit a sitcom script pertaining to your show, "*Make Me Laugh*."

I understand you normally do (or, do not) accept submissions and I would like very much to present my script as a demonstration of my writing ability.

I have enjoyed your show, studied the characters and I believe I can make a substantial contribution to the success of the show.

May I send my WGA registered script for your evaluation?

Thank you for the opportunity to submit.

Sincerely,

James Russell

James Russell
P.O. Box ICUP
Portland, OR 00000
701-000-000

> **WHAT IS WRONG WITH THIS LETTER?**
> Each paragraph begins with the word "I" which should be avoided as much as you possibly can. Try to rewrite this so "I" is not habitual, as it stands out like a sore paw. It's the sign of an amateur. Read a book on how to write business and sales letters. Learn how to write good letters.

____ Send script ____ Send synopsis of your script.
____ Additional instructions _____.
____ Pass at this time.
____ Please do not send us future mailings.

Note: You may want to mention you are enclosing a resume. If you have show credits certainly do mention them. If not, just keep the letter brief as demonstrated above and let your script do the selling. Remember to keep your query letter brief with an uplifting feeling for the reader that you will be a benefit to the show's success. If you do not have a completed script, only an idea for a show, develop a treatment to send. Once the producer accepts the treatment, you'll be hired to write the script. You can't do this unless you have already demonstrated you have the ability to write and complete a script.

To break into television, you should have a completed TV script you can use as a calling card. In this case, a sitcom script for the actual show, "*Make Me Laugh*" or "*Cry Elsewhere*" show. A general rule of thumb is to write a competing sitcom for a writing sample so the producer can see you have varied writing skills and so s/he can be entertained reading it (they get tired of reading, "*Make Me Laugh*" material).

Not all shows are open for submissions. It never hurts to try anyway, you may just get lucky. Don't describe the script's content on a cold call letter unless you send a general release. Still, I wouldn't recommend taking that approach. You should write for submission guidelines. See "*Written By:*" magazine for TV shows seeking scripts.

Fig. 1-16

SAMPLE QUERY LETTER SEEKING AGENCY REPRESENTATION

October 28, 2005

Diane Goodman
Hall of Fame Agency
2846 Gold Fever Alley
Burbank, CA 90122

STAY ON TRACK
STICK TO THE FACT

Dear Diane Goodman:

Having written two screenplays I am seeking agency representation. My drama screenplay "*Midnight*" placed as a semi-finalist in the Get Rich Quick Screenplay Contest. A frightening story of the nuclear holocaust that almost became reality as Russia mobilized to attack the United States.

My screenplay, "*Love Master*" is a thriller/comedy of college girls pursuing marriage only to find disaster as a serial tickler is on the loose. A total farce of the Friday The 13th horror genre.

Enclosed: synopsis of "*Midnight*" for your consideration.

Thank you.

Sincerely,

James Russell

James Russell
P.O. Box SCRNPLAY`
Hollywood, CA 00000
818-000-000

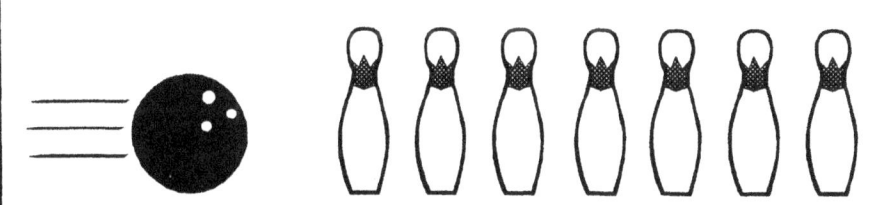

THERE IS NO MAGIC BULLET OR FORMULA TO SCORE A STRIKE EVERYTIME. SAME AS WITH QUERY LETTERS WHATEVER WORKS... WORKS.

____ Send "Midnight" script.   ____ Send "Love Master" script.
____ Additional instructions _____.
____ Pass at this time.
____ Please do not send us future mailings.

Note: There are many ways to query an agent for representation. Here we are plugging the "Midnight" script enclosing a synopsis. We are also letting the agent know you have another script in the wings, so you're no one-script wonder. We are not sending two synopsis, only your best work is presented here. If you have more than one script, you could send a log line listing or just mention the fact you have written six screenplays and would be happy to forward log line listing of your projects upon request. You can include a personal biography or a resume to indicate your seriousness of pursuing a writing career. Most agents want writers who are dedicated for the long haul. The more scripts you have, the more dedication is revealed. Still, getting an agent is a daunting task under the best of conditions. Just keep on trying. Try different query letters. Notice each paragraph above does not begin with the word, "I". Try to avoid: I am, I would, I'd like, I can, I will, etc.

Screen & Stage Marketing Secrets   **Fig. 1-17**   Page 154

SAMPLE QUERY LETTER TO AGENT WITH SYNOPSIS

October 28, 2012

Samuel Goblingab
Heck On Wheels Agency
4838 Private Parts Expressway
Beaver Falls, ID 65729

> In your query letter, don't capitalize character names as you would in the script. It's tacky and unprofessional.
>
> **Example:** That's BILLY CALCUTTA for you...
> Follow the example given in this query letter.

Dear Samuel Goblingab:

If I could spank you, I would!

Poor me, poor ol' me. That's Billy Calcutta for you, always seeking sympathy in all the wrong places. This time he'll get his desserts because he's in prison for his stupid crimes. Yep, the convicts like good old Billy Calcutta. He's the perfect dupe for the escape of the century.

```
                    BILLY
     I ain't a talkin' no more.

                    CONVICT
     I feel for you, you sad sack of
     living misery.
                    BILLY
     You think I'm a whiner?  Huh?

                    SECOND CONVICT
     We got plenty of pruno, Billy.  All
     you can drink.  Here, sip a little or
     I'll insert my shoe where it hurts.
     Drink it.  All of it.  That a boy.

                    BILLY
     I feel ill.  My eyes are fuzzy.  You
     poisoned me.  I trusted you.  Help.
     Call the cops!
```

Enclosed; synopsis of *Spank You* for your consideration.

James Russell

James Russell
P.O. Box 000
Eugene, OR 97440
701-000-000

____ Send "Spank You" script.
____ Additional instructions _____
____ Pass at this time.
____ Please do not send us future mailings.

> This is only a sample of a creative approach to tickle the reader's interest to request the script. One thing any agent will agree is that the approach is "different" than all the other queries that arrived in the mail today. It may or may not work. Try it. It just may do you right.

Screen & Stage Marketing Secrets   **Fig. 1-18**   Page 155

SAMPLE OF A QUERY LETTER TO PRODUCER/PRODCO

XYZ Productions
Julie Rich / Producer
234 Avenue of the Stars
Hollywood, CA 90000

October 30, 2008

Dear Julie Rich (or Story Editor):

I am requesting permission to submit a comedy feature film script pertaining to three men chucking jobs and wives to become bums on the railroad. Without disclosing further details, I have enclosed a general release.

May I send this WGAw registered script to you for your evaluation?

Thank you for the opportunity to submit.

OR

I am requesting permission to submit log lines and synopses of my available feature film scripts. I currently have eight scripts covering comedy, drama, and action genres. All scripts WGAw registered.

Please enclose your release form in the S.A.S.E. and I'll send you a listing of my projects.

Thank you for your consideration.

Sincerely,

James Russell

James Russell
P.O. Box 1012
Eugene, OR 97440
701-000-000

Be concise and professional and your scripts will end up here for consideration.

____ Send listing of log lines ____ Send synopsis of your scripts.
____ Additional instructions _____.
____ Pass at this time.
____ Please do not send us future mailings.

Note: Never reveal the core of your story unless you submit a release form as in the first example above. Use the handy check list at the bottom of the letter so it makes it easy for the producer to respond. You can easily customize letters like this in the "ACT!" contact manager program. When you write to agents or prodcos never sound desperate in your letter. Enthusiasm is okay, but it's a fine line to cross. Being brief, as shown above, is professional and easy to read. Odds are, considering the long-winded letters producers often do receive, they will respond to a short business-like letter as indicated above. Less is more! The screenwriting magazines often give examples of query letters and discuss the purpose. It is important that you subscribe to these magazines to obtain knowledge of the industry and to keep your spirits up when the rejections begin to roll in like tsunami waves. Check your spelling! Always run the spell checker just before you print your letter and read the letter before you mail it. Spell-checkers do not discriminate between words like, "your" and "you're" as both are spelled right, but may be grammatically wrong.

Screen & Stage Marketing Secrets   Fig. 1-19   Page 156

TEST

Mark each question True or False.   See Fig. 1-20 for answers.

1. When querying an agent you must send a release. ____
2. When querying a producer you must send a release. ____
3. When querying a prodco you must send a release. ____
4. Never send a shopping list to an agent or prodco. ____
5. Always include SASE with any query letter. ____
6. A log line is a single sentence synopsis of the story. ____
7. Query letter should be brief indicating the script is WGA registered. ____
8. If prodco advertises to send script, send the script. ____
9. I have an agent. I don't have to market scripts. ____
10. "Requested Screenplay Enclosed" is on envelope. ____
11. Staple a separate release on each script you mail. ____
12. Use a brass color gold trim cover to bind script. ____
13. Use #2 size solid brass brads to secure script. ____
14. V.O. is used sparingly in description. ____
15. O.S. is sounds made by characters off screen. ____
16. Put "Continued" on every header and footer. ____
17. Dialog reveals character. ____
18. If it can't be seen don't write it in description. ____
19. Use camera angle instructions sparingly. ____
20. Use color stationary on cover letter or query. ____
21. Major studios will accept log line submissions. ____
22. Okay to send log lines to producers and prodcos. ____
23. Check with Post Office before using Special 4th Class stamp to comply with postal regulations. ____
24. Numbers under 100 should be spelled out. ____
25. "Cut To" is used on all scene transitions. ____
26. Identify the artist when calling out for music. ____
27. In heated character conversation, don't break it with descriptive action. ____
28. Sitcom pacing per page is 2 1/2 minutes. ____
29. All agents sell stage plays. ____
30. Insert commercial breaks in a MOW. ____
31. Certain words should never be used in a script. ____
32. Send a release with all scripts you mail. ____
33. Prodcos won't read a script if not copyrighted. ____
34. V.O. is used when character is not seen, but heard. ____
35. Marketing scripts requires great skill. ____
36. Synopsis must include a General Release to agent. ____
37. Prodco advertises for synopsis, always send release. ____
38. Readers can spot an amateur's script fast. ____
39. Write synopsis and query before writing the script. ____
40. Prodco ask for script. Tell your agent to send your script only. ____
41. Mailing lists helps reduce competition. ____
42. The internet web site is a safe place to list log lines. ____
43. Parenthical directions are okay to use. ____
44. Directions should be no more than 4 lines. ____
45. Prodco means independent production company. ____
46. Studio means major production company. ____
47. It's okay to use words ending in "ing" occasionally. ____
48. You can query major production companies. ____
49. Use black ink on all query and cover letters. ____
50. "Act" is a recommended database to market scripts. ____
51. It's okay to exceed 120 pages in a feature film script. ____
52. Timing the market is a proven method to sell script. ____
53. Query and cover letters should be very brief. ____
54. Dialog should push the story forward. ____
55. Every script should have some comic elements. ____
56. Your name should be on the cover of the script. ____
57. WGA number should be on the title page of script. ____
58. No spelling and grammar errors in the script. ____
59. Check script for missing pages before mailing. ____
60. Never send an unsolicited script to anyone. ____
61. Dialog is the most important element in the script. ____
62. Always send scripts in the U.S. mail. ____
63. You must include SASE to return the script. ____
64. Obtain an agent signatory to the Writer's Guild. ____
65. WGA agency list, lists all signatory agents. ____
66. You can send a stage play direct to theaters. ____
67. Use lavender color paper for General Release. ____
68. Some agents simply will not respond to any query. ____
69. Many good scripts fail due to poor marketing. ____
70. Negative responses mean you are a lousy writer. ____
71. Writing a MOW is a good way to sell a script. ____
72. Print list of characters and sets in a feature script. ____
73. Always address letters to a person's name. ____
74. Use a dedicated script formatting program. ____
75. Always use complete slug lines. ____
76. Use ellipsis (...) as much as you want. ____
77. Major characters are capitalized when introduced. ____
78. Sound effects are capitalized in feature scripts. ____
79. (--) symbol is used to reveal interrupted dialog. ____
80. (...) symbol reveals character's change of thought. ____
81. Informal mass query letters never work. ____
82. A thousand rejections will not make me quit. ____
83. A script should have lots of white space on page. ____
84. Break up long description blocks with dialog. ____
85. Never send a multiple submission log line list. ____
86. Show don't tell. Cut out all unnecessary dialog. ____
87. Address all informal letters to; Story Editor. ____
88. (- -) symbol used for series of shots in description. ____
89. You can buy rights to a true story for $1. ____
90. Use stationary multicolored #10 SASE envelope. ____
91. There is no magic formula to market a script. ____
92. Everyone has different opinions how to sell scripts. ____
93. State in cover letter not to return script. ____
94. Ask for permission to submit to prodcos/actors. ____
95. Write with enthusiasm on cover letters. ____
96. Tell the prodco not to send script to a reader. ____
97. Please the reader with brilliant dialog. ____
98. Write the script from the heart, what you care of. ____
99. Consider market appeal when writing script. ____
100. Hire an agent when you sell a script. ____
101. Subscribe to screenwriter magazines. ____
102. Submit scripts to screenplay contests. ____
103. Agent asks for script. Send it next-day delivery. ____
104. Keep rewriting query letters until they get results. ____
105. Less you write, more professional query will be. ____
106. Selling scripts is a terrible ordeal. ____
107. Tyvek envelopes are the best to ship scripts. ____
108. Producers don't want to be bothered with scripts. ____
110. Never send a script to a movie star. ____
111. Be polite if agent calls and rejects your work. ____
112. It's okay to call agents and prodcos. ____
113. Send six query letters in one envelope to agent. ____
114. Keep conversations brief when calling agent. ____
115. Write your script for a specific actor. ____
116. Write a low budget script for best results. ____
117. Screenwriting can't be learned, it's a gift. ____
118. It may take you 10-years to sell a script. ____
119. Write books or magazine articles too. ____
120. Don't rely on computer spell-checking software. ____
121. A college degree in writing ensures success. ____
122. Develop a resume or biography. ____
123. You must have a treatment to sell a script. ____
124. Story software is a valuable asset to write script. ____
125. Laser printer at 300 d.p.i. is imperative to use. ____
126. Keep budget cost in mind when writing script. ____
127. Write different genre scripts to enhance market. ____
128. Use script evaluation services for better results. ____
129. Tell people you are a screenwriter. ____
130. Copy the format of a shooting script. ____
131. Read as many books as you can on screenwriting. ____
132. Avoid computer programs with copy protection. ____
133. You must write more than two scripts. ____
134. You must never query a director. ____

Screen & Stage Marketing Secrets — Fig. 1-20 — Page 157

TEST ANSWERS
T = True   F=False

1. F. But it's okay to do so.
2. T. Always include a release, always.
3. T. Absolutely send a release.
4. F. Send brief log lines and you'll be okay.
5. T. Always include SASE with all letters.
6. T. It's a high concept pitch like a TV guide listing.
7. T. Always mention the script is registered with WGA as many will not read script if it is not registered.
8. F. Send a query letter. Include a release too.
9. F. The more marketing you do the better for you.
10. T. So recipient knows script was requested.
11. F. Use paper clip to attach each release to each script.
12. F. Plain cover only. Don't use anything fancy.
13. F. Use #5 size solid brass brads to secure feature script.
14. F. V.O. is used in Character Cue line only.
15. F. O.S. is for sounds not voices and used in description.
16. F. It's not used anymore, especially in author's scripts.
17. T. Absolutely, and to push the story forward.
18. T. Learn to write visually. Cut out the junk.
19. F. Don't use camera angle instructions at all.
20. T. But not too splashy. Keep it simple.
21. F. They will accept nothing. Best to not query them.
22. T. Okay to send log lines or query, but include a release.
23. T. Rules can change. Some postal employees themselves are not certain of the rules & adds to confusion.
24. T. Be consistent if you do throughout the script.
25. F. You don't have to. Takes up space, distracts reader.
26. F. Use "similar to" then name the song title.
27. F. Break it up with action. Otherwise you'll end up with a "T" page that upsets timing of the script.
28. T. Approx 46 pages per 30-minute sitcom script episode.
29. F. Many do not sell stage plays.
30. F. Not needed. Just know where they should be.
31. T. Certain words will kill a script.
32. T. It can never hurt even when sending to an agent.
33. F. Prodcos won't read a script if not WGA registered
34. T. V.O. is used when character is not seen, but heard.
35. F. Marketing scripts requires instructions how to do it.
36. F. Agents don't need release, but it okay to send one.
37. T. Even if they don't ask for release, send them one.
38. T. Oh, yes. Readers can spot an amateur's script fast.
39. T. It will help you in writing the script.
40. T. Always tell your agent to send your script only, otherwise, agent will send his shopping list to the prodco.
41. T. You are not competing with an advertisement.
42. F. Not yet. Internet can be risky as ideas are stolen.
43. T. But use parenthical directions sparingly if at all.
44. T. Two lines of direction is even better.
45. T. For use in this manual.
46. T. For use in this manual.
47. T. But use sparingly if possible.
48. T&F. You can send a request to submit letter.
49. T. You could try brown ink, but black is the standard.
50. T. "Act" is this author's recommendation.
51. F. Rarely can you exceed 120 pages. Not more than 125.
52. F. Timing the market is a proven method to fail.
53. T. Busy people have little time. Be professional.
54. T. And reveal character.
55. T. All movies do. It's necessary.
56. T. Always.
57. F. You can, but it's not necessary. Opinions differ.
58. T. Check your spelling and grammar or your doomed.
59. T. Printers can insert, delete, or smudge pages.
60. T. Always send a query first.
61. T. Dialog is most important to the reader.
62. T. Don't use express mail unless requested.
63. T. If you want your script returned.
64. T. Large studios won't deal with non-sig agents.
65. F. List is often out of date not listing all.
66. T. You can, but a query letter is still cheaper.
67. F. Legal documents must be on white paper.
68. T. Some agents will not respond at all. Rude.
69. T. Marketing is half the battle to win the war.
70. F. This is not true. Don't believe it.
71. T. Odds are better you can sell true stories.
72. F. Never. Just write the story.
73. T. If possible. If not, send to; "Story Editor."
74. T. It will save you many hours of grief.
75. T. Include DAY or NIGHT.
76. F. Use ellipsis (...) when absolutely needed.
77. T. This is for cast purposes. It's standard.
78. T. But you don't have to cap all sounds.
79. T. Use (- -) when something interrupts speaking.
80. T. Don't... overuse... or... you... sound... dumb.
81. F. They do work. You have to when starting out.
82. T. Expect rejections and you won't quit.
83. T. An airy feeling to the eyes. Easy to read.
84. T. Always break long description with dialog.
85. F. You can. Just don't send multiple synopsis.
86. T. Write visually only what can be seen on screen.
87. T. A name is nice but we often don't get them.
88. T. (- -) can be used on SoS description paragraph
89. T. As long as you're the only one bidding.
90. F. Not necessary. You can if you want to.
91. T. Nobody has the formula to market a script.
92. T. Opinions differ. Whatever works, works.
93. T. If you don't want script returned, say so.
94. T. You should most of the time.
95. T. Just don't brag or get weird. Be upbeat.
96. F. Don't say stupid things like this.
97. T. Dialog is what catches the reader's excitement.
98. T. Don't write for money or the market trend.
99. T. Consider genre and size of market.
100. T. They can get you more money, now or later.
101. T. Definitely subscribe. More the better.
102. T. This will help your writing & marketing 100%.
103. F. Send script by First or Special 4th Class mail.
104. T. Experiment until you find a winning result.
105. T. Exposes less errors in your writing. Easy read.
106. T. Selling scripts is not fun. It's hard work.
107. T. Tyvek envelopes are best, but not only option.
108. F. Producers are always looking for scripts.
110. T. Send query to a movie star's agent/manager.
111. T. Be polite no matter how insulting it feels.
112. T. But mail is most professional.
113. F. Only if agent specifically requests to do so.
114. T. Don't be a pest. Respect the agent's time.
115. F. Not a good idea. Limits your market.
116. T. Opens up the market broad and wide.
117. F. You can learn it like many others have.
118. T. Fair warning. It's not a get rich quick game.
119. T. You can make money writing so do it.
120. T. Read it! Software is not reliable.
121. F. Many writer's failed English and sell scripts.
122. T. Some agents want them. Some don't.
123. F. Many writers don't use treatments. Many do.
124. T. Dramatica Pro & Blockbuster are good.
125. T. Don't use a cheap printer. It will stop sales.
126. T. It will help you sell the script.
127. T. Opens the market. Opinions differ.
128. T. Can help you see the errors you'll never find.
129. T. Don't be shy. Believe in yourself.
130. F. Write the author's script.
131. T. More the better. Each has knowledge to share.
132. T. May cause problems with hard disk drive.
133. T. More the merrier. Increases odds of success.
134 F. You can query anyone except major studios.

Screen & Stage Marketing Secrets

Fig. 1-21 A
Letter To Movie Star's Agent

Page 158

October 1, 2002

Star Management, Inc.
David Shushnookie
100 Dollar Bill Road
Culver City, CA 9000

Re: Screenplay, "*Fires Within.*"

> This letter is advertising a challenge to the actor, that this character's role may be a bit tough to handle, but we have faith in you! Actors love to be challenged!

Dear David Shushnookie:

Enclosed find a synopsis and release form to be submitted to (actor's name) for consideration.

The story's charactor is quite different than the usual films (actor's name) has performed, though I believe is fully capable of executing.

I look forward to hear from you soon.

Sincerely,

James Russell
James Russell
1 Fan Club Drive
New York, NY 00022
303-000-0000

> Did you enclose the S.A.S.E.?

Follow Up Inquiry Letter

Fig. 1-21 B

February 1, 2003

Star Management, Inc.
David Shushnookie
100 Dollar Bill Road
Culver City, CA 9000

Dear David Shushnookie:

Back in October 1, 2002, I submitted a synopsis and query for (actor's name) for consideration.

Please inform the status of the decision pertaining to the screenplay, "*Fires Within.*"

Thank you.

Sincerely,

James Russell
James Russell
1 Fan Club Drive
New York, NY 00022
303-000-0000

> Don't forget the S.A.S.E.

> FOR A HANDY CONTACT RECORD TO KEEP TRACK OF YOUR SUBMISSIONS -- SEE FIG. 1-30

Did you find the spelling error in 1-21 A? Charactor should be Character.

Screen & Stage Marketing Secrets   **Fig. 1-22**   Page 159

QUERY LETTER TO MOVIE STAR's AGENT

October 28, 2008

John Gilly / Agent
CU47 Talent Management
1 Avenue of the Stars
Los Angeles, CA 90122

Dear John Gilly:

Having written a script for actress, Diane Fabulous, I am requesting permission to submit for consideration.

Without revealing specifics, the script is a comedy based on the main character's powers of love blinding every man, except the man she loves. "*X-Ray*" is a romantic comedy that may interest Diane Fabulous.

The script is WGA registered. A general release is enclosed.

Looking forward to hearing from you.

Thank you.

Sincerely,

James Russell

James Russell
Love To Write Lane
Sparks, Nevada 89517
775-000-000

KEEP YOUR LETTERS BRIEF & TO THE POINT

____ Send "X-Ray" script.
____ Additional instructions _____.
____ Pass at this time.

Note: You write to the star's agent, not to the star. This way you avoid getting lost in the fan mail circuit. The agent may request the script, perform coverage, and notify the star if the script measures up to expectations. There is no law saying you can't enclose a personal letter to the star. You can do this if you want, but there is only one drawback to this... you may be viewed as a fan, not a professional writer, depending on how you compose your letter. I'd advise not to do it until later on in the process when and if the script is optioned. It is likely you'll meet the actress anyway in the development process. For best results, keep business, business. If you receive absolutely no response from the agent in 60 to 90 days, write to the production company who has shot films for the star, the producer or director. Never write a script just for one star, as it limits your market. However, you can write a script and later say you had the star in mind for the role as the above query letter suggests. Keep the letter simple and don't compliment the star so as to induce "Fan Mail" flags. Do not harass the star. If they are not interested, let it be. They may contact you next year. Be professional.

Screen & Stage Marketing Secrets **Fig. 1-23** Page 160

SAMPLE FOLLOW-UP INQUIRY LETTER

January 3, 2025

John Gilly / Agent
CU47 Talent Management
1 Avenue of the Stars
Los Angeles, CA 90122

Dear John Gilly:

On October 28, 2008, I submitted a query and release on my script "*X-Ray*" for Diane Fabulous's consideration. Obtaining a letter of intent would greatly increase the marketing effort.

Having not heard from you, I am inquiring if a decision was made.

At your convienence, please let me know if I can submit "*X-Ray*."

Thank you.

Sincerely,

James Russell

James Russell
1 Production Avenue
Burbank, CA 84135
501-000-000

____ Send "*X-Ray*" script.
____ Additional instructions _____.
____ Pass at this time.

Note: In the above example a "letter of intent" is being requested. This is part of the "packaging" process you can use to "attach" a movie star to your script. This may happen if the star likes your script. Usually, producers obtain these intentions, but you can too, or at least try to. They will open many doors if you do succeed. You shouldn't be writing movie stars until your script has received high rankings in screenplay contests or excellent coverage with script evaluation services. Be patient. Writing to star management is not a means or method for the novice with only a couple scripts in hand.

You can use this letter's basic idea to create follow-up letters to agents and prodcos who are late in responding to the results of the script you sent them. Be certain you wait approximately 60 days before sending such a letter. Don't be a pest. Patience is required in this business. When you are waiting for a response you should be busy contacting other prodcos and agents and writing your next script. Don't sit around fretting as it will drive you up the walls. Keep moving forward. Don't look back.

Screen & Stage Marketing Secrets   Fig. 1-24   Page 161

TRUE COST OF MAILING <u>ONE</u> QUERY LETTER

HIGH

Fine stationery .32
Fine envelope .10
S.A.S.E. #10 envelope .10
Stamp for S.A.S.E. .32
Stamp for #10 envelope .32
Label for #10 envelope .01
<u>TOTAL</u> $1.17

LOW

Economical stationery .025
Economical envelope .01
S.A.S.E. #10 envelope .03
Stamp for S.A.S.E. .32
Stamp for #10 envelope .32
Label for #10 envelope .01
<u>TOTAL</u> $.715 cents

<u>SAVE 45 1/2 CENTS</u>

NOW LETS TAKE THESE FIGURES INTO THE REAL WORLD
Here's the cost involved to query 600 agents for 5 scripts.

<u>SINGLE QUERY MAILING</u>

600 agents X $1.17 = $702.00
$702 X 5 mailings = $3,510

$3,510

<u>MUTIPLE SUBMISSION QUERY</u>

600 agents X $71.50 = $429.00
$429 X 1 mailings = $429.00

$429

<u>SAVE $3,081 DOLLARS</u>

For $429 you can query 600 agents with five of your scripts by using the multiple submission log line approach. If you add three more scripts, you can market 8 scripts to 600 agents at the <u>same cost</u>. For each script you market with a single query, it may cost you $702. The multiple submission method may not be deemed politically correct, but it certainly is economically brilliant.

Now, assume 400 agents or prodcos reject the log line submissions and 200 respond by returning your S.A.S.E. Of the 200, only 10 request a script. You have certainly broken down firewalls at the lowest cost denominator and you have 10 scripts in the pipeline. There is absolutely no guarantee if you use the single submission approach you will obtain better results. Increased costs do not improve the response rate.

In fact, the odds increase against you if you use the single query submission. Why? Because many of us do not know how to write the "Golden Bullet" query letter. Send a poorly written query and you'll wish you had just sent a log line. Reserve your queries for agents and prodcos who are advertising for scripts in the screenwriting magazines. For mass mailing, use the multiple submission log line method.

-- YOUR EXPENSES ARE TAX DEDUCTIBLE --

Screen & Stage Marketing Secrets   **Fig. 1-25**   Page 162

SAMPLE OF A BRIEF QUERY LETTER PUSHING ONE SCRIPT

February 28, 2008

Billyboy Mecallayalater
Bonanza Strike Enterprises
911 Frantic Road
Virginia City, NV 90638

Re: Your ad in Millionaire Screenwriting magazine. Exclusive submission.

Dear Billyboy Mecallayalater:

"*Fastrack*" - a wild ride of con artists operating international fraud rackets, cracks corporate America's financial network, creating stock market instability and ultimate melt-down. Only one person has the expertise to defuse the ticking financial bomb and that's "Ahab Va'Moose III" who is a CIA double-agent planted within this evil crime ring. Ahab has miraculous powers as a guru and medicine man, along with his guardian angel nobody can see.

The comedy feature script is WGA registered and ranked #3 in the Get Rich Quick Screenplay contest.

Looking forward to hear from you.

Thank you.

Sincerely,

James Russell

James Russell
10 Screenplay Street
Anywhere, Europe A14 G97
0-01-991-000-000

____ Send "*Fastrack*" script.
____ Additional instructions _____.
____ Pass at this time.

KNOCK 'EM DOWN WITH A QUICK PUNCH

You could easily go overboard in a query letter because your excitement level is so high you want to explain as much detail as possible, but that is a mistake. Agents don't want long letters, they want a simple paragraph describing the essence of the story. No more, no less. Plus, you can't condense a 2-hour movie into a 1-page synopsis anyway. Just write the best single paragraph you can. It takes practice and it never seems to be right.

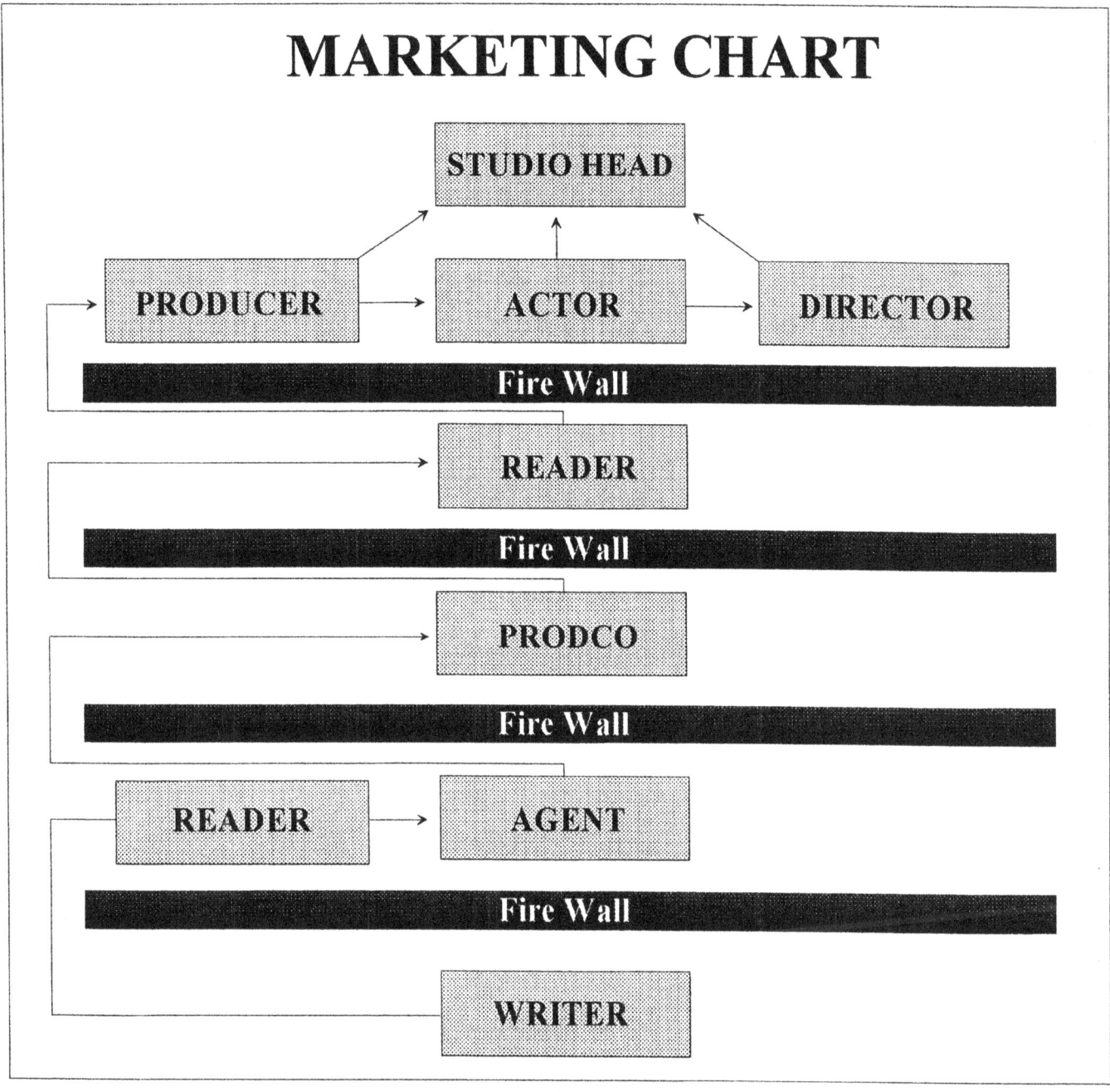

The above chart is a simple diagram revealing the firewalls in place between each phase of the marketing process a writer must penetrate to gain the sale of the script. This chart is only an example, there are many other variations. However, the chart reveals basic barriers. In this book, you have learned how to effectively side-step the agent and go direct to the production company, the director, producer or actor. These individuals have the influence and the power to purchase scripts or to get movies made.

You will notice readers stand in the way. They are the ultimate firewall to penetrate and the most trying to please. Ultimately, only a good script will be given by the reader to be forwarded on to the studio head, but this is not always true. Bad scripts are often bought and bad movies are often made!

In your marketing plan, you should write out a basic chart, like you see here, that fits your specific method of submission. The important thing is to get your script "out there" being read. If the script is good, in time -- often years in circulation -- your script should sell. Industry personnel turnover is high, so keep submitting at least once per year to agents and prodcos. The next guy who just moved in may love your script!

Screen & Stage Marketing Secrets **Fig. 1-27** Page 164

SAMPLE OF A BRIEF QUERY LETTER FOR STAGE PLAY

September 3, 2012

Miss Kitty Cat
Literary Director
The Drama Stage
1 Broadway
New York, NY 00002

You don't have to indent the first line of each paragraph when sending a letter with short sentences. It's optional. You can justify left, as shown.

Dear Miss Kitty Cat:

Enclosed a synopsis of my comedy 3-act play "*Stage Play*" for your review.

Stage Play is a low-budget stage-setting similar to the TV show, "*Cheers*" with a proprietary theme, plot, and characters. The script is WGA registered and authored by a Dramatist Guild member.

This story was written to bring the fast pace television sitcom to the stage. Reason being, the expanded audience draw will boost theater attendance.

I believe you will find *Stage Play* entertaining and furiously comical.

Thank you for the opportunity to submit. I await your early reply.

Looking forward to hear from you.

Sincerely,

James Russell

James Russell
12 Broadway Avenue
New York, NY 00011
214-000-000

NOTICE HOW STREAMLINED THIS QUERY IS. NOT HEAVY AT ALL. IT TEASES THE READER TO REQUEST THE PLAY SCRIPT.

____ Send "*Stage Play*" script.   Send ____ pages of the script.
____ Additional instructions _____.
____ Pass at this time.
____ Please do not send us future mailings.

THERE ARE SOME VARIATIONS

Marketing the stage play is much less restrictive than screenplays, as you can write directly to the theaters but some rules still apply. Read submission guidelines and adhere to them. Don't call or pester and don't send unsolicited scripts. Normally, you don't need to send a release to theaters. You may send a release to any producer, director or actor. Be patient! Theaters require months to a year to evaluate scripts.

COVERAGE REPORT

GOOD   FAIR   BAD

CHARACTER
- Personalities developed and consistent?
- Motivations and attitudes clear?
- Needs developed and expressed?
- Did you care about the character?
- Interesting protagonist?
- Strong first impression for each character?
- Good contrast between characters?
- Strong inner obstacles to overcome?

DIALOG
- Reveal emotions of characters?
- Convey the action and advance the story?
- Fit the characters and was realistic?
- Enhance the drama and action?
- Weaved into the fabric of the story?
- Amplify relationships?
- Add rhythm and pace to the story?
- Words spoken out of character?

VISUAL EXCITEMENT
- Opening scene grab attention?
- Action unique or typical duplication?
- Scene settings interesting?
- Action gets in the way of characters?
- Action scenes feel strong and proper?
- Too little action?
- Script written visually?
- Characters not moving or talking too much?

PLOT
- Conflict starts early and clearly developed?
- Is there a beginning, middle and end resolution?
- Action and reaction flowed logically?
- Conflict builds as story progresses?
- Did you feel suspense? Grab your attention?
- Credible plot with no plot holes?
- Did the crisis get worse or fall flat?
- Each scene moved story forward?

WRITING QUALITY
- Standard format correct?
- Lean and easy to read?
- Pages balanced with action and dialog?
- Descriptions concise and clearly understood?
- Too wordy? Needs rewrite?
- Writer writes visually?
- Grammar and spelling errors?
- Did you like the writing style?

YES   NO   RECOMMENDATION
- Is script marketable?
- Pass.
- Recommend further review?
- Strongly recommend?

Each agent, producer and prodco has their own coverage reports. This example is typical.

It's a shame you can't get these coverage reports so you can make changes to the script.

Sometimes, if you ask, you may get lucky and the coverage will be sent to you.

Keep in mind, it is only one person's opinion and it is highly subjective. Another analyst may like the script while another may despise it.

It never hurts to try to correct the script's weak elements when you do get a bad review.

USE THIS COVERAGE REPORT TO CHECK YOUR OWN SCRIPT!

YOU MAY EVEN USE THE REPORT TO GIVE TO ANOTHER WRITER SO HE/SHE CAN FILL IT OUT AFTER READING YOUR SCRIPT.

TAKE ADVANTAGE OF THIS!

Screen & Stage Marketing Secrets — Fig. 1-29 — Copyright by James Russell

CHECK LIST - SUBMISSION PACKAGE

- [ ] **#10 S.A.S.E. ENCLOSED WITH BUSINESS POSTAGE APPLIED.**
  See Illustration Fig. 1-12.

- [ ] **SPELLING AND GRAMMAR CHECKED ON SCRIPT & QUERY LETTER.**
  Don't Rely on Software. Proofread it From a Printed Copy.

- [ ] **QUERY & LOG LINE POWERFULLY WRITTEN - WITH SIGNATURE.**
  Keep Revising and Testing. Make Sure it is Easy to Read and Brief.

- [ ] **SYNOPSIS ENCLOSED SPELLING / GRAMMAR CHECKED -WITH SIGNATURE.**
  Synopsis is One Page, Not Two or More Pages! Keep it Short & to the Point!

- [ ] **SCRIPT S.A.S.E. ENCLOSED WITH BUSINESS POSTAGE APPLIED.**
  Script S.A.S.E Not Required if Mailing Query Letter Only

- [ ] **NO MISSING PAGES IN SCRIPT. PAGES IN PROPER ORDER.**
  Remove any blank pages the printer may have inserted.

- [ ] **ALL ELEMENTS ASSEMBLED AND PACKAGED AS SHOWN IN FIG 1-13**
  Do Not Make Mistakes! Use This Checklist to Avoid Rejection!

- [ ] **REQUESTED SCREENPLAY NOTICE ON SCRIPT MAILING ENVELOPE .**
  See Illustration Fig. 1-13

- [ ] **S.A.S.E. ENVELOPES PROPERLY RETURN ADDRESSED.**
  See Illustration Fig. 1-12 and 1-13

- [ ] **TWO BRADS USED TO BIND SCRIPT. NO FANCY SCRIPT COVER.**
  See Illustration Fig. 1-1

- [ ] **QUERY OR S.A.S.E. ENVELOPE IS A STANDARD WHITE BUSINESS #10 SIZE.**
  Make Certain You Send a #10 S.A.S.E.. Larger Size is Okay, But Never Smaller.

- [ ] **STATIONARY IS OF A SIMPLE DESIGN - NOT TOO COLORFUL.**
  Stay Clear of Using Colorful Stationery. Keep it Simple.

- [ ] **CHECKLIST INSERTED ON QUERY LETTER.**
  See Illustration Fig. 1-27

- [ ] **RELEASE FORM ENCLOSED.**
  Release Only Required If Mailing To Prodco or the Agency Requires a Release. See Fig. 1-3

- [ ] Follow up with Agent / Prodco on: _____ . See Fig. 1-21 B and Fig. 1-30

- [ ] **S.A.S.P. ENCLOSED? THIS POSTCARD IS YOUR RETURN RECEIPT**
  Generally, the S.A.S.P. is Used Only When Submitting a Script, Not a Query.

- [ ] _____.

- [ ] _____.

- [ ] _____.

The Blank Areas Above Are For Your Own Special Criteria.
Go ahead and copy this form to use, and give one to your friend!
Any Major Bookstore Can Order *Screen & Stage Marketing Secrets*

Screen & Stage Marketing Secrets

Fig. 1-30

CONTACT RECORD
AGENCY

PAGE # _____.

AGENCY:_____. DATE: _____.

CONTACT:_____.

PHONE:_____E-MAIL_____WEB_____.

QUERY SENT: _____. RESPONSE_____.

SCRIPT SENT: _____. RESPONSE_____.

SPECIAL INSTRUCTIONS:_____
_____.

FOLLOW UP SENT: _____. RESPONSE_____

AGENT REQUIRES RELEASE FORM: Yes. No. AGENT REPRESENTS MOVIE STAR: _____.

BEST MONTH TO SUBMIT: J. F. M. A. M. J. J. A. S. O. N. D.

WGA AGENT: Yes. No. AGENT REQUIRES READING FEE $_____.

OTHER CRITERIA: _____.

CONTACT RECORD
PRODCO / OTHER

PRODCO:_____. DATE: _____.

CONTACT:_____TITLE:_____DEPT:_____.

PHONE:_____E-MAIL_____WEB_____.

QUERY SENT: _____. RESPONSE_____.

SCRIPT SENT: _____. RESPONSE_____.

SPECIAL INSTRUCTIONS:_____
_____.

FOLLOW UP SENT: _____. RESPONSE_____

GENERAL RELEASE FORM OKAY: Yes. No.   FIRM REQUIRES OWN RELEASE: Yes. No.

BEST MONTH TO SUBMIT: J. F. M. A. M. J. J. A. S. O. N. D.

PREFERS SUBMISSIONS FROM: _____. PAGE # _____

OTHER CRITERIA: _____.

 Go ahead and copy this form to use, and give one to your friend!
Any Major Bookstore Can Order *Screen & Stage Marketing Secrets*

ORDER FORM
(Okay to photocopy this order form)

MAILING LISTS
Approx 600 agents, producers and production companies

☐ Send me the mailing list of **PRODCOS** and **AGENTS**. A paper print out. $30.

☐ Send me the directory of **PRODCOS** and **AGENTS** on PC Compatible Computer Disk ACT! Database File Format. Now On CD-ROM disk. $30.

1. SUB TOTAL _____.____

SCREENPLAY Author's script. Not a shooting script. Sold <u>without</u> production rights.

☐ Send me the "True Bums" comedy screenplay, so I can learn how to write a condensed visual style. $34.95 (Visit an Internet Bookstore for other James Russell script selections).

2. SUB TOTAL _____.____

COLLABORATION AGREEMENT

☐ Send me the **COLLABORATION AGREEMENT CONTRACT** to purchase rights to a person's life story. I've enclosed $12.00

3. SUB TOTAL _____.____

Method of Payment

4. TOTAL (add 1 thru 3) _____.____

☐ Personal Check #_____ enclosed.

5. NV add 7.25% sales tax _____.____

☐ Money Order #_____ enclosed.

6. $4 Shipping & Handling _____.____

☐ Your phone number (optional) _____

➪ **7. GRAND TOTAL** _____.____

Ordered by: (Print very clearly)   **Ship to: (If shipping address is different)**

_____   _____
_____   _____
_____   _____

Shipping charge of $4 only applies to the screenplay. Other items on this page are shipped postage paid. Allow 3 to 4 weeks for delivery.

Mail this order to: James Russell
780 Diogenes Drive
Reno, NV 89512

Fig. 2 - 1

SAMPLE LETTER TO REQUEST COVERAGE REPORT

February 22, 3001

Box Office Agency
John Doe / Literary Agent
20 Gold Strike Lode Road
Tiverton, Rhode Island 02730

Re: Coverage Report / *Fastrack* Script

Dear John Doe:

Thank you for reviewing my screenplay *Fastrack*.

I know it is not customary for writers to receive a copy of the coverage report, but I was wondering if you can make an exception to the rule so I may correct the errors in my script.

Rest assured, I will not rebuttle comments in the report and it will remain in strict confidence. Thank you for understanding. S.A.S.E. enclosed.

Sincerely,

James Russell

James Russell
100 Strikes Out Lane
Ventura, CA 91233
888-991-000

NO GUARANTEE

There are no assurances this request for coverage report will give you the report from all agencies or production companies, but no doubt you will receive a few reports. Just getting one or two reports will be of great value to you, so you can tune up your script to please the next reader. As a courtesy, consider sending your next query of the rewritten script to the agencies and prodcos that gave you the coverage report.

STAY CALM AND BE PROFESSIONAL

When you do receive your coverage report, be thankful for it, as it is a valuable tool to use to get your script into marketable form. These coverage reports can be very harsh to read and may even be outright insulting. They are not meant to be given to the author! It is an inside communication not designed for your eyes to see. Consider yourself priviliged if the coverage report is sent to you. Keep your cool, no matter how terrible the report may read. Do not complain or write rebuttals. Resist these temptations! Just get back to work on cleaning up the script. There are valid reasons why a report passes on your script, so take full advantage of this great opportunity. Many writers wish they had these coverage reports!

Fig. 2-3

SAMPLE LETTER TO REQUEST REFERRAL

March 15, 2017

Jeff Hotwriter
50 Beverly Hills Mansion Dr.
Beverly Hills, CA 90212

Re: Referral

Dear Jeff Hotwriter

Having read your script and seeing your movie *Casino Fools,* I'd like to congradulate you for a job well done.

I am a writer with four screenplays, trying to break in, but the going is tough. If it all possible, when time permits, may I send you my romantic comedy *Win A Wife For Life* for a referral? The script ranked #10 in the Hollywood Avenue of Fame screenplay contest.

I will respect your decision in a professional manner and I will not call or write you for explanations, etc. If the script meets your standards, a referral would be greately appreciated so I may obtain representation. S.A.S.E. enclosed.

Sincerely,

James Russell

James Russell
1 Gotta Break In Blvd.
No Opportunity, MA 02743
508-991-000

 Referrals are powerful marketing tools. They can be difficult to aquire, as you are in direct competition with the writer giving the referral.

⇨ SHORT, SWEET AND TO THE POINT

Don't draft a long letter. Don't send a synopsis or treatment and do not send the script until the writer has asked for it. The above letter sample will work just fine. There is no incincerity in the letter, no overblown compliments and it's right to the point. The letter is drafted in such a way that the writer will feel like giving you a chance, since you promise to not harass the writer and the screenplay has ranked high in a contest.

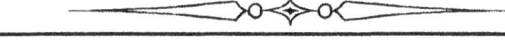

⇨ KEEP YOUR PROMISES

No writer is under any obligation to you to give you a referral. In fact, it could even jeopodize the writer's career, if you are later found to be unprofessional and unreliable. In the above letter you mention promises, so keep them, to the letter! If the writer fails to respond, do not write or call that writer again. If the writer sends you a rejection, leave it alone. Send a thank you letter. Clean up the script and try again. Any writer who gives you an open door to submit, count your blessings, as it is hard to get. Never pester the writer or send gifts, etc. All you need is one writer to get your referral and the doors of Hollywood swing wide open. Do not send your script to any writer unless it has ranked in the top 50 in a screenwriting contest. Don't blow this opportunity by sending scripts that fail to meet high ranking in contests. Be professional!

Screen & Stage Marketing Secrets **Fig. 2-4** Page 171
SAMPLE LETTER FOR PACKAGING

July 4, 2025

Don Takeachance / Director
2000 Fremont St.
Los Angeles, CA 90212

Re: Packaging. Exclusive submission.

Dear Don Takeachance:

You are receiving this query along with actor John Pain, Donna Tears, Big Deal Agency, ABC Productions.

I am packaging a comedy script "*Crashing To Heaven*" and requesting permission to submit. Enclosed is a release form and S.A.S.E. The script has ranked #25 in the Fabulously Talented Screenplay Contest.

This exclusive submission is valid for 30 days. Please indicate your interest.

Sincerely,

James Russell

James Russell
1 Desperate Street
Help Me Please, FL 87653
477-552-000

INSTRUCTIONS

This letter is drafted to a producer or director. Simply change the order of the individuals in the letter to submit to other entities. This letter must be sent to all individuals at the same time. If you have no agent, just leave out the agency reference. Once you get one tagged on to the project, it becomes easier to interest others, then the ball begins to roll. At that point, getting an agent is easy.

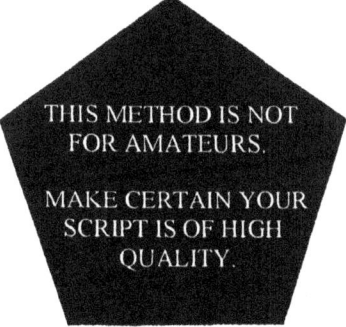

THIS METHOD IS NOT FOR AMATEURS.

MAKE CERTAIN YOUR SCRIPT IS OF HIGH QUALITY.

ANGLE OF ATTACK

Agencies package scripts and principles, not writers but there is no rule that you can not do it! In fact, networking is routine and this is simply gathering interested individuals to look at a script. It helps if you do a bit of research to insure all the individuals work well together before selecting your cast.

When you have exhausted traditional marketing avenues, this packaging plan may very well be the key to generate the heat required to kick-start your script. The benefit is that the reader is placed in a situation to respond, and to do so quickly or lose out on a potential profitable venture others may jump on.

Fig. 2-5
SAMPLE COVER LETTER FOR AGENT LISTING IN BOOK

November 20, 2035

CBA Entertainment Agency
Diane Dealqueen
52 Howdy Drive
Beverly Hills, CA 91204

Re: Book Listing Submission.

Dear CBA Entertainment Agency (or contact name):

I am a reader of the *Screen & Stage Marketing Secrets* and submitting in accordance with your special listing in the book.

Enclosed: query for *Heaven In Detroit*, a feature film romantic comedy screenplay (or sitcom teleplay) with S.A.S.E. and a logline listing of my other projects for your consideration.

This screenplay is my second (or seventh) script and has ranked #15 of 6,000 entries in the "Great Balls of Fire" screenplay contest. Enclosed: copy of an evaluation from ABC script doctor.

Thank you for the opportunity to submit my work.

Sincerely,

James Russell

James Russell
777 Slot Machine Jacpot Ave
Reno, NV 89513
775-346-000

> YOU MAY INCLUDE A BRIEF BIO IF RELEVANT TO SCREEN WRITING.
>
> JUST ADD IT IN A SMALL PARAGRAPH HERE.

INSTRUCTIONS

Use this cover letter format when you contact agents listed in this book. Make certain you read the letter carefully and insure no spelling mistakes are present. Keep the cover letter brief, as shown. You don't need to include a script doctor evaluation, but it will help. Make sure you sign the cover letter and you have included all mentioned elements before you mail it. Write it, wait one day, then read it again. If it still sounds good? Mail it. If you follow the above sample guideline, you'll be okay.

MAILING

Assemble all items in order as they are called out in the cover letter. Assemble with a large paper clip and insert into a large 9x12 envelope, so the submission materials are flat and clean to read. Don't fold and stuff the elements into a #10 envelope for this special submission!

WHAT NOT TO SEND

Since this is a special listing of agencies who are willing to give you a chance, they won't mind if you send a bit more than just a query letter, but not too much more. Don't send an entire script or treatment. Don't send a resume. Don't send gifts, make promises or try to cut a deal. Don't send a query letter, this cover letter is your query letter!

WHAT YOU CAN SEND

You may send this cover letter, two pages of your script, copy of contest certificate, evaluation from script doctor, logline listing, one page synopsis. Don't go beyond this. Anything more the submission will be too heavy to read.

... A WORD OF ADVICE ...

SLOW, STEADY AND <u>SURE</u> TO WIN !

Most writers, especially the new writers, are way too much in a hurry. They rush everything and it shows up in the script, in the query letter, in the synopsis, etc. Desperation reveals itself like a runaway train. Clearly, the motivation is money causing this, *"I must sell my scripts!"*

It is okay to have the desire to make money. After all, that's why writers write; for the joy and financial reward writing can bring. This book can speed up your action scenes, but at the same time, eliminate the panic factor. Now you know how to develop contacts and perform professional submissions. This book even supplies you with agents that are willing to give you a chance!

Now relax. Take it easy. Don't be hard on yourself. You know how to get the job done. There is no reason to be in a hurry. Each day, mail a query, write a bit more and everything will fall into place. Take your time now to rewrite your scripts and submission materials bringing them into line with industry standards. The slower you work, the more accurate you will be. Agents and producers will sense your expression of calm professionalism and feel comfortable dealing with you. Writers that exhibit an aura of tension and panic (desperation) actually drive people away from themselves.

Remember, a professional is calm, cool and level. Do not express your inner emotions of extreme happiness or sadness when an agent or prodco tells you good or bad news. Be in control! Take it all with a grain of salt, as if you really don't mind which way the decision came out. In fact, be more concerned in comforting the agent or producer who is telling you the news... you will gain respect!

Now The Fun Begins ! Now you can apply yourself with great inner calm and portray your professional image in your writing and marketing endeavors. You no longer have to pump yourself up with that uncontrolled railroaded feeling of having to make it at all costs. Marketing the script now becomes fun! Writing becomes fun! There is an old secret to happiness and the solution is quite simple, *"Be happy!"* You will need this advice before and after you sell your screenplay!

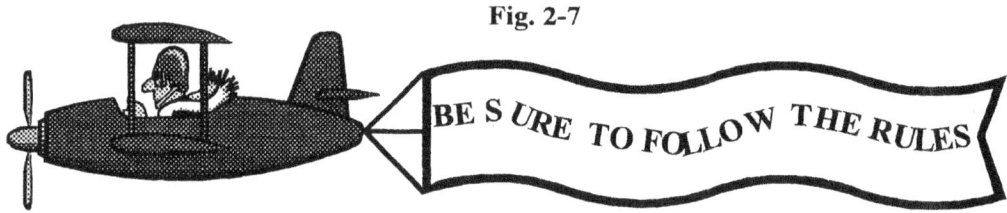

Fig. 2-7

#1. Timing can be important to submit scripts. Many agents set specific months they will accept scripts for submission. The ACT! database program can notify you when to make your submission automatically. Also, if you have a Western film and you see a new Western movie, it's too late to submit. You should have read The Hollywood Reporter a year ago and you would have seen producers requesting Western scripts! You will see the trend as the magazine lists the films in production. This is the only viable method to time the market.

#2. The link in the chain is the writer's marketing strategy and procedures. Many script rejections are issued due to following improper procedures and not adhering to industry standards. Your query must be targeted to agents that specifically handle the genre your script represents. This is a fatal error many writers make time and time again!
Your query letter must not be boring and contain long paragraphs or it will only be repeatedly rejected. Agents have no time to read a story in your query letter, it's got to be abreviated to a minute or less. Make your query letter powerfully small in size before you mail it. You have only seconds to grab the agents interest. A long query is a death sentence and a certain indication an amateur is making the submission.

#3 Does your query and cover letter reveal a sense of explosive excitement? Does it have a strong indication of professionalism? Are you asking the agent to request the script, but not begging in any way? Does it purvey an image to the agent this script could be the one they are looking for, without saying it in those words? Can you reword the log line to import more visual power to the storyline? What makes your script better than anything else ever written? Try to incorporate these powerful elements in your query. The query should create an image in the mind of the reader. What image is yours creating?

#4. To unlock the doors to Hollywood there is no one certain method. Every script purchased finds its own way. Some by agents, others by friends of those in the industry, some by actors, producers, directors, managers, entertainment lawyers, even the secretary! Most writer's rely too heavily on trying to get an agent when they should be aggressively marketing their product to all of the entities mentioned above. Only you have the key to unlock those doors! If you want to sell your screenplay or stage play, you have to get on the ball and get to work making hundreds of query submissions. Marketing is more important than writing the script! A product can not sell if it is not marketed. Your query letter is an advertisement flyer and it has to be compelling to the reader. It must "tease" the mind so the script will be requested from curiosity. Keep polishing and improving that query letter!

#5. Everybody is in the same boat and it's sinking! Everybody wants to sell a script and see it on the silver screen or on stage. The ship is sinking because it is overloaded with too many writers. Many become desperate and resort to gimmicks to try to stand out from the crowd; fancy stationary, colorful script covers, etc. It only backfires on them with *more rejections!* Do not resort to such tactics. The way to break in is with good writing! That is the most surefire method every agent and producer will tell you. Good writing means great visual writing! The ability to create images from words and formulate a compelling story that is exciting to the senses. Your query letter is your major advertisement brochure. It is here you need to focus on in great detail to market your script. The query is the most powerful device you have to get your script sold!

Screen & Stage Marketing Secrets

THE MARKETING PROCESS IS FORMULA!

ITH 97% SKILL & 3% LUCK.

You must learn the theory and rules of entertainment marketing procedures and it's here in this book book!

Fig. 2-8

#1. Focus strongly on producing a winning query letter. Too many writers fail to understand the importance and power of the query. It gets the script requested!

Rewrite your script to get rid of the "danger words" that weaken the flow of action and upset readers! Make your scipt lean an mean and easy to read.

Timing is everything! Develop a marketing plan you will employ each week without fail. You <u>can</u> shotgun the market!

#4. Quickdrawing is responding promptly to script requests! You have to read the writing magazines and respond to the ads requesting scripts, fast! These windows of opportunity remain open only for short periods of time. *The Hollywood Reporter Magazine* is one of the best mags for connecting with production companies seeking scripts. It's a loophole in the firewall system. Prodcos that advertise, will read your script with or without an agent. Be quick to respond to these ads! Competition here is way less than responding to annual agency surveys in writing magazines.

Fig. 2-9

Screen & Stage Marketing Secrets

VISIT JAMES RUSSELL'S WEB SITE
www.powernet.net/~scrnplay

NO COMPUTER OR INTERNET? NO PROBLEM...
VISIT YOUR LOCAL LIBRARY AND THEY WILL GET YOU ON-LINE FOR FREE!

- **FREE SHOOTING TIPS - OVER 500!** GET ANSWERS TO YOUR SHOOTING PROBLEMS! LEARN HOW TO SHOOT WAY BETTER THAN YOU DO NOW... AND IT'S ALL FREE!

- **INFORMATIVE DETAILED ARTICLES!** EVERYTHING FROM WHAT TO LOOK FOR WHEN BUYING A NEW GUN TO BEING A GOOD SQUAD LEADER... TIPS ON HOW TO MANAGE CONCENTRATION, SEE TARGETS, ETC.

- **COMEDY - TRAP SHOOTING JOKES.** MEET CLARANCE BAGASAND III, AND LEARN HOW YOU TOO CAN BE A PROFESSIONAL SANDBAGGER! FUNNY INTERVIEWS... SEE THE LIGHTER SIDE OF TRAPSHOOTING!

- **LOOKING FOR A GUN PART?** A NEW GUN? NEED A SHOOTING INSTRUCTOR TO LIFT YOUR SCORES? WANT TO TAKE A CLAY TARGET SHOOTING VACATION? SEE OUR "LINKS" SECTION.

- **THIS WEB SITE IS HUGE...** OVER 120-LONG FORMAT PAGES OF TRAPSHOOTING TIPS, ADVICE, PROBLEM SOLVING INSTRUCTIONS. THIS IS <u>THE WORLD'S LARGEST TRAPSHOOTING WEB SITE</u>. DON'T MISS IT!

- **YOU WILL LEARN TRAPSHOOTING TECHNIQUES YOU HAVE NEVER READ BEFORE IN ANY MAGAZINE,** BOOK OR SAW IN ANY VIDEOTAPE. TIPS THE TOP OLYMPIC & ATA PROFESSIONALS USE... GUARANTEED!

- **NEW PRODUCTS ARE REVIEWED** WITH ADVICE ON HOW TO USE THE PRODUCT TO INCREASE YOUR SCORES! CHECK OUT THE 'EASYHIT' SHOTGUN SIGHT THAT CAN HAMMER TARGETS AND SHOW YOU WHAT YOU DID WRONG INSTANTLY IF YOU MISS, SO YOU WON'T MISS AGAIN! WE CALL IT THE $40 MIRACLE!

THE MORE YOU LEARN... THE MORE YOU EARN...
AND THE MORE FUN YOU'LL HAVE TRAP SHOOTING!

... NEW ...   ... NEW ...   ... NEW ...   ... NEW ...   ... NEW ...   ... NEW ...

TRAP SHOOTING BOOKS

WHO ENDORSES THESE TEXTBOOKS?

DARO HANDY - ATA Top Gun in USA & Shooting Instructor
PHIL KINER - ATA All-American & Shooting Instructor
LUCA SCRIBANI ROSSI - Olympic Gold Medallist & Team Coach.
Shotgun Sports Magazine - USA
Clay Shooting Magazine - Europe
Gun Web Magazine - USA

> "Number 1 of the top-10 books
> Trap Shooting Secrets
> by James Russell!"
> Clay Shooting Magazine

100's of <u>Competition Trapshooters</u> reading these books see an immediate pick up in scores. Like having a shooting coach by your side telling you exactly what to do!

These are the first technical trap shooting books ever published. They don't just talk about trap shooting... they tell you how to shoot!

You will learn many of the inside secrets professional trapshooters use to annihilate targets... and it's quite easy to learn too!

WHERE TO GET YOUR COPY
Barnes & Noble bookstores
Amazon.com & Varsity.com internet bookstore
BooksAMillion bookstores
Walden Books bookstores
Borders bookstores
Shotgun Sports Magazine call 800-676-8920
ATA Trap & Field Magazine
Clay Shooting Magazine
Any Bookstore can order the books!

BORED? TRY TRAP SHOOTING
Visit our Web Site.
URL Address is listed above.

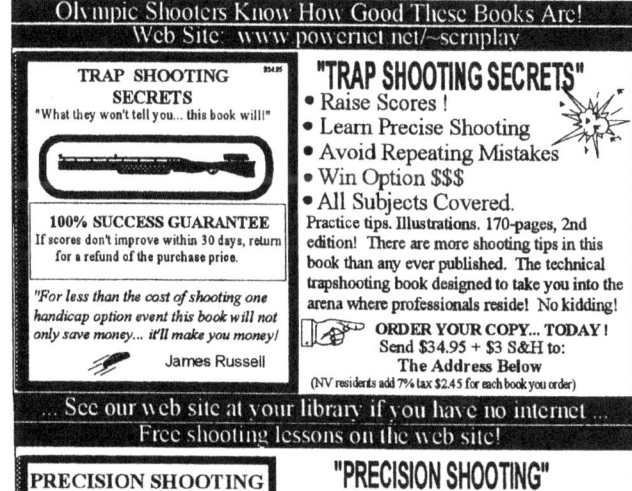

Screen & Stage Marketing Secrets

THE 7 DAY PLAN TO BE A BETTER CHRISTIAN!

SUNDAY -- This is a day of rest (see Saturday) of which no work is to be performed. Take full advantage of it! However, extend extra means of kindness to others. Read the Word and watch Christian TV for faith comes by "hearing" the Word of God.

MONDAY -- Drive your vehicle with patience towards others. Be changed at work. No more gossip, complaining, bad jokes. Just start being nice -- Biblically correct! Be cooperative. Can you do this for just one day?

TUESDAY -- Forget Me! Do a good thing for another. Open doors, buy someone a meal or gift, feed a stranger's parking meter. Give so you will receive. Give something! The Lord gives, so should you.

WEDNESDAY -- Compliment Day! Say something nice to someone, including one who may not like you. Be sincere about it! If someone needs help, go their aid. Make someone smile today!

THURSDAY -- Distribute a Bible track. No tracks? Make or buy some! It is time you begin your ministry to the Lord to share the Good News. There are many hurting people who need the Lord and it is your responsibility to introduce the Lord to them. Using tracks make the job easy!

FRIDAY -- Day of forgiveness! When you forgive others transgressions, you are released from the anguish within yourself. It is easy to do! Start the process today! See Tuesday's and Wednesday's instructions. Life is so much easier to live and great mercy and blessing arrive when you forgive!

SATURDAY -- Rest if this is the Sabbath you honor or donate; time, items, food, or money to the homeless shelters. Do not forget the poor! Visit or call a relative or friend. Express your appreciation for what the Lord has given you! Share with others what you have and the Lord will give you even more!

EACH DAY

START the day right by greeting the Lord and giving thanks for all He has done and what He will do for you in the future. **END** the day right by expressing your gratitude to the Lord.

SPEAK often to the Lord as He were your best friend. Remember, He wants to handle every detail in your life for you, even the small stuff. Do not become so busy in your day that you leave Him out of your life.

WHEN you pray just speak as you would to a friend. There is no need for theatrical displays of emotions or insincerity. If you fall short, do not turn your face away from the Lord and hide. Take the issue to Him.

WHAT will you give to the Lord if He grants your request? Will you simply say thank you and forget Him until you need something else later? The Lord sees the suffering of the sick and poor. Why not pledge to help them? Make your promise and keep it! Do it now before you recieve. This is faith in action.

SPREAD the Word of God. You may not be a minister, but you can distribute tracks. Leave them everywhere you go. Keep some on your person each day. Your reward shall be great!

TITHE to the Lord. Give and you shall receive even more! Give to churches, ministries, homeless shelters, or anywhere there is dire need. A perfect expression of love for others! God's System Never Fails!

*** COPY THIS PAGE AND DISTRIBUTE IT! ***   *James Russell*

SCREEN & STAGE MARKETING SECRETS

LEARN HOW TO

- ☑ GET AN AGENT OR SELL SCRIPTS WITHOUT ONE
- ☑ SAVE $$$ ON MARKETING EXPENSES
- ☑ WRITE POWERFUL RESPONSIVE QUERY LETTERS
- ☑ AVOID SCRIPTWRITING FATAL MISTAKES
- ☑ PROTECT YOUR WORK AND SUBMISSIONS
- ☑ OBTAIN A HIGH-RESPONSE FROM LITERARY AGENCIES
- ☑ CONTACT PRODUCTION COMPANIES WITHOUT AN AGENT
- ☑ INCREASE PRODUCTION COMPANY RESPONSES FOR YOUR SCRIPTS
- ☑ PROMOTE YOUR PROJECTS PROPERLY AND PROFESSIONALLY
- ☑ ACCESS THE TELEVISION MARKET
- ☑ CONTACT MOVIE STARS
- ☑ GET MORE REQUESTS FOR YOUR SCRIPTS
- ☑ LIST OF AGENTS WILLING TO GIVE YOU A CHANCE!

AND MUCH MORE...

| THIS | COULD | BE | YOUR | FILM | Written by: |

www.ingramcontent.com/pod-product-compliance
Lightning Source LLC
Chambersburg PA
CBHW081420230426
43668CB00016B/2300